Embraced and Engaged

Embraced and Engaged

Grace and Ethics in American Foreign Policy

Ron Kirkemo

WIPF & STOCK · Eugene, Oregon

EMBRACED AND ENGAGED
Grace and Ethics in American Foreign Policy

Copyright © 2010 Ron Kirkemo. All rights reserved. Except for brief quotations in critical publications or reviews, no part of this book may be reproduced in any manner without prior written permission from the publisher. Write: Permissions, Wipf and Stock Publishers, 199 W. 8th Ave., Suite 3, Eugene, OR 97401.

Wipf & Stock
An Imprint of Wipf and Stock Publishers
199 W. 8th Ave., Suite 3
Eugene, OR 97401
www.wipfandstock.com

ISBN 13: 978-1-60608-335-2

Manufactured in the U.S.A.

To my Grandchildren
May their lives contribute to a better world

Contents

Preface ix
Introduction xi

1 **WAR AND RENEWAL** 1
   The Diplomats of July—Hans Morgenthau and the Sisyphean World Order—The Science of War and Peace—The Reach for Transformation—Cycles and the Promethean Temptation—The Folly of Prometheus—Reality and Renewal

2 **SCRIPTURE AND GRACE** 35
   Scriptural Foundations—Scriptural Examples—Courts—The Kingdom of God—Emmaus and Troas—Theological Framework—Reformation Theology—Grace and Personal Stages—Grace and Goodness—A Model of Grace in Our Lives—Embraced by Grace—Grace and Governance—Two Test Cases—From Grace to Ethics

3 **DIPLOMACY: THE PROFESSIONAL FRONT LINE** 73
   Diplomacy—Grace and Diplomacy—The Foreign Service—The Service at Work—The Department of State—Organizational Culture—The Personal Face of Diplomacy—Two Examples—Success Strategies—Engaging the World—A Meditation on Revelation 2-3

4 **INTELLIGENCE: BREAKING THE THREAT CHAIN** 109
   The Threat Chain—First Steps—The Institutional Context—Analytical Operations—Clandestine Operations—The Personal Context—Examples—The New Global Context—Organizational Culture—Covert Operations—Counterintelligence—Ethical Dilemmas—Grace and Operations—A Meditation on Psalm 137

5 **DEFENSE: MINDS AT WAR** 146
   Strategic Doctrines—Fourth-Era, Fourth-Generation Wars—Academics in Defense—The Defense Industry—Scientists and Technicians—Public Administration: Program Manager—Lobbyists—Conclusion—A Meditation on Isaiah 47

6 **POLITICS: THE POLITICAL WORLD OF CONGRESS** 185
   The Structural Context—Example—Reaching for Congress—Building a Campaign—The Christian Vote—Campaign Ethics—A Platform for Impact—Politics Is Personal—Ethics in Congress—Christians and Congress—Legislative Example—Three Key Words—No Guarantees—A Meditation on Judges 9

7 **BEYOND THE CAMPUS CULTURE** 222
   The Locust Years—The Rhodes Ideal—To Reinvent Yourself—Gender Issues—Example—Internships—Distinguished Scholarships—Personal Statements—Matthew, The Prodigal, and the Preacher—A Meditation on Jeremiah 4:19–22

Bibliography 253

Preface

THE PREACHER WRITES, "Of making many books there is no end." Why another? Numerous books exist for laying out purported Christian moral principles *for* the policy of foreign affairs, principles for war, peace, poverty, human rights, intervention, and many others. Few deal with the ethical issues faced by Christians *in* foreign policy. Arguments over policy raise the Great Questions in liberal arts classrooms, often followed by the Great Answers. Not so here.

There are boundaries and choices. What if a young Foreign Service Officer (FSO) disagrees with a policy he or she is instructed to carry out? They may defend it anyway, remain passive and do mediocre work, lobby and argue against it within the Department of State, move to a different region or department, or resign. Where are the ethical boundaries for a Christian operating as a clandestine intelligence officer? There are no Great Answers to those kinds of questions, but they are fraught with questions of personal ethics. Normative ethics must at last become applied ethics. Principles may be asserted from the safety of a campus or pulpit, but Christians live by grace not law, by the leadership of the Holy Spirit as they journey with Scripture through the uncertainties, risks, and shadows of foreign affairs. So equipped the young person can bring his or her creative and ethical best to the issues at hand, to the machinations of organizational jockeying, and to their personal efforts to impact this nation and the world by being means of grace in the arena of power and self-interest.

This book has three goals. The first is to describe the institutions and the processes of foreign affairs, including diplomacy through the State Department, clandestine operations of the Central Intelligence Agency, the competition between national defense industries, and methods of impact through the U.S. House of Representatives. The second goal is to inspire young people to consider careers in foreign affairs, for we are living in an era of great challenge and threat, and the country needs to respond better than merely well. My third goal is to explore the issues of applied ethics that Christians will face if they take up a career serving their nation in such a capacity. In pursuing those three goals I hope to also give valuable insights on strategies for both professional and spiritual success. The biblical context for this book is life in Christ, or life in the Spirit as Paul portrays it in Romans 8, while the political context is our rapidly changing world, embodying a potential pivot point in the history of the United States.

I want to thank those who knowingly and unknowingly helped me understand and review these issues, who read drafts and suggested new ideas. They are many, inside government and out. Special thanks to Tom Bandy, Richard Buangan, Sarah Dunn, Cliff Fisher, Kent Hill, Will Inboden, Sterling McHale, Kenny Marchant, Elizabeth O'Casey, Cristen Renick, Don Spanninga, Robert Wang, and Rosco Williamson. Several classes and many students come together in this argument, as do colleagues, with a special thanks to Herb Prince and Reuben Welch. A special thanks also to my copyeditors, Jennifer Rogers and Susan Carlson Wood, for their work. Limitations or errors in this book are mine alone.

I want to thank the Wesleyan Center for 21st Century Studies for a research grant. I also want to thank the Churches' Center for Theology and Public Policy for accommodating me during an earlier sabbatical, and the provost, president, and trustees of Point Loma Nazarene University for that and a more recent reading sabbatical. Some of these issues were first explored at several of the biannual conferences of the Christians in Political Science organization, where my Wesleyan orientation was usually at variance with the more common Reformed tradition. I make no claim to speak for Wesleyans, but my approach to Scripture, theology, and ethics are certainly informed by that tradition.

I also need to note my privilege of knowing former President W. Shelburne Brown and acknowledge the profound impact of his life and work on me. In response to the leading of the Lord and against all odds and near universal criticism, including my own, he moved a college from a dying fate in Pasadena to a renewed and dynamic future in San Diego. Providential history intersected with institutional history, with risk, and with the trajectories of individual lives. What he received in return was terminal cancer. What I received was an appreciation of God's movement in history, the leadership of the Lord in the individual lives of his people, including my own decision whether or not I would join the venture in San Diego, an appreciation of the possibilities of renewal, and the knowledge that my analysis is not always right.

The Lord can work even in blind dates. I thank the Lord for my wife, Patti, and I thank her for her love and tolerance during another period of my preoccupation.

Introduction

The View from the Thirty-fourth Floor

IN THE SPRING OF 2006 I taught a course on rebuilding devastated states, and during that time a hundred men a day were discovered dead on trash heaps in Baghdad. Killing was horror enough, but to torture and throw the victims on a trash heap was far beyond the bounds of most inhumane and bloody insurrections and civil wars. Worse, it was a second-order consequence of our nation's action—its invasion of Iraq and destruction of the ruling party—that allowed the formerly repressed to extract both revenge and sectarian cleansing. Disturbed by such depravity, I seriously questioned why I was teaching in this field. Surely one could find other academic fields more conducive to a humane and thoughtful Christian.

Such depravity erupts from the kinds of dynamics of division, exclusion, hatred, and self-righteousness that are normally only latent in the more orderly forms of politics in this world. The ability to awaken, mobilize, and shape them into forces that tear at the normal operations of societies and create new political orders based on hatred of the United States represents but one threat to our nation's well-being. This country needs professionals working to rebuke, restrain, reconcile, channel, and ameliorate those dynamics to prevent them from becoming serious threats to our lives. It would have been wrong for me to turn my back on the field of international politics and foreign policy for a more friendly academic discipline. The people and the well-being of the world need Christians to engage those dynamics to make the world safer and more humane. At home the same is true. This country needs you for the same reasons. While career positions for engaging this world may seem beyond realistic reach from where you sit in the classroom, they are not. This book provides a Christian rationale and strategies for success for engaging this world.

As Director of the Institute of Politics on my campus I host an annual Insiders Seminar for political science students, featuring political staffers and lobbyists who share their insights on success strategies in political affairs. The seminar is conducted at San Diego's University Club, on the thirty-fourth floor of one of the city's high-rise buildings where one can see most of the city. At the beginning of the seminar I ask everyone to look out the floor-to-ceiling windows and see the city as a whole, its natural beauty, its constructed world, and the visible evidence of human systems of power and aspiration. "Why do I bring you here?" I ask as I point out the window. "There is your future, not the campus. Think beyond the campus and plan now for your involvement in the world."

I understand the reaction of many to this challenge: "That sounds like the third temptation of Jesus when Satan showed him all the nations of the world and tempted him to bow down!" In that and the other temptations Jesus struggled within himself over how to bring the kingdom of God to earth. The third was the temptation to use his power to achieve world fame and honor. It may also have been the temptation to use his power for moral ends on earth, to abolish the greed and exploitation and brutality on which the glories of nations rest. Jesus had the power to make that transformation; we do not. We have to work through political structures. True, nongovernmental organizations (NGOs) are an option, and an attractive one because students think they can do good in the world without getting their hands dirty in "politics." That is not true, however, for NGOs have to be political to raise funds, to deal with host governments, to compete with multiple other NGOs to be selected for operations, and to coordinate with them to avoid duplication. Moreover, they promise a career untainted by government bureaucracy. The good they do, however, is limited, more like Band Aids on festering problems than the structural benefits that government policies and programs can produce. So, for significant impact, one must engage the worlds of politics, government, and U.S. foreign policy.

From the thirty-fourth-floor window San Diego Bay is visible as well, home to three aircraft carriers, several nuclear submarines, and numerous other navy warships. This sight brings another pressing question to mind: "How does a Christian college talk about political morality in plain view of warships? The church is to stand against the powers of this world. It must be God's witness against the patterns of violence and domination."

The clash of arms during the two world wars and their four successors, fought in Korea, Vietnam, and twice in Iraq, all used brutality in service to the national self-interest. Despite this fact, however, the church ought not separate itself from the realities of foreign policy. The world and its victims deserve a more effective response than simply having the self-righteous throw verbal grenades in a passive role as "witness" to the world from the safety of their counterculture community. Christians ought to work for the shalom peace of reconciliation and goodness, but they ought to work for the non-war peace that ends killing and terror and genocide also. Christians need to engage the politically constructed world, not just God's world of nature and grace but also the world of human systems—the systems of wars, spies, duplicity, and domination. They need to engage the institutional systems of bureaucratic culture, the innovative systems of science and technology, and the academic systems of competition and achievement through national competitive scholarships.

Rejecting that witness-only criticism certainly places this book in the so-called modernist camp, with those who believe in the value of the Enlightenment's legacy of reason as opposed to dogma or blind fate or group-think, who believe in the values of observation, definition, and experimentation, and the values of liberal democracy and tolerance over social/religious authoritarianism. This book assumes Christians in the United States are inescapably members of two communities, the kingdom of God and the American national experience. While it assumes the existence of providential history, its basic thrust is at odds with escapist postures of both the eschatological theology that justifies pacifism and the resident alien (emphasis on alien) theology that justifies withdrawal into an authoritarian church community. It differs on the point of the importance of the individual in relation to the group. It also differs from those who believe a Christian theological framework or an alternative Christian "worldview" can be imposed on the history and politics of foreign policy.

It is as individuals that we find our salvation, our loves, and our careers, and decide which religious community we join, and each of those choices shapes, limits, and redefines us on our life's journey. This book addresses the exercise of foreign policy, that is, the personal and ethical issues facing the young person who enters an unmarked building to take the initial test for acceptance into the Central Intelligence Agency. He or she possibly just graduated from a Christian college with its many service groups, prayer and support meetings, chapel worship, and explication of doctrine. The campus community was warm and congruent with her part-time job as a waitress or his volunteer work with immigrants at the local International Rescue Committee. Although he had fallen in love with a fellow student and the relationship failed, or there was insincerity or cheating along the way, there was little else in their university experiences to prepare them for the moral and ethical challenges of serving their country in a period of high danger, in a career of high risk.

The experiential reality in which a foreign policy career takes place is far removed from community life on campus. Careers in foreign affairs engage friends, adversaries, and the dangerously menacing. Foreign policy is conducted within the interplay of the world as a community, and as a theater of duplicity, repression, and violent conflict. It is a world of transparency and shadows, a world of serving humans in need and a world of suspicion and risk. In this field a person of faith lives with the purpose of protecting and promoting the needs and interests of this nation, the victims of policy, and an elevated conception of humanity. Hopefully that can be done in cooperation with others to deepen congeniality in the world, but alone and in opposition to the groups and values of others if necessary. At the personal level, singleness of purpose is the definition of being holy. But for those choosing a career with a sworn loyalty to this country and its constitution, there is no singleness of purpose, no single-mindedness, but neither is there singleness after one has sworn love and loyalty to a spouse or heard one's child coo in the other room. One must be holy while living with multiple loyalties.

If the doctrine of the college student was one of dual morality, he or she might be able to compartmentalize personal faith and public service, though the moral boundaries in a purely public morality can become soft and a moving target. If the doctrine asserted that government is a delegated authority from God for justice he might be able to see himself doing God's will for the world. That is relatively easy for political policy within a nation with some degree of unity, functioning government, and enforcement of laws. But in the high-stakes rivalry and dangers of foreign policy between governments, in a fractured global system rather than within a domestic one, God's justice seems much more parochial and out of reach. A college ethos that promotes character ethics, derived from the authoritative training of young people in a campus culture that considers Christians to be resident aliens, is too anchored in opposition to modern life to bridge the gap to the values of national security policy.

The Christian life isn't simple. And so this book. Its topics go to the heart of the nature and ethical issues of foreign policy, including diplomacy, intelligence, defense, and legislative policy-making. This book is not about the macro issues of policy as policy, but about the micro worlds of pursuing careers in foreign policy. Running through the book is a concern for the ethical issues that are likely to confront a young person entering one of those worlds in the first decade of his or her career.

From the thirty-fourth floor we see a world of change, conflict, winners and losers, wealth supporting high-end shopping, not-so-hidden poverty, construction cranes of urban development, resentments over election returns, and purpose-driven power. These are but a small sample of the cultures, conflicts, and changes impacting foreign policy. And in the first decade of a career these will be joined with a young person's own ambitions, ethics, journey with the Scriptures, and responsiveness to the leading, strengthening, and character formation of the grace of God.

Two issues are not addressed in this book are pacifism and the ethics of serving in the military. Pacifism is a well-explored and argued topic in numerous other books. This book assumes there is religious legitimacy for coercion and duplicity. Similarly, a wealth of writing exists on Christians and the ethics involved in enlisting and serving in the armed forces. My concern is the middle range of issues between these two.

Theology, theory, and experience must converge. This book will attempt to join all three with core understandings and mediating concepts. A concept of grace will be developed as the mediating concept between theology and theory, derived from journeying with Scripture. From these can come a sense of self as a Christian and a public servant, and a set of applied ethics. In order to survive as a Christian in one of these careers, the life of the young man or woman has to be rooted in experience, reflection, and the Scriptures, grounded in the presence of God's grace, and lived out in moral actions that unite mind, body, and spirit. That is the definition of a full and fulfilling life!

The career may be very professional and marked by few ethical issues, or at times take place with the personal core strong but with shadows wherein ethical boundaries of the Sermon on the Mount have been stretched or blurred. Personal and professional needs may deviate from the sermons of pastors, and the sense of self may become stretched to accommodate the shadows as the personal core embraces contradictions. To do so may well become a self-justifying process. There must be clarity about the dangers, for political choices in a world of risk are neither politically easy nor morally simple. Moral absolutes can be too detached, and choosing the lesser-of-two-evils can be quite slippery. At times there are situations of murky morality and moral blind alleys where no choice is morally obvious or possible. Also, there are times when the choices between options carry second-order and third-order consequences where the percentages of good and bad are too nearly equal. Leaders' orders, actions of colleagues, misunderstood information, frustrations of your recommendations being rejected in favor of less favorable options—all these and many other scenarios contradict the oft-intoned prescriptions of purity, love, humility, and self-sacrifice. Where are the margins? What is the definition of national necessity? Where is the protection from the seduction of reversing sides? How long can masks be worn before the self is damaged?

The strong do what they will, Thucydides asserts, but Rousseau reminds us that the strong are never strong enough unless they turn strength into right. Moral values are necessary to give purpose to politics, a purpose focused on the good of the nation and its people and society. Given too much national identity, prominence, and scope, however, those values turn nations into exclusivist communities and sacred crusaders, rejecting all self-limits and cooperative measures and thereby endangering the rest of the globe. The world needs a morality that limits brutality in means, domination in goals, and duplicity in partnerships, and that provides a commitment to humane values and international cooperation. Situations of serious or lethal danger can unite and consolidate legitimacy, but they can also weaken the common moral commitments between nations. In both cases the world needs moral persons to pursue those goals and demonstrate the shape of a better world.

This is the world and the moral dialogue that Christians need to engage, being willing to face the moral challenges of defending their nation while building a better world. They accept the challenge out of commitments to their nation and their relationship with God through the Holy Spirit. They accept that such a living relationship can be exhilarating—sometimes a source of leadership for decisions and actions, sometimes the basis for the recognition and faith that "things worked together" to reach a high point. Sometimes that relationship is the anchor against the storm breaking around us.

The basic assumptions of *Embraced and Engaged* are that Christians need not confine themselves to nongovernmental organizations and their limited measures to be "pure." Rather, the theme of this book is that Christians can fully engage this world through governmental and political means with impact while living "in Christ" and embraced by his grace. Based on that assumption, and the risks and dangers of this world, this book seeks to inspire young people to consider careers in foreign affairs.

We are born into this world at this time and place, a nation of reason, liberty, and equality in a world of power, paradox, and fate. Chapter 1 explores several theoretical approaches to understanding that world and the international/historical context in which we live, and the values of art, science, hope, and fear, the temptations of a Promethean policy, and the need for renewal as a nation and as a new generation.

Chapter 2 explores stories from Scripture and offers a theological model of the work of grace in our individual lives and in the elements of foreign policy, then tests that model against the outbreak of World War I and the avoidance of war in the Cuban Missile Crisis. From that model the chapter offers a framework for applied ethics.

The next chapters leave those theoretical worlds for the more personal realities of institutions and operations. Chapter 3 examines the professional world of diplomacy. If war is the continuation of politics by other means, then the policy and personal stakes of diplomacy carry the highest of stakes. The chapter explores the operations of diplomacy, roles of grace in diplomacy, and the challenges and choices for a person who comes into deep disagreement with established policy.

The risks involved in foreign policy require leaders to have a clear understanding of the policies, motivations, and capabilities of other nations and be able to detect and deter the chain of events that lead to attacks on this country and elsewhere. Such information is rarely displayed openly, so the United States must uncover the secrets of other nations and groups. Chapter 4 considers the role of clandestine officers involving means that require living a Christian life at the margins of morality.

Should information shortage and diplomatic maneuver fail, the nation will rely on its military for protection, however broadly defined. The common statement that the military prepares to fight the last war cannot be permitted in this age of fourth-generation wars. Chapter 5 considers the need and shape of a new defense framework, and the moral issues of risk and consequences facing those working within the defense industry as engineers or lobbyists.

While foreign and military policies are the prerogatives of the executive branch, both depend on the funding and legislative authorizations of Congress. Politics is another world within which Christians may impact foreign policy, and chapter 6 describes the electoral and legislative processes of the House of Representatives and the moral issues of multiple loyalties.

The book leaves the issues that will arise in the future and concludes with a chapter much more personal with immediate relevance to students. Chapter 7 questions the relevance of the commitment of Christian colleges and universities to the values of the now popular "servant leadership" model of a Christian life as a foundation for engagement and leadership in the worlds of foreign affairs. It suggests instead the commitment to public service for engagement, and a Rhodes Ideal as a model for achieving one's personal best. As part of that discussion the chapter describes the value of national scholarships relating to foreign affairs, advice on preparing applications for them, and the ethics of elitist scholarships.

There is a master theme to this book, and it is the Christian life well lived in grace and dilemma, in reason and competition, in humility and penitence, in ambition and impact, in loyalty and fulfillment.

1

War and Renewal

> These policy intellectuals ... once in high office, keen to carve out new policies—started to tout and embrace the ideas as if they were elixirs, not merely useful tools. They grew entranced by the new kinds of power—the new kind of world—that these ideas might bring into being. The ideas morphed into a vision, the vision into a dream. After September 9/11, they took their dream into the real world—acted it with open eyes—and saw it dissolve into a nightmare.[1]

THE UNITED STATES IS at war, and the continuing risks that confront this nation are evolving faster than our responses. This war is not just the military wars in Iraq and Afghanistan, but also a war with the future, a war with the movement of history, and a war of America with itself. This is a moment of urgency, a time pregnant with divergent outcomes, only some of them good. It is a political, diplomatic, and clandestine war of freedom against fate, progress against decline.

To say it another way, America faces a crucial turning point in its place in the world, with severe consequences for making wrong decisions. A sudden and deep economic recession destroyed wealth and limited the nation's options as war in Iraq and Afghanistan stretched the military to the breaking point. Serious national rivals are moving to displace American influence in Asia, Africa, and the Middle East. North Korea may sell nuclear weapons technology to other nations and perhaps terrorist groups, and terrorist and drug groups pose a threat not prepared for in our military doctrine and forces. Religious sanction for suicide bombers makes the proliferation of nuclear weapons even more serious than the nuclear threat from the former Soviet Union. Secretary of Defense Robert

---

1. Kaplan, *Daydream Believers*, 5.

Gates said weapons development in North Korea is "a harbinger of a dark future."[2] This is a serious point in our history, and our foreign policy requires serious people, policies, and actions, not daydream believers. This is our time, and we must respond to the challenge and shape our future.

David Boren, former governor, U.S. senator, and now president of the University of Oklahoma, relates his experience of asking applicants for the Rhodes Scholarship, "How long do you think the United States will be the world's leading superpower?" The students all fumbled through an answer, having never thought about the loss of the nation's stature nor focused on the things that will determine our future.[3] Whatever should be the appropriate policies to answer Boren's question, those who choose to become involved in the policies will confront ethical issues that arise from the realities of international politics and history as well as their own assumptions about those realities.

Foreign policy is a human endeavor. Larger forces are in play and constrain the scope of action and offer opportunities for those human endeavors. Consequences and responses by leaders in other countries are not always understood, and unexpected turns of events are not rare, from 9/11 to the protest reactions to the disputed election in Iran. The margin of freedom varies over time and issue. Still, it is people who act, and do so in the service of others through their commitment to the nation, which can create ethical dilemmas.

Those larger forces will be explored through four theoretical approaches to understand the world of international politics and some of the ethical issues they imply. A theory of international politics is an attempt to provide definitions, categories of actions, ends and means linkages, and a systematic exercise in marshalling data. Given those, a theory then asserts explanations of the past, understanding of the present, and expectations of the future, hopefully to guide policy and action. Academics and policy makers, however, live in different worlds, and frustrate each other. Policy makers react to events on the basis of their own beliefs, however general or detailed, the pressures of time and unfolding events, and whatever policy programs and action are available and practical to use. We need a theory to bridge the gap between the theorists and practitioners. No one theory is likely to explain everything—that would be too much like

---

2. Quoted in Jakes and Joshi, "Gates: North Korea Nuke Progress Sign of 'Dark Future.'"

3. Boren, *A Letter to America*, 4–5.

an ideology. What we shall seek is to find a "hard core" of a theory, that is, a central and fundamental view of how international politics works, to which other lesser theories relate. The series of concentric circles of theories and evidence out from the hard core increases the scope of the hard core, giving a working theory for understanding and policy.[4]

Historical events and lessons can also provide auxiliary data to validate and expand the hard core, or reshape it, or invalidate it. The historical material on the outbreak of World War I and the subsequent efforts to reconstruct the world in the peace conference of 1919 are full of potential lessons. We begin with the diplomats of that crucial July of 1914, then visit Winston Churchill's understanding of the coming of the war, and then Woodrow Wilson's vision of global reform.

THE DIPLOMATS OF JULY

With only two exceptions, Europe had been at peace for nearly a hundred years since the defeat of Napoleon in 1815 and the restructuring of the system at the Congress of Vienna and the creation of the Concert of Europe. The rules of war were codified in the Hague Peace Conferences of 1899 and 1907, assuring that future wars would be fought "fairly" and prisoners and civilians protected. Industrialization brought economic growth and international trade ties between nations. War seemed like an illusion.

War was not an illusion. Germany was born as a unified nation in the Franco-Prussian War of 1870. Having achieved his goal with his war, Bismarck, its architect, now needed to avoid a war launched by someone else. He needed a Germany that was moderate, that would not provoke fear and a new continental arms race and security dilemma. The mere presence of such a dynamic nation directly affected the geopolitical calculations of the other nations, particularly in stimulating closer relations between France and Russia. Of primary importance was the fact that France did not accept the loss of territory to Germany in 1870, and an enduring rivalry developed that could well break out into a war between them. Germany was surrounded: France to the south, Austria-Hungary to the East, and Russia in the north.

---

4. This approach is based on the methodology of Imre Lakatos. For its particular relevance to international politics, see Elman and Elman, "How Not to Be Lakatos Intolerant," 231–62.

Strategically, Bismarck needed to avoid any combination among those three that would confront Germany with a two-front war, and his goal was to insure Russia and Austria-Hungary would be allies and not join France, which he achieved in the Three Emperors League. Bismarck was fired in 1880, and Russia withdrew from the League. Imperial Germany launched a massive naval arms race with England by constructing ever-larger battleships, moving from the sixth-ranked navy to the second by 1914. Russia's pragmatism was undercut by its support of the Slavic peoples against Austria-Hungary in the Balkans, a domestic social value more important than a pragmatic alliance with Germany. Russia made a secret alliance with Serbia, and, more ominously, with France. Bismarck's fear now came to pass as Russia and France lined up against Germany and Austria-Hungary. The alliance system of Great Powers established basic parity among them and polarized the structure of diplomacy. To complicate matters, there were at least five rivalries in the neighborhood, and key nations and empires were experiencing growth or decline, all creating the insecurities for statesmen that arise in such situations. Decisions that seemed rational were about to turn out to be gambles, for the interactions they created caused unforeseen consequences.

Southeastern Europe was troubled in 1914. Austria, a partner in the dual alliance of the Austro-Hungarian Empire, annexed Bosnia, leaving Serbian leaders incensed. Russian leaders, having been humiliated by Japan in 1905, took a renewed interest in the Balkans. The assassination of Austria-Hungary's Archduke Ferdinand in Sarajevo provoked an ultimatum for capitulation by Serbia. The leaders of Austria-Hungary thought a *fait accompli* against Serbia would be accepted by other nations. Other leaders rejected that and thought a local war was acceptable to save Serbia, and maybe even a regional war between Austria-Hungary and Russia. No one wanted a continental war, and a world war was completely unacceptable.[5]

One of the key gamblers at the center of events was Dr. von Bethmann-Hollweg. As chancellor of Germany, Bethmann had to make serious strategic calculations. He dutifully confirmed his kaiser's agreement on July 5 to support Austria-Hungary if they attacked Serbia. He assumed Austria-Hungary would strike before Russia could mobilize,

---

5. The following is taken from a variety of sources, including Remak, *The Origins of World War I*, 97–128; Thomson, *The Twelve Days*, 99–102; and Lafore, *The Long Fuse*, 210–62.

but he was wrong. He faced the dilemma that Germany needed its alliance with Austria-Hungary, but the latter always acted like they were pushed into activities if Germany supported them, and if Germany urged restraint, they were accused of abandoning their ally. Worse, if Germany did not support them now, he argued, they might look elsewhere and that might weaken Germany's alliance with them. No discussions were held on what price a policy of support of Austria-Hungary would require, or what the costs would be if they failed to reach their goal.[6]

Despite reports proving Serbian officials were not involved in the assassination, Austria-Hungary wanted the war and moved to the argument that the assassination was just another provocation to the empire that had to be stopped. Peace needed occupation. Serbia agreed to nearly all the demands of the ultimatum, but Austria-Hungary broke relations anyway as a step to war.

When Sir Edmund Grey of England proposed a Four Power conference, Bethmann refused to attend, did not tell his boss the kaiser, and refused to send the proposal to Austria-Hungary. He wanted to support his ally in what he expected to be a quick and cheap little war and feared the kaiser might agree to a deal if he attended a Four Power conference. He was also receiving information that Russia would not fight and that England was unlikely to fight because of the strong pacifist influences in the British cabinet.

Events depended on Russia's good judgment not to mobilize its military and threaten Germany. If Germany responded, France would have to respond. They all did. Common borders and alliances quickly diffused the war throughout Europe and then around the world, and magnified the magnitude of the war. Bethmann had bad intelligence about Russia and England, was mistaken about the nature of the coming war, and was completely wrong about his ability to contain it to a small regional war. The casualty rate was high—9,000,000 people killed, three empires gone, terrible dislocation and despair, and assumptions about rationality severely weakened. The generation after the war is sometimes called the "lost generation."

---

6. New documents from the former East Germany are leading some historians to claim that Germany was not caught off-guard but had definite war aims. See Lieber, "The New History of World War I," 155–91, and the resulting correspondence by Snyder and Lieber, "Defensive Realism and the 'New' History of World War I."

Winston Churchill's history of the First World War is less well known than his history of the Second, but is just as insightful and erudite. It glimpses what was to come as he attempted to answer who was to blame for the failure to control events. "There are no simple answers," the historian and participant wrote. Contributing to the failure were the "limited minds of even the ablest men," as well as the pressures of public opinion and governmental "wheels within wheels." The historical problem was so vast in scale and detail that it escaped their control; events shaped a certain line that soon could not be derailed; and the leaders "lived simultaneously in two different worlds," the actual visible world and "a world of monstrous shadows moving in convulsive combinations through vistas of fathomless catastrophe."[7] With a shortage of control over events all were caught in a terrible fate.

Could a similar fate in the future be avoided by reforming the processes of world politics? The United States did not stay isolated; it intervened late in the war and threw the balance to the allies. When the war was over, President Woodrow Wilson was determined to reform world politics and end the machinations of imperial, dynastic, and aristocratic rule. He believed structural problems allowed these shadow movements and inscrutable decision-making processes, particularly the restlessness caused by empires, secret treaties, back-door diplomacy, and international odds that promoted risk taking. The peace conference in Paris lasted from January to July in 1919, and Wilson worked in Paris to make changes, represented by his Fourteen Points.

Those fourteen points were revolutionary, based on the assumptions that people are reasonable and peaceful. Three empires were gone—Germany, Austro-Hungarian, and the Ottoman—and replaced with the revolutionary ideas of national self-determination. Repressed people rebel; thus comes war. Now there would be a just world order with a right regard for the aspirations of people. Outside Europe the imperial control of peoples would be replaced by the protection of the League, which would assign the colonies "in trust" to one or another great power, justified and overseen by the League's mandate system to prepare those peoples for nationhood and independence. Imperial power would be replaced by responsibility. All diplomacy (after Paris) had to be open so people would know what their leaders were committing their nations to; governments were to be republican in form so people could prevent their

---

7. Churchill, *The World Crisis*, 6, 14.

leaders from undertaking an unpopular war; and a League of Nations was formed that would create a collective security system to remove all odds that a threatening aspiring power could launch a war of aggression with minor opposition.

When a nation's ambitions erode its self-restraint, external disincentives or collective restraints must be applied. The League and the general Wilsonian reform effort were based on the assumption of a common interest among nations that, when identified and mobilized, could provide incentives for cooperation. He was not seeking the realization in politics of a common humanity but an international commonwealth among the nations where agreements on rules and responsibilities allowed the establishment of a regulatory mechanism to help independent states (not colonies) settle differences and avoid a new war.

The vision Wilson brought to Paris had neither support nor details for application. Europe was in ruins and so was optimism for the future. Wilson was hailed as a savior by the people in Europe, but France wanted Germany weakened, reparations for the cost of the war, and guarantees of future protection. Great Britain wanted the German navy neutralized and control over enough of the former Ottoman lands to protect the Suez Canal. While Britain and France divided up the Middle East, the Emir Feisal was at the conference to minimize their grip on the region. Japan sent a delegation to protect the islands it gained from Russia and China, with instructions to oppose the League unless it contained a racial equality clause. There were military issues to decide, the construction of a Balkanized Eastern Europe from the ruins of the Austro-Hungarian Empire and a Poland from Germany, the reconstruction of the Middle East, and more. Wilson refused to detail how his Fourteen Points would be implemented, and they were quickly recast in a common interpretation that robbed them of most of their content.[8]

The plenary session of the peace conference was far too large for any decision making, so a Council of Ten emerged to try to speed up proceedings. When that did not work, it was replaced by the now-famous Council of Four. During the proceedings Wilson returned home to find demands for the protection of America's sphere of influence called the Monroe Doctrine, a clear violation of his Covenant of the League of Nations. The

---

8. There are numerous memoirs and commentaries from the participants. Two recent histories include the prize-winning Macmillan, *Paris 1919*, and Mee, *The End of Order: Versailles 1919*.

Republican Party had taken control of Congress, and the European leaders read American politics well and knew they faced a weakened Wilson.

In the end, Wilson received agreement from the conference for his League of Nations, but not the reformation of world politics. Despite Wilson's efforts, both the allies in Europe and opponents in Congress refused to implement such revolutionary ideas. The allies took their revenge on Germany, traded territories and colonies among themselves, and made the mandate system a sham. Congress refused to allow the United States to join the League of Nations, a victory for isolationists over the internationalists and a political strategy designed for the next presidential election. Wilson became a prophet without honor because his vision was irrelevant, devised as it was in a nation without understanding of the stakes of foreign policy for nations bordering each other or for nations without vast resources. Could it have been made relevant? Perhaps, but for his ideas to find traction and for the diplomats of Paris to make a transition from the Westphalian System to a Covenant System, the prophet needed to become a serious and skilled diplomat abroad and party leader at home. He failed at both.

Despite the absence of the United States, international law was expanded, conflict resolution procedures brought from labor-management relations into the global world, a Permanent Court of International Justice was set up to settle disputes judiciously, and an arbitration system was set up to settle disputes not taken to court. Reasoned discussion would bring all issues into the open, discourage bullying, and develop consensus on what was right and just in any issue. All depended on a national commitment to the common interest over the national interest. During the decade of the 1930s when Japan attacked Manchuria and Germany attacked Poland, the nations acted on their own self-interest rather than the common interest.

In the second and third decades of the twenty-first century the United States still needs a foreign and national security policy that is ethical and effective in meeting the current crisis. Russia is rebuilding its military and its dictatorship; Iran has hegemonic designs on the Middle East; China will emerge as the dominant power in the Far East and perhaps the world; and Pakistan, while a crucial ally to the U.S., is also a fearful nuclear neighbor to India and the home of Islamic radicals, reactionaries, coups, assassinations, and executions. These are issues of power, historical movement, and surprises. The signposts of *realpolitik* are inescapable, and Hans Morgenthau developed the theory and policy direction of a power-politics approach.

HANS MORGENTHAU AND THE SISYPHEAN WORLD ORDER

Except for Wilson, the diplomacy of 1914 and 1919 had much in common with the theory of realism developed by Hans Morgenthau, who became the "father" of the field of international politics with his 1948 seminal book *Politics among Nations*. Morgenthau wanted to move beyond the interesting quotations and personal insights of historians to a more systematic approach to thinking. The key was to define and link the core concepts of power, national interest, and balance of power. He broke with the earlier texts that were merely descriptive of current conditions and/or were normative-oriented in calling for reform.

Churchill was forty years old at the outbreak of World War I and understood empires, while Morgenthau was only ten years old and came of age during the collapse of the Wilsonian efforts to reform global politics. Nations cheated on the arms control treaties; the League of Nations failed in the Far East and Europe; and Morgenthau fled to the United States in 1937 as he saw the Nazis turn German civilization into an anti-intellectual, ethnically exclusivist, and predatory nation.

Morgenthau's views accepted the reality of the Westphalian System, named for the Treaty of Westphalia that ended the Thirty Years War and provided the final death to the imperial world orders of Rome and its successors. Power in the emergent system was decentralized into individual states, given free play for states claiming sovereignty or the absence of accountability to any other nation or order. They are free to be and do as they choose in their internal and external affairs. Much has changed since the system's emergence as nations created international laws and organizations to increase rationality, reduce uncertainty, and promote co-operation. Still, however, the basic structure remains: power is central to relationships, nations must agree to collective restraints, and so the only real restraint on nations is self-restraint.

Morgenthau wanted to save the world from the kind of European nationalism that the Nazis took to extreme and to persuade the World War II leaders not to repeat the mistakes of the Wilsonians who tried to build a new international structure of peace on flimsy rationalistic grounds. In a classic statement Morgenthau wrote, "International politics, like all politics, is a struggle for power." It was a continuation of the argument he began two years earlier with his *Scientific Man Versus Power Politics*, in which he argued that the rationality of the scientific world was misplaced in politics. "Politics is an art and not a science," he wrote, "and what is required for its mastery is not the rationality of the engineer but the wisdom and the moral strength of the statesman."[9] Morgenthau was neither glorifying nor extolling power; power is a reality, and self-restraint and goodwill are insufficient to resist those nations and leaders utilizing power to achieve their goals at the expense of others. The task of foreign policy is the art of realistically and prudently using power to make allies and block adversaries. It is also the art of having a correct definition of the national interest and skillful assessment of how to protect and defend it. Realism for Morgenthau is both a theory and a practice; ethics is both normative for the nation and applied for the practitioner.

Nations and power are central to foreign policy, and whatever their size and culture, Morgenthau argued, all nations have individual interests that define their safety and independence, and these exist regardless of the opinion of publics and ideologies of rulers. Four levels of national interest exist: survival, vital, major, and peripheral. The distinction between vital and major interest is crucial, for it defines the line that separates the interests over which a nation will go to war (vital) as distinct from those interests that are of major importance but not sufficiently important to fight to achieve. That is an important line of differentiation. A terrible waste of blood and treasure follows from confusing the two.

Morgenthau was a strong critic of the architects of the war in Vietnam because of their artless and imprudent moralism for freedom and democracy, which was more peripheral than vital, and their refusal to accept the fact that different communist countries had different national interests, so all their actions did not constitute threats to our vital interests. That confusion was only made worse by using intelligence to provide justifying facts to support the policy rather than inform and assess policy.[10] The art of politics was lost in bad knowledge and lack of restraint.

Differences in power provide great powers with opportunities, temptations, and insensitivity. Nations too small or weak to resist the strong alone must seek protection by banding together with other nations to form

9. Morgenthau, *Politics among Nations*, 27, and *Scientific Man Versus Power Politics*, 10.

10. Morgenthau, "We Are Deluding Ourselves in Vietnam."

a balance of power. Even strong powers will find the need for partners in a growing crisis to deter the growth and designs of another strong power. Though Morgenthau was never clear whether balance meant equal power or overbalance, the essence of the two concepts of national interest and power is that nations will recognize a rising threat and band together to protect themselves and the global system of freedom.

In this *realpolitik* world, the national interest precedes the common interest, order precedes justice, power precedes cooperation, prudence precedes gambles, and skilled statesmen are necessary to make the most logical decisions. Realism demands that a nation calculate its safety in terms of power, and be willing to partner with whatever nation is necessary at the time to counterbalance dangerous shifts in relative power. Nations are never permanent friends or enemies, and the real dangers are permanent alliances that polarize and rigidify the system.

Realists, given the necessity for coldly calculating interest and power, insist on professional diplomats, professionals with the art and skill of diplomacy. Bismarck was the professional who understood geo-strategy, but he was replaced with an amateur who lacked the finesse to artfully guard Germany's national interest and was outmaneuvered by the French and Russians. There is also the naiveté of the uninformed public. Politicians in a democracy pursue the local and short-term interests of their constituents, the basis of their reelection. Given that, can a democracy pursue an effective policy for the good of the nation, or the collective good of the globe? George Kennan wrote in his study of World War I that democratic nations are like dinosaurs, which frolic in the primeval mud unaware of any danger until they get whacked in the head; then they thrash around in anger, destroying everything around them. Kennan lays out what the nations should have done in the years prior to 1914, but admits the people would never have agreed to such exertions, and concludes by saying that we need to recognize the limitation of a democracy operating in the reality of world politics.[11]

Even the policies of Kennan would not have ended the dangers of war in Europe, merely avoided them in 1914, to be readdressed later when power shifted further and new disputes expanded to crises. The theory of realism has much in common with the myth of Sisyphus; diplomacy is a constant struggle for peace, never finally achieved. Always the stone

---

11. Kennan, *American Diplomacy 1900–1950*, 62–65.

of peace has to be moved up the mountain, only to fall back and require another generation's effort in diplomacy.

This theory of realism is not an immoral jungle. Morality is important for Morgenthau, but it is the morality of statecraft—prudence, not moral betterment. He begins with the duality of human nature, its humane and normative aspects, and its sinfulness, selfishness, and quest for power. Statesmen seek moral goals of a better world, but any refusal to take sinfulness into account leads to moral optimism or to crusades. The "long road from Versailles to Pearl Harbor," he wrote, is "cluttered with the whitened bones on crusades that failed."[12]

That dual nature is a moral dilemma for Morgenthau—no social action can be completely free of egotism. "For man's aspiration for power over other men, which is the very essence of politics, implies a denial of the very core of Judeo-Christian morality—respect for man as an end in himself."[13] The other duality concerns loyalty to one religious beliefs and to the nation, for the nation can never be the highest moral goal; even in wars the conflict is fought for some higher purpose.

We are left then with merely prudence. Caution will preclude undertaking significant efforts to reform world politics through such goals as development or human rights, and also precludes any concern about any reforms in the domestic structure of the nation. We are also left with an overly stylized vision of world politics. Morgenthau conceives of nations as essentially "black boxes" or billiard balls that must deal with foreign policy issues on strategic grounds. Power issues are central and domestic issues are not. Crusades for democracy or domestic reactions like "no more Vietnams" cannot be allowed, or else the nation will not be able to respond correctly to the foreign policy challenges. Morgenthau also sees nations as basically alike, with no recognition of failed states and internal insurgencies, no consideration of internal stability for a nation ruled by an autocratic religious regime of old men with old ideas while half of its population is under twenty-five years of age and chafing under repressive conditions.

Any participant in foreign affairs must accept the factor of national self-interest and the absolute necessity for success in managing survival and vital interests. While the leaders and workers of General Motors or Chrysler may preside over the loss of market share and the growing insolvency of their firms, and accept bankruptcy or merger with a foreign firm,

---

12. Lefever, *Ethics and United States Foreign Policy*, 18.
13. Morgenthau, Introduction, xvi.

those are not options for foreign policy officials. Any short-term losses have to be isolated and offset by long-term gains.

The role of power in world politics also has to be accepted and supported as a central factor in protecting and promoting national interests. So long as one serves the United States and its global role rather than a global stature and role like those of Switzerland or Canada, threat and coercion will always be policy options. Power always magnifies the ever-present factor of risk in the interplay of nations, so ethical issues will always arise in strategic calculations. Prudence is wise and important, but it is not the same as risk-aversion or doing no more than the minimum. Moral goals are crucial to a nation's self identity and its domestic legitimacy, but those goals must be restrained to avoid becoming ideological. Morgenthau reminds us that reaching for some exalted moral goals may involve risks far beyond the power of the nation; following the example of the banking firm of Morgan Stanley into deep commitments to risky loans for the sake of easy profits and then collapsing as a firm is not an option for the United States.

Realism may be appropriate for survival and vital interests, but the work of diplomats also takes place on lower-level issues where nations can compromise, can go along with the consensus, can restrain themselves from a preferred policy, and can make agreements that involve domestic costs but achieve a larger national or global goal. That expanded or generous attitude can only take place when vital interests are not at stake, for when humane interests conflict with national self-interest, the latter prevails.

The ethics, like the art, of foreign policy take place in a global system that resembles a web; action to one nation has implications for many others. Other nations look to their own national interest and reputation and will not allow themselves to be dragged into damaging political activity. Policies must be accepted or at least tolerated by those allies, and their reaction may be based as much on the attitude of U.S. officials as on the policy itself. There needs to be a moral consensus within that web to hold it together.

THE SCIENCE OF WAR AND PEACE

Churchill saw limited minds, public pressure, "wheel within wheels" in government, and two worlds, one visible and the other a shadow world. If this view of the diplomats of 1914 is correct, then the realism of Morgenthau is inadequate to preserve peace. The signpost of national interest is too often misread and the resort to force too frequent. The major nations were pursuing policies of national interest, power, and balance of power up to the year of 1914, and the policy did not prevent a war but actually made it worse and nearly destroyed all of them. Realism may work for a while, but when it fails, too much is destroyed.

Given the world that will likely emerge by 2025, war and peace are too important for diplomacy to be considered an art alone; despite the views of Morgenthau, diplomacy needs a deeper rationality. It needs a foundation of science. The interests of the United States cannot be confined to the individual views of whoever happens to be president, or to the floating majorities in Congress; it needs the continuity of a more rationally scientific foundation.

Empirical scholars have carried out statistical studies and findings from databases covering a much larger time span to produce verifiable probabilistic laws describing empirical regularities in war and peace. Such studies require precise definitions, like the definition of war itself. No such precision exists for the national interest. The goal is to discover understandings about which policies under particular sets of conditions are more or least likely to culminate in crisis and war, and with that information alert decision makers and try to blunt the velocity of an impending crisis. Moreover, such information can help overcome negative factors such as bureaucratic inertia and a narrow-minded sense of control of history.

The central database for this empirical foundation of studies of war and alliance events has been the Correlates of War Project (COW). The project initially identified all the wars between 1815 and 1965 and later extended to 1992. The population and armed forces of each participant was identified and entered, along with their length of time in the international system and which nation initiated the conflict. The conflicts themselves were studied in terms of when and where the war was fought, number of deaths, and outcome. This project was developed by J. David Singer and Melvin Small as an empirical database for systematic observation and empirical analysis of war with replicable analytical procedures. Singer came of age during World War II and the nuclear age, and for him war can no longer be considered merely a tool of diplomatic policy or the result of bad logic and gambles; the hope of the COW project was to find the knowledge base to discover danger points and so avoid the self-defeating actions that lead to war.

From the COW database we know that some nations are war prone. There were 144 nations between 1815 and 1965, and a frequency distribution shows that one nation, France, was involved in 12 wars, and Italy and the Ottoman Empire/Turkey were involved in eleven. Seventy-seven nations were involved in no wars, 25 in one war, and 23 in two wars. Clearly war is not evenly distributed among the nations, and global politics are not the anarchy the realists assume. War has been common in Europe but not in Latin America, the highest percentage of wars have been initiated by large developing nations, and there is some correlations between war and a highly centralized executive, and high levels of militarization, and the number of alliances.

We also know wars can be contagious in the neighborhood, spreading to nations not involved in the initial conflict. That was certainly true in 1914 and in Southeast Asia in the 1970s. Besides contagion is contiguity. The rate that war breaks out between contiguous states is 35 times higher than for noncontiguous states. Other factors are also important, but when combined with contiguity, the territory of the nations is at risk and so issues take on vital and survival status. Other factors may be underlying causes, but contiguity is the sufficient cause.[14]

The fact that both Pakistan and India have nuclear weapons should make this probability an extremely high concern for the United States, which needs both as allies. The data also demonstrates that alliances do not deter war, but instead, by including more nations, they make the war more severe, with 1914 being a prime example.[15]

The studies were advanced and refined by many other scholars. Stuart Bremer and Thomas Cusack study the cases of deep crises short of war. They emphasize the coming of war as a process in which the sequence of events and choices are important. Bremer's process model actually involves several external interaction transitions. One nation may see the issues of a dispute as a vital interest and invoke or threaten the use of force, becoming what is called Militarized Interstate Dispute (MID). Only 5 percent of those MIDs reach the point of conflict—a relief to know. If several of those MIDs occur within the span of ten or twelve years the pattern is called an enduring rivalry. War is not foreordained but dependent upon the sequence of choices and interactions. There are multiple

14. Vasquez, *The War Puzzle*, 127.
15. Bremer and Cusack, *The Process of War*, 13–14.

paths to war, and the history of choices can produce an erratic and weakly patterned sequence of events.

The studies document that long periods of hierarchy exist between major wars and that the presence of preponderance reduces the likelihood of war while power parity is associated with war. Within rivalries the presence of a power transition among the nations increases the probability of war by more than 21 percent. Wars may occur prior to one nation overtaking another, or afterwards, but the probability of war is higher prior to and less severe on that upward slope, while wars on the downside are less probable but more severe.[16]

It is like the crossing of two S curves, one S reflecting the growth in power of an aspiring nation and a reverse S reflecting the decline of a global nation. At those two ends of a period of peace, realism becomes prominent, and if diplomacy is inadequate to manage the transition, war can occur. Iran, China, and India are on an upswing, and the United States must not move into a reverse S curve.

The importance of understanding the probabilities that flow from structures of power and dispute is clear, but so is the importance of time and process. There is movement in power, status, and reputation over time as events and consequences occur continually. Nations that do not react to events affecting them or to a growing contagion of events find that time has been lost and a time of troubles is upon them. With populations highly politicized and communications instant, a global nation must maintain a full-time scan of the events horizon.

The coming of war is a process, and John Vasquez used the data to develop a Steps to War process model, which identifies the seven steps to war.

- Step 1: Making a Dispute. An issue becomes a dispute when one nation assigns it a new level of priority.
- Step 2: Strategic Diplomacy. Nations harden their positions and take actions that aggravate tensions.
- Step 3: Expansion. Leaders mobilize their domestic public and bureaucracies with "rally 'round the flag" efforts to support their policies. In the midst of a crisis the leaders interpret events on the basis of what they believe to be the lessons of history, and most policy

---

16. See Kugler and Lemke, "The Power Transition Research Program," 128–63.

advocates derive their views from their reading of what policy was successful in the past.

- Step 4: Making a Crisis. The nations now seek alliance partners and enter an arms race, and the theory of realism locks them into intensifying actions that make further steps hard to resist. The evidence does not support the view that arms races cause war; enduring rivalries lead to war whether or not there was a preceding arms race. Arms races recognize a reality clearly revealed in Spain in 1936: if one side builds up forces and the other freezes theirs, the latter loses when conflict comes.
- Step 5: Crisis Diplomacy. At this point there may be a shift (election, coup) to hard-liners in the government who employ bullying tactics and simplistic demands abroad. At home they develop policy "stabilizers" in the form of media "spin" and appointment of lower-level officials who support their views. This internal political dynamic emerges as a crucial element in the move toward or away from war. Now the leaders make the final decision on whether this issue is a major or a vital interest. If they choose the latter, the crisis moves to step 6.
- Step 6: Militarized Dispute. One or both nations introduce the threat or limited use of force, crossing a threshold from which it is difficult both internally and externally to back away. Now the margin of freedom to step back is severely reduced.
- Step 7: Crisis Management. War is now likely as two or more crisis events occur, causing crisis escalation. If neither side wants war, their crisis-management leadership teams may dampen fears and find an exit option. If one or both sides want the war, it will usually occur during the third crisis.

The factors of time, process, and probabilities are important dynamics, and the rhetoric of policy disputes and the politics of leadership selection make the content and boundaries of ethical issues more complex to understand. Steps 2 and 4 and 5 are crucial points for both the leaders and the public. These scientific findings were well known in 2003, but the rhetoric of the 2000 election masked the nature of the foreign policy administration that would be brought to power.

The Persian Gulf War of 1991 succeeded in reversing the innate aggressiveness and threat of Saddam Hussein but left him in power. The resulting Militarized International Dispute lingered without resolution during the Clinton years, and then a Step 5 occurred with the election of the George W. Bush administration and his team of hard-liners who claimed Iraq had weapons of mass destruction that threatened peace and who led the development of stabilizers in the foreign policy establishment and in Congress. The 9/11 attacks telescoped time and sped up the process to Step 6 and a "rally 'round the flag" effort in the public. Our best human and technological intelligence were unable to prove a negative (that there were no weapons of mass destruction) in the face of Hussein's calculated dissembling over whether such weapons existed.

This empirical study of war also assumes the philosophical stance of a reality apart from inherent ethics and values. Facts and values are separate worlds, so commentators and leaders add their values to the factual realities and the correlates and probabilities of war. The study may be value-free, but the purpose of the studies has a clear value, which is preventing war by finding the empirical realities that can inform policy analysis. The scientist has an ethical obligation to use his or her scientific studies to reveal the correlates and probabilities as time and process produce the events that become a moving history with risks and consequences.

The optimism for the diplomatic rewards of a science of war has yet to be validated. In fact, the failure of war avoidance lends a degree of fatality to the history of war, and the traditional historical study of concrete cases leaves one with the impression that none of them were necessary. Despite his faith in empirical studies, Daniel Geller, another scholar who works with empirical studies of war, also points out that while academic theories remind us that whatever the external "givens" of structure and issues and interests, there is the human element. Academic theories and the empirical studies may be informative and helpful, but the human factor makes the last and decisive step to war indeterminate.[17] When the professionals like Bismarck are dismissed or disregarded, decisions are made without understanding that those decisions can create a momentum which then pushes decision makers into events they did not want and which they no longer control.

THE REACH FOR TRANSFORMATION

Can the world as it is, with nuclear weapons and religious conflict, be left to the unpredictable human factor, to passion and false heroics that

---

17. Geller, "Explaining War," 445.

warp rationality in the name of the national interest? Can we hope for a better world? The Wilsonian tradition of liberal thought and practice has been strong in American diplomatic efforts of creating rules of international law and organizations in collective decision making and has tempted some leaders to try to restructure world politics itself by promoting "zones of peace" and a strategy of "transformational diplomacy" to install democracies in potential adversaries and rogue states.

Academics and activists produce fine visions of alternate reconstructed worlds. The World Order Models Project at Princeton in the 1970s was a serious effort to define and move toward a just world order. Led by Richard Falk, Samuel S. Kim, and Saul Mendlovitz, the project produced a series of readers and monographs, but it ultimately failed because it could not resolve the "transition problem." How does one get from here to there? The hopes that popular revolutions against tyrants would lead to humane and good governance were dashed by the Iranian and Nicaraguan revolutions.[18] Falk hoped that an educational effort at reforming consciousness, "awakening the reason of men to the idea of wholeness as the basis for individual or collective action" would help.[19] When religion burst upon the world after the Iranian Revolution, Falk hoped that the emotional commitment one gives to religion could become a basis for a socially and politically responsible globalization. None have led to a transformation of the central features of the Westphalian system.[20]

Postmodernists go beyond the hope for reform by advocating transformation. They begin by rejecting the positivist or "objective" thinking of the Enlightenment because we cannot escape our cultural context. Thinking itself and the concepts we use are not detached and objective but socially constructed. Drop the emphasis on inductive or deductive reasoning, since no one can find "objective reality." Start over from the reality on the ground, with personal experience, and make values central. That view has a lot in common with those who find the cause of war not in the structure of world politics but in social psychology. Ideas and images construct reality and are keys to understanding conflict. Nationalism defines the "we" and the "other," which leads to distorted and demonic images, which generate conflict. Certainly the views of the world and im-

18. Falk, Kim, and Mendlovitz, *Toward a Just World Order*, 13–16.
19. Falk, "Reforming World Order: Zones of Consciousness and Domains of Action," 195.
20. Falk, *Religion and Humane Global Governance*.

ages of the "other" will differ for people schooled in a liberal arts college, a communist college in the former Soviet Union, or an Islamic madrasah. Some of those views and images expect and therefore promote conflict. Recognizing and reconstructing those images is the path that postmodernists see as the approach to peace.

The deepest constructionist critique of the realist and scientific approach is the feminist critique. For feminists, the casualty numbers from World War I, bad as they are, still do not count the true costs of the war, the cost to surviving mothers and children, the widows who have to face child-raising alone in despair and in a severely damaged society. War is not confined to men, machines, and battlefronts but also includes widows, children, refugees, rape victims, and prostitutes. There are other costs to women. War industries are discriminatory in labor practices, and women are virtually invisible in diplomacy except as supportive wives and hostesses. The invisibility is especially galling, and they insist women be recognized for their roles even if such roles would be considered marginal. Women are involved in foreign policy as secretaries to officials, tourists taking foreign exchange to needy Third-World countries, as assemblers of commodities for export, domestic servants, all the while coping with the definition of beauty. Such discriminations and invisibilities are exposed and explored by Cynthia Enloe's *magna carta* of feminist international relations, *Bananas, Beaches and Bases: Making Feminist Sense of International Politics.21*

Emily S. Rosenberg uses cultural analysis of two films, *A Foreign Affair* (1948) and *The Man in the Gray Flannel Suit* (1956), to demonstrate the connections between foreign policy and cultural construction of values of male dominance. In the films we see women and their "foreign affairs" creating troubling international involvements. The role of "responsibility" for men in a society is also reflected in U.S. foreign policy in the Cold War, where containment of the Soviet Union is associated with the containment of American women in a subordinate domestic role. The mental health of men after the trauma of war is not considered the responsibility of the nation but of women, of wives who need to take the lead in being subordinate, understanding, and pampering.[22]

---

21. Enloe, *Bananas, Beaches and Bases.*
22. Rosenberg, "'Foreign Affairs' after World War II," 59–70.

Feminist thinking in foreign policy and international politics is not about adding women and the historically excluded domestic sphere to the field but about restructuring the very foundation of the field and its boundaries. There is no single view, for conversations and dialogue continue within feminism. Still, the state is a starting point in two ways. First, since women find themselves marginalized in politics, citizenship itself is problematic. Second, the concept of the national interest is far too narrow and shallow since the state does not provide adequate security in its multilevel and multidimensional terms. So the state cannot be the starting point of our analysis. Whereas Morgenthau begins his theory with the nation and its national interest, feminists assert that "the state itself is so pathological a polity that no hope of decent order—domestic or international—is possible without profound change in its political structures."[23]

That pathology is reflected in its skewed priorities, such as the monstrous investments in war industries rather than childcare and education, and its preoccupation with violence between nations rather than domestic violence against women. Moreover, the state itself is a consequence of conquest by men, including women who could not defend themselves adequately while having to care for their children. That initial conquest is then structured and legitimized. The concept of sovereignty, so central to the state, is a concept of control, a masculine concept that is easily carried over into domestic politics and the social structures of gender.

Reasons for this political pathology vary but are commonly linked to disorder in men deriving from the shaping power of their conquest-based cultural context. In a mild form, Betty Reardon finds the need for power and violence in the psychic wounds created by the socially constructed concepts of men and women. That wounded psyche is repressed but generates violence, and acts of war are but a location on a continuum of violence that includes sexual abuse, battery against women, and rape.[24]

Traditional thinking about theory is distorted by what feminists call the Enlightenment Project, which believes in finding truth, or at least reality, in objective scientific approaches to study. Carol Cohen sought to undercut the supposed rationality of nuclear deterrence theory by demonstrating the preoccupation of strategic language with sexual imagery—vertical erector launchers, thrust-to-weight ratios, soft lay downs, deep penetration, spasm attacks. Frank Costigliola points out the unnoticed

23. Harrington, "Feminists and Foreign Policy," 360.
24. Reardon, *Sexism and the War System*.

sexual language of George Kennan in his *Memoirs* and the famous Long Telegram.[25]

J. Ann Tickner orients her approach to research toward issues useful to women or feminist questions. Women are creators of knowledge, and she argues that personal experience should be taken as evidence. While traditional international relations scholars seek to explain the behavior of states, which can then be used to understand the global order and appropriate foreign and national security policy, feminists want to investigate the lives of women within the global order in order to change or reconstitute them. Knowledge for feminists has a different purpose—to be used by women to change whatever oppressive conditions they may face.[26]

Evidence is also different. The opinions and experiences of women are the real evidence of reality, superior to the statistical data of the COW project, and must be given precedence. The concept of the national interest must be redefined to a more multidimensional set of interests, and political science should cease to define itself as a distinct field and instead open up its boundaries to bring in other fields.[27]

Two questions arise for those involved in foreign affairs. First, are nations in conflict because images are distorted, or are images distorted because nations are in conflict? Though the two are not mutually exclusive, and degrees may vary by situation, the difference is crucial in deciding where to locate the line between reform and transformation, between the possible and impossible. If one assumes that images cause conflict, how does one make transformation in a world of risk? The "transition problem" that bedeviled Richard Falk is a brick wall here too. Societies have been radically reconstructed, but the reconstruction has been imposed from the top down, not from the bottom up through voluntary changed thinking.

The second question is where to locate the line between the national interest and the public interest. How many soldiers are expendable in a war for a vital interest? How much loss of social capital and infrastructure can be tolerated in the national interest? Feminists raise important issues about the gendered assumptions and true costs of war and foreign policy,

---

25. Carol Cohen, "Sex and Death in the Rational World of Defense Intellectuals," 687–718; and Costigliola, "Unceasing Pressure for Penetration," particularly pages 1316–18 and 1333–39.

26. Tickner, "What Is Your Research Program?" 1–22.

27. Tickner, "Hans Morgenthau's Principles of Political Realism," 429–40.

but efforts to find a position on those issues must take the first question into account.

Jean Bethke Elshtain uses some of the feminist critique analytical tools but also takes a broader view in her chapter "Just War as Politics: What the Gulf War Told Us about Contemporary American Life." Elshtain explored the use of the just war morality by George H. W. Bush and noted its narrowness, how it overlooked the human consequences of the war, and how this use of morality was never extended to evaluating domestic public policies on families and communities.[28] She is not an anti-war feminist, however. Though she deconstructs the images, rhetoric, and iconography of war for men and women in *Women and War*, her recent book *Just War against Terror: The Burden of American Power in a Violent World* argues there are times we must use force to stop evil and help establish (or protect) a civic order.[29]

Reformers have made gains in developing a better world. Common efforts and global organizations have developed international norms and regimes of international law, programs to fight poverty and disease, regulations on a variety of subjects from ocean travel to copyright protection, and international efforts toward resolving conflict and rebuilding failed states. If the concept of global governance seems not yet appropriate, the opposite concept of international anarchy is clearly antiquated. The efforts of many people, scholars and diplomats, who hoped to build a better world have been validated and rewarded.

CYCLES AND THE PROMETHEAN TEMPTATION

America needs the hopes of Wilson, Falk, and Tickner to avoid the status quo and the mere prudence of Morgenthau. Feminists would like to change the future, but statistics point to a future that is more apt to be a reflection of past world orders with different leaders and crises. American foreign policy takes place in the moment, but also within a much broader sweep of cyclical history. History is a series of elongated bell curves. Each begins with an S curve of upward growth in a few nations. After a great war among rising and established powers, the emergent great powers form a hegemonic or power oligarchy and establish the rules and values of the system for a long cycle of hegemony. This specific system remains intact as a long

---

28. Elshtain, "Just War as Politics."
29. Elshtain, *Women and War* and *Just War against Terror*.

cycle for sixty to one hundred years, so long as the founding oligarchy stays in power through coercion and deterrence, or convinces other nations to support it and its policies in an expanded oligarchy and partnership.

Peace, then, is constructed by the oligarchy of great powers and the moderation of forces operating within it, until it stretches itself too thin and begins a downward reverse S curve, and rival forces arise to challenge and overthrow it in a power transition to a new oligarchy and long cycle. That outcome is not foreordained. The fate of any long cycle rests with the possibility of a renewal S curve among the oligarchs to forestall the reverse S.

Two historians first laid out the shape of this theory: Oswald Spengler, in his *Decline of the West*, saw such undeniable repetitions as convincing evidence that history can only be understood as mechanically deterministic. Fate rules history. Arnold Toynbee saw the same cycles, but he also saw evidence that some civilizations were able to renew themselves. Spengler ignored why civilizations rose and fell, but Toynbee thought that in seeking to understand why, there may be a margin of freedom. Toynbee saw in World War I a crisis similar to that of the Greek world at the time of Thucydides. That insight brought all history together, destroying the difference between ancient and modern, and making clear the potential disintegration of Western civilization. The key dynamic in this process of rise and decline is the process of challenge and response. History is not a closed and determined process, for a small minority can respond to the historical crisis and renew the energy and achievement of their civilization. "My own view of history," Toynbee wrote, "is that human beings do have genuine freedom to make choices. Our destiny is *not* predetermined for us; we determine it for ourselves."[30]

Within the long-cycle process there is freedom for renewal at any point in the cycle, during the period of dominance or even after the decline has begun, pulling a nation out of its decline and into a new era of power if not dominance. Moreover, halfway through his work Toynbee had a spiritual experience that led him to revise his view of history. Within the cycles of history Toynbee now saw the slow and painful but increasing recognition of God. The study of history is incomplete without a transcendent vision of God, for history is not self-contained with its own values and ethics, but is teleological, moving toward the goal of a more perfect recognition and communion with God. "The meaning be-

---

30. Toynbee, "Why and How I Work," 23.

hind the facts of History, toward which the poetry in the facts is leading us, is a revelation of God and a hope of communion with Him."[31] God is one, and so is humanity, and so should be our life together.

Those ideas moved Toynbee to value unity. The salvation of Western civilization from another ruinous world war was to reunite Europe, to unite the other nations of the world into a world confederation, and to unite the religions of the world into a common aspiration to understand God. This new global civilization and religion would give the people of the world the chance to move beyond parochialism and find a new unity of knowledge, meaning, and hope. If not Eden, then at least not Babel.

Toynbee's work was impressive but suffered from serious defects, both historical and interpretive. Yet his historical themes of culture and cycles live on in revised forms and hope for a better world. In the intervening years they have been updated by several scholars of international politics. Toynbee's focus on civilizations was reintroduced to international politics by Samuel Huntington's thesis that the dynamics of world politics are becoming less national and more cultural, resulting in a clash of civilizations. Huntington urged an expanded view of global politics that includes seven cultures: the West, Orthodox, Islamic, Hindu, Confucian, African, and Latin American. According to Huntington, states will remain important, "but their interests and conflicts are increasingly shaped by cultural and civilizational factors."[32]

Huntington documents the decline of the West and the growing impact of Islam. Non-Muslim governments took control of some ninety-two portions of Muslim territory between 1757 and 1919. By 1995, sixty-nine of those territories were again under Muslim control. Some, like President Bill Clinton, he wrote, "have argued that the West does not have problems with Islam but only with violent Islamist extremists. Fourteen hundred years of history demonstrate otherwise."[33] Huntington's message is to recognize that new nature of history so a "West versus the Rest" polarization does not emerge. His thesis was widely criticized before 9/11 as untenable because of the nebulous concept of culture, and Westerners were not expected to understand other cultures anyway.

---

31. Quoted in McNeill, *Arnold J. Toynbee*, 220.
32. Huntington, *The Clash of Civilizations*, 36.
33. Ibid., 209–10.

Many scholars view economics as the key to understanding the cycles of history. Economic growth translates into foreign policy capabilities and leads toward greater power and status. Over time a disparity in growth rates occurs between the great powers and the emerging powers with their new technologies. Great powers find themselves with stagnant or declining growth rates while they have to increase spending on foreign policy and military forces in their efforts to resist the growth of others. That growing "overreach" strains the economy, limiting its ability to resist and prevail. Paul Kennedy's *Rise and Fall of the Great Powers* popularized the idea that the major shifts in the world military-power balance have always followed alterations in the "productive balances" and that in the rising and falling of various empires and states "victory has always gone to the side with the greatest military resources."[34] Kennedy wrote *Rise and Fall* to warn the United States that it faced inevitable relative decline and it needed what Bismarck called "skill and experience" to manage its fate in "the stream of Time."[35] A foreign policy of overreach jeopardizes a nation's future. This was true of the Soviet Union, and it collapsed first, which gave the United States a chance to start a renewal S curve, which is now in jeopardy again.

Kalevi J. Holsti rejects the economic determinism thesis of rise and decline in his survey of five hegemonic periods since 1648. The eternal question of why nations fight is not answered definitively, but he identifies the issues that generated the five periods and wars and then rates their importance. Knowing those, Holsti then compares the settlements following these wars to eight factors he develops that are involved in a lasting peace settlement. Though he is inclined not to think there will be another world war in the nuclear age, he does contend that his eight criteria can guide policy makers and negotiators to anticipate and devise means to cope with the future, and perhaps more importantly, to guide thinking about the causes of war and the peace settlements flowing from lower-level regional wars.[36]

This approach has the value of accommodating realism in the S curve periods when Morgenthau's struggle for power is central, and it accommodates Wilsonian ideas and ideals during the period of hegemonic

---

34. Kennedy, *The Rise and Fall of the Great Powers*, 439.
35. Ibid., 540.
36. Holsti, *Peace and War*, 307, 340, 353.

dominance. The approach is not limited to great powers but also accommodates other nations on upward paths of economic growth and power acquisition. They may be satisfied allies or dissatisfied rivals of the oligarchs. The dynamics and implications that move the transition process are the change not only in power but also in their degree of satisfaction and dissatisfaction within the existing international system. In this second tier of nations there is openness, secrecy, and shadows. In 1914 Germany wanted to move from second class to parity with Great Britain; the Austro-Hungarian Empire was striving to preserve its stature; and Russia wanted to check the power of that empire, while the Ottoman Empire was in domestic decay and global decline. The unintended world war sparked by a minor incident was too early for Germany and destroyed the two empires. Today nations like Iran and China clearly want to change their position in global affairs, with the degree of hostility toward the United States openly displayed or implicit in their actions.

Wars occur when a dissatisfied nation approaches power parity with the dominant great power. Ascending nations may be dissatisfied with the oligarchy and its values and represent an evolving threat to the system, creating structural undercurrents in the system. Nations experience lag times between recognizing changes in the link between their ends and means. A nation's rising power may outpace its readiness to assume roles and responsibilities in the system, while an oligarchy continues its policies and goals without recognizing a decline in its power.

These four approaches have not included transnational issues from international crime to pandemics, from global governance mechanisms to regional economic unions and common markets. Instead the material here has specific features of international politics, including from Toynbee the inevitable nature of change, from Singer and Churchill the existence of patterns in the outbreak of war but also the context of uncertainty, and from Morgenthau, Wilson, Falk and Tickner the central issue of power and the narrow margins for reconstructing the Westphalia system. International law, organizations, and regimes are social constructions by the participants to bring some order and predictability, cooperation and progress, but they remain self-enforcing and hostage to changes in the power structure of the hegemonic nation or oligarchy.

Little can be done to prevent a nation from becoming powerful if it has the means of doing so. There is fate in that inevitability. In 2008 China was the fourth largest economy in the world; in 2009 it displaced Germany as the third largest. In time an ascendant nation may be satisfied with accommodation to the existing great power and join them as a partner hegemon, or it will reach a point where it determines to seek revisions or more fundamental change in the international system. It may also make a Promethean try to establish its own singular dominance in the globe.

Change comes with time, for the reigning hegemonic power will reach a point where its power begins to decline in actual and not just relative terms if it does not keep up with economic and technological change. Or the effort at global reach and impact will stretch its men, money, and material beyond its limits in the determination to hold its global role. The trajectories of dissatisfied and ascending nations will create rivalry with the hegemon. This process occurs over time. There may be an early crisis, but more likely the downward slope of a reverse S curve can be gradual while the international system becomes more multipolar and strong interconnections remain within the oligarchy and with other nations. At some point a nation's internal political will or economic capabilities reduce its commitment to hegemony, or the purpose and power of another nation become more threatening. Either development accelerates fate as the slope of the curve becomes more severe, and more critical as the point of equality or parity is reached. In the thirty years before 1914, every member of the central powers experienced at least one critical point on its power cycle.[37]

History is not linear but cyclical, meaning that a nation's stature and the resulting benefits of its position are not permanent. Therefore fear should always be a background motivation in foreign policy, for the immediate and long-term costs of decline and fall of a nation or oligarchy are very high. Foreign policy requires skill and art, recognition of time, process, and probabilities, and the hopes and fears that can motivate people and leaders to pay the price necessary for success. It requires more than mere prudence, more than a context-denying individualism, and it requires the self-restraint from trying to transform the world. It requires an economy with vitality and a foreign and national security policy that can divide opponents, preserve allies, and defeat enemies. Those are choices.

---

37. Doran, "Confronting the Principles of the Power Cycle," 332–68.

THE FOLLY OF PROMETHEUS

This chapter began with the individual policies and decisions that led to World War I and then looked at the reality of structural factors and the potentialities of changing those factors to arrive at better decisions and policies. Transformation of the Westphalia system is beyond the reach of the structural probabilities, but structural factors are not fully determinative, for renewal can take place within structural opportunities and move the trajectories of structural history. It is time, therefore, to return to the human factor.

The United States and its NATO allies were the hegemonic oligarchy after World War II. They established the United Nations system (with the veto power in the Security Council), including the free-market Bretton Woods Agreement and the Charter of Human Rights as the ruling structures and values of the post-war world. An alternative rival substructure was the enduring rivalry with the Soviet Union and its allies. The collapse of the latter left the United States as the sole superpower.

The Promethean dynamic came to power in the U.S. government with the election of George W. Bush in 2000 and his foreign policy architects who believed the Cold War was merely an interruption in the century-long rise of American power to dominance in the world. With the collapse of the Soviet Union, and with a military budget exceeding more than the next ten nations combined, U.S. superiority was uncontested.

What to do with the new position? This much was sure to the administration—no more was the U.S. to be a Gulliver tied down by treaties and organizations like the United Nations and the "old nations" of NATO. As the title of one book put it, America was to be unbound.[38] From its exalted position it could promote conditions of peace that would be good for us and promote our conception of democracy around the world through elections or forced regime change. That policy would convince other nations to reform themselves and quiet their foreign aspirations.

After the 9/11 attacks the United States added to its reach for global hegemony the engineering of global transformation, a move far beyond Morgenthau's prudence. The invasion of Iraq was to be quick and easy, with the Hussein regime replaced by a new group of friendly and grateful rulers, and American troops returning within six weeks. That demonstra-

---

38. Daalder and Lindsay, *America Unbound*. See also Halper and Clarke, *America Alone*; and Mann, *The Rise of the Vulcans*.

tion of American might did not become a transforming moment for the Middle East but a long fourth-generation war against insurgents within a bloody civil war.

Concurrently the administration adopted a deficit tax and deregulation policy designed to benefit the increasingly intertwined finance, insurance, and real estate (FIRE) sector of the economy as a way to strengthen the power of the nation. Without the tax revenue to support the war the administration financed the war "off budget" through bonds sold abroad, particularly China. The "deficit hawks" and those advocating a balanced budget amendment to the constitution in an earlier decade were marginalized and silenced. The consequences of the Promethean overreach were revealed to the nation and the world in the collapse of the debt-financed economy in 2008. The U.S. reputation abroad, which Americans expected to reflect the goodness of the country, plummeted. What is most striking is how anti-Americanism has spread among its allies. The Promethean Bush policies turned from daydreams to nightmares.

No other nation in the early years of the twenty-first century's second decade will match the power of the United States, but there will be powerful rivals of the U.S. and its interests in Asia, the Middle East, and Central Europe. The United States stands at the pivot point in the reverse S curve and is in need of a renewal S curve, a multiprong effort to revitalize its economy, restore confidence in the government, rebuild its military forces, and renew its image abroad. In this period of challenge, the United States must use its margin of freedom to create a national response that breaks the power of the challenges that are not yet deterministic.

REALITY AND RENEWAL

What does the nation need for its future? Intellectually it requires a core theory of international politics and the role of related theories that fit into a concept that defines an appropriate and positive role for the nation. This chapter posits power transition theory as a theoretical center. The United States is somewhere on the continuing movement of a long cycle of hegemony, meaning that it faces the options of decline or renewal in the next quarter century. At stake in the dynamics and events of foreign affairs is not just the national interest but also the longer-term fate of the nation as a world leader. At stake in that leadership is a Western and Enlightenment-based world order of secularity, rationality, democracy, the rights of women, globalization, growth in wealth, respect for international law developed through collective action on collective problems, and protection against rising revolutionary nations.

Young men and women who decide to become engaged in foreign affairs should understand that within that cyclical construct, the reality of a power struggle is clear during a period of power transition. Power, competition, and conflict based on national self-interest are inescapable parts of reality. Practitioners need to come to their own conclusions on Huntington's "clash of civilizations" thesis as the United States deals with the rise of Iran and radical Islam. An ideological clash can become a military clash in an effort to prevent or promote a power transition.

The concept of the national interest is a fundamental concept. Practitioners should understand that while it has been defined too narrowly, it cannot be so broadly defined as to weaken the ability of the nation to prevail in crises and conflicts. The trade-off between guns and butter is a perennial problem, and human needs may be expendable in times of survival and vital-interest conflicts to avoid the fate of failure and loss of future ability to deal with domestic interests.

Awareness of the steps to war allows a practitioner to understand the times and places for greatest impact for slowing or halting the process of war. Time becomes an important factor as practitioners find themselves short of time or find time has been lost and with it the chance for impact. Step 5 is singularly important because it involves the integrity of the election process for leaders, and the integrity of the democratic processes of discussion and debate on a policy, and the means of promoting and defending to the public.

Practitioners need to understand the limits of Morgenthau, for there are opportunities during a long cycle to build means of cooperation and humane values. They also need to understand how even this greatly modified Westphalian structure creates inescapable and significant problems for transitioning to a significantly different world order as exemplified by Richard Falk.

All these elements of foreign policy raise important ethical issues.

Morally the nation needs a renewal of hope for the future. Not a future limited to prosperity, but a future and a renewal of appreciation and support for the country, which must begin with a new attitude toward government and public service. The current skepticism of everything political is fed incessantly by cable news and commentary programs constantly seeking to expose hypocrisy, idiocy, and deceit. The same is true of publications.

We must understand that those who serve the public must be accountable to a high standard, but in so doing the public ought not to forget that politicians are no worse than the leaders who drove this country's top corporations into failure while taking enormous salaries and perks, and with no responsibility to the strength and vitality of the country beyond their market share and shareholders. Nor does one hear of major religious leaders who call for national righteousness and condemn politicians and policies ever calling a press conference of major media and exposing themselves to their questions. Prophets believe in one-way communication; condemn politicians and "bureaucrats" with demands for purity but leave it to others to act. Unlike prophets, practitioners have to act and bear the responsibilities for the consequences.

As advised by George Kennan, we must recognize the difficulty of a democracy attempting to be effective in foreign policy. He notes that the public is too self-centered and takes too little interest in the strategic necessities of foreign policy. Beyond that, however, are built-in factors promoting public skepticism of government.

Skepticism is fed by the very structure of our unique government. People expect results, but the government has two houses of Congress elected by different constituencies for different terms, three branches of national government, and two political parties, all sharing power. The bipartisanship that once ameliorated much of that division over foreign policy was killed off by the division over Vietnam and the political polarization that arose in the 1990s. Add to those the fact that the media acts as a separate but indispensable fourth branch of government, while itself divided and competitive, which further divides, slows, and complicates the governing process.

Skepticism has been bred by two wars that delivered much less than promised despite enormous costs, and the seeming impossibility of the rest of the world ever living in peace. There seems to always be threats, insurgencies, civil wars, genocide, repression, corruption around the world, so the promises of political leaders that this policy or that will lead to a better one ring hollow.

One element of hope comes from the current economic crisis that has ended the former decades of "the government is the problem" attitude. The individualism fed by easy credit, cell phones, entrepreneurial religion, and the new technologies may run into the reality of a common fate of rising prices and rising unemployment if America's place in the world economy as the world's largest debtor nation does not change.

An approach to hope is that young people will recognize what this chapter has argued, that reality is made up of the four perspectives, that of Morgenthau's art of power-diplomacy and Singer's science of recognizing probabilities and process, of Falk and Tickner's hope for reform and the fear represented in Toynbee's inevitable decline if responses are not adequate to meet the challenges. There are no easy answers because the fourfold nature of reality involves risks and uncertainties, and recognizing that will hopefully preclude a daydream approach to participating in foreign affairs. This book assumes that the basic structure of the Toynbee and Holsti and Kennedy argument of cyclical history is the best center for understanding, or potentially a hard core of a working theory of international politics and foundation for foreign policy when one selects the factors driving that history.

Consequently there needs to be a fivefold renewal within the next generation leading to public service. When young people understand that basic structure of fate they will (1) be more interested in the David Boren's question, (2) have a high regard for their nation, (3) then find their personal stance on the relative priority for power and reform, (4) use their personal, political, and spiritual freedom to engage the world, and (5) thereby serve the nation and its people.

There is a counterargument, that Christians should be "very skeptical of patriotism" and "reject the call to love one's country."[39] That view rejects the reality that our lives and the values we cherish depend upon a nation strong enough to protect itself and provide space for skepticism, and democratic enough to allow freedom of religion. A nation is not a being that can protect itself; it depends upon people willing to serve their fellow citizens and their common values through public service. The emerging reality of a common fate needs to lead American citizens to hold a new and positive attitude toward the American nation and its government and policies. In Toynbeean terms, this country needs to make use of human freedom and political freedom to create new responses to its challenges, but that can only come in lasting form if supported by a renewed sense of shared values, shared responsibilities, and shared destiny.

---

39. Van Geest, "Deepening and Broadening Christian Citizenship," 107.

A massive World War II type of land war that can galvanize, energize, and unify the public behind the nation is not going to happen, and renewal by tragedy is not even desirable. Instead, this book hopes the challenges of the near future will inspire a creative and concerned segment of this emerging generation to take a renewed interest in the nature of international politics, a renewed sense of shared responsibility, and a renewed interest in public service. Any agenda for reform, of which there are many, will disappear unless embraced by a generation with a renewed sense of leadership for their country and its fate. Infatuation with the supposedly nongovernmental organizations and their micro and Band-Aid programs needs to be supplemented with young people turning to the public agencies that can have a deep impact that will not only renew this country but will do so in a way that builds a better world.

2

Scripture and Grace

DIPLOMATS, SPIES, AND WEAPONS makers—how do history, guns, and spies go together with Scripture and theology? Though most of us came to believe in Christ through a church, our beliefs and those of whatever church we attend are both based on Scripture. They were written long ago and far away, but they are the self-disclosure of God and the primary source of our religious beliefs. How and to what extent can these beliefs be applied elsewhere—including foreign policy? Understanding the Bible requires both faith and reason. Blind faith can lead to radicalism, and soulless reason can lead to pessimism. Too much certainty leads to mistaken literalism, easy indictments of others, and mistaken application of Scripture to events, while limiting the relevance of Scripture can leave too much space for modern idols and too little space for spiritual power.

SCRIPTURAL FOUNDATIONS

The Bible is a library of historical documents and memories as well as poetry, prophecy, law, war oracles, and sermons on grace. Scripture did not fall down from heaven intact, full of God's first-person statements, with all chapters and verses equally inspired and important for an asserted single message. A parochial and nationalistic perspective replaced the global perspective on humanity in early Genesis, though the global reappears later. The books and messages of the Bible are historically contingent and emerge from the stimulation of historical circumstances, or some personal reaction or insight, or from a religious or political need. They were put together over hundreds of years, with many conferences, discussions, and decisions by the Jewish and Christian worlds. It was not until the Council of Trent in 1546 that the church in the West formally and finally declared the contents of the canon.

Christians believe God was involved in shaping the understanding of the writers in a process of self-disclosure as well as in the development of the canon, so the Scriptures are revelatory and normative and represent the tradition of Christian orthodoxy. Scripture, like Jesus, is both divine and human. There are layers and depths of meaning that require reasoned analysis and contemplation, resulting in various interpretations, usually institutionalized into church denominations or communities. Efforts to make the Scriptures simple run the dangers of being too selective, as one reads into the Scripture what one wants the Scripture to say. For example, those who focus on the deliverance from Egypt as indicative of God's good grace conveniently overlook the massacre of Egypt's firstborn sons and the Canaanite Genocide that followed.

We bring our experiences to the Scriptures. "I had faith until I got to Iraq," said National Guard Specialist George Schmidt. "I haven't gotten it back since. Once you get there, you wonder how God could allow anyone to go through that."[1] We do not start our reading from the point of experience, but the divine disclosure must be brought into dialogue with our experience. No one has moved a mountain by faith alone, and Christians get killed in battle despite the promises of Psalms.

After recognizing and assessing the human aspects and elements of Scripture, the reader must return to them with love and a desire to learn, and accept with openness their role as the Lord's self-disclosure and as material for the leadership of the Holy Spirit. While written long ago and far away, with various levels of inspiration, even the histories of the Old Testament as well as the Gospels and letters of the New Testament become alive and immediate when the Holy Spirit personalizes them to us for insight, inspiration, and instruction. They become ours in times of study and search, routine and crisis, a means for insights that open new vistas of understanding, leadership in times of choice, or critique and judgment.

To link the Scriptures to present-day foreign policy realities we have to "journey with the scriptures," living in them as the inspired self-disclosure, but also reading them in complex conversation with one another. How does the warrior God of the Old Testament fit with the Sermon on the Mount in the New? Are the two testaments complementary, or does one replace the other—or was there "progressive revelation"? We also read them in complex conversation with the natural and social sciences, and

---

1. Quoted in Conant, "Faith under Fire," 28.

we reflect on them in the present and in the overall mosaic of our lives, the times of joy and grief, triumphs and suffering in our lives and world.[2] From them come images and metaphors that cross time and space, historical stories that relate to politics, prophetic and wisdom perspectives on human dealings, and the description by Jesus of the kingdom of God. These the Holy Spirit can personalize into our specific circumstance.

Life in foreign affairs is adjusting to events, surprises, miscalculations, suspicions, double agents, new technologies, and career train wrecks. We journey with the Scriptures during the journey of our career, and the Holy Spirit is present in those journeys to create a living dialogue with us about how to live in history. In the following scriptural passages we find inspired political insights to bring to bear on American foreign policy.

SCRIPTURAL EXAMPLES

No historical evidence validates the Tower of Babel story, but it is not unreasonable to expect something like it took place as a failed building project of an early empire when the empire could not integrate the conquered groups into an efficient workforce. The biblical writer reads into its failure a divine action, and then uses it to understand divisions in humanity and the futility of any effort to reconstruct universal (as opposed to consent-based international) political values and structures. It becomes a metaphor for the Westphalian system, explaining the seeming curse of the world's political divisions. "The political life of mankind," Paul Ramsey writes, "goes on perennially under the sign of the verdict at Babel."[3]

There is no sense that God ordained their coming together into an early government as his delegated agent on earth. God created the garden, a metaphor picked up by various writers to define God's good creation and an image of humanity as a global family. The first city, on the other hand, was built by the condemned figure of Cain, and all the cities are ambiguous places of refuge, striving, and self-absorption (Babel, Babylon). There is no sense that God is in control of human history because humanity had become so violent by chapter six that God was grieved and pained and decided to terminate the human project. After Noah and the new start came new cities. The story of Babel is the last of the five stories in the first eleven chapters of Genesis that show the inability of men and women to

2. Jones, "Formed and Transformed by Scripture," 21, 24–25, 28.
3. Ramsey, "A Political Ethics Context for Strategic Thinking," 102.

build peace and justice among themselves. The call of Abram in the next chapter is the beginning of the work of God to call humanity to a saving relationship with him. That is why Matthew begins his genealogy of Jesus with Abraham rather than Adam.

Government in the early days of Israel's state formation was primitive and politics fluid, not too unlike the *realpolitik* of global politics today. Saul was king, but David had been secretly anointed to be king, a successor-in-waiting. Saul launched raids to end the threat to his throne and dynastic house, forcing David to flee. David believed he would be king in the future but for a period lived and operated within the foreign territory of the Philistines. He built a marauding fighting force from family members and some discontented folk and carried out massacres against the traditional enemies of Israel, all the while avoiding being overtaken and defeated by Saul and his forces, and duping the Philistines on whose good graces he depended for survival.

David was in his mid-twenties, conducting a life of blood and duplicity. His skill and cunning were necessary survival skills in his world, while his goal of becoming king and his ethnic loyalty gave moral purpose in a world of danger and suspicion. Even so, it seems his moral boundaries were hazy. The Scriptures hold David righteous because of the purposes of God's providential history, rather than David's daily actions in this formative decade of his life. But the historians who wrote this story go on to demonstrate how his violence and duplicity continued on through his reign as king and infected his family, becoming a base for empire and royal pretensions. He was pious and pragmatic. His dying advice to Solomon was to follow the ways of God but murder those against whom he had carried grudges for years—Joab and Shimei. David was flawed, but we are told he was also favored, a man after God's own heart. David was not a catalog of virtues and vices but an affirmation of the ambiguity of history and the equivocal nature of human beings. Flawed and favored, pious and pragmatic—a man in foreign affairs and a man in the need of grace.

COURTS

History is in part a projection of the historian and reader, with the analysis of both impacted by their reason and experience. That was true for the historians of the events below and of the present author's attempt to understand these people, particularly Joseph, Joab, Jeremiah, and Esther.

They are engaged in political history in the courts of kings and reflect the moral complexities and the successes and failures that come amidst personal and historical choices.

Joseph woke up one morning as something like prime minister of the ancient empire of Egypt. Raised in a dysfunctional family as one of the youngest boys who found his identity in dreams of superiority, Joseph was sold to an Egyptian after his older brothers grew sick of him. He clearly had managerial skills and was given high authority in the household before being thrown into jail after a false accusation of sexual misconduct. Determined to get ahead, he made connections with other high officials in jail, which paid off when he was asked to interpret Pharaoh's dream. His forecast of a coming famine crisis was astute, and then he took his chance and suggested a policy solution. The pharaoh was impressed and made him a high official to oversee it.

Joseph found himself in the pharaoh's court but in a vulnerable position. Other officials were incensed after having served the king for years with no such reward. Joseph remembered how twice before others tried to destroy him. His position depended on the good graces of the pharaoh. What does Joseph the administrator owe the pharaoh and the people of Egypt?[4] He served the king at the expense of the people, and solidified his position by advising the king to require the people to give up their land and goods in return for food, which made the pharaoh an even greater despot and left Egypt in a worse state.

Joseph sought to live his personal life as a young man of integrity, but in office and in matters of state he was ambitious and morally passive. He limited his ethics of public administration to being efficient and effective. His was a privatized morality, with no ethical principles of serving the people or making decisions as if people mattered. He had the personal moral sense or character to resist sexual seduction, but his lack of a public moral sense led him to confuse his self-interest and identity politics with the good of the pharaoh. He succeeded; he finally had power and kept it, never again cast down by enemies. He lived a life of honor and wealth and power, yet he left a legacy of administrative evil, and the people of Egypt suffered for the narrow ethics of his personal political ambition.

A central figure in King David's court was Joab, who received his promotion to captain of the army after he seized the fortress on Mount

---

4. Wildavsky, "What Is Permissible So That This People May Survive Survive?" 779.

Zion for the future monarch. From that position he served both king and country, and they often conflicted. The death of Saul left Israel divided, north and south, with fighting between the forces of Saul in the north and David in the south. Abner, the military chief of the north, likely had ambitions to command the forces of a reunited country while he carried on the war against the Philistines and against David and his forces. He installed one of Saul's sons as leader of the north, probably out of loyalty and as a temporary measure until he could make his own claim to the throne. That cooperative arrangement soured when the son accused Abner of having an affair with one of his father's concubines, which Abner probably did to lay claim to Saul's heritage, as Absalom did to David's harem. In revenge Abner made overtures to David, who welcomed him. They made a deal to reunite the two sections under David, if Abner could persuade the northern tribes to switch their allegiance to David.

Joab as leader of David's forces was caught by surprise. Not knowing the events that led to Abner's diplomatic initiative, he assumed in his military risk analysis that Abner was gaining information on David's strength and plotting an attack to seize the south. Joab may have also feared being replaced by the new favorite of the king. Even more personally, Abner had killed one of Joab's brothers in an earlier battle. Joab arranged a secret meeting with the unsuspecting Abner and murdered him. Self-interest, national interest, and lack of good intelligence got tangled with shadows, biased analysis, and duplicity. With Abner gone, two minor military leaders in the north murdered Saul's son and brought his head to David, assuming they would be well rewarded in the new united nation. They were wrong—northerners would resent David for any involvement in the murder of their king so David wanted no part of the assassination. The two were executed for regicide, and David brought together sectional leaders in a summit meeting to reunite the country.

Whatever the strain in relations between David and Joab, the king still needed his commander, especially after David's own son Absalom staged a palace coup and David had to flee under Joab's protection. Now they both used spies and double agents in Absalom's leadership circle to gain the intelligence needed to set the stage for a counterattack. When the decisive battle came, and against David's specific orders, Joab killed Absalom, knowing Absalom would always be a threat. When David mourned too long, Joab demanded it cease before David lost the loyalty of his people.

Joab arranged the death of Uriah to cover David's adultery, but when David seemed to develop expansionist ideas, which would provoke a security dilemma with Egypt and Assyria, Joab strongly counseled against David's order to take a census for his military forces. He lost that argument and did what he was told. His was a political morality, and he found that the ethics of serving both king and country were complex.

Joab did not have intelligence agents in the court when David died, and he assumed dynastic succession would take its prescribed course leading to the inauguration of David's son Adonijah as the new king. He missed the court conspiracy by the strange alliance of Nathan the prophet and Bathsheba the adulteress. Solomon carried the day and Joab was killed for treason.

Jeremiah is a third court advisor. Much later in history Israel was attacked, defeated, and forced into submission by Assyria, the hegemonic empire of the region. As that empire declined, Egypt sought to replace it as the empire of the region, but was pushed back by the growing power of Babylon, and control of Judah passed from Assyria to Babylon. Unable to defeat Babylon in a conventional war, Egypt determined to weaken it for a future confrontation, and one way to do that would be to convince subject states to rebel against Babylon. A pro-Egypt court faction in Jerusalem advanced that policy, and urged the king to break with Babylon, a risky gamble for a small state. Jeremiah, who had been preaching against the idolatry and moral degeneration of Judah, opposed the plan as too dangerous. Egypt was Israel's ancient enemy and would be too unreliable. He lost the argument, the break was made, and Jeremiah's fears came true.

During the siege of Jerusalem Jeremiah claimed Babylon was acting as God's agent to punish Judah for its unfaithfulness, and therefore Jerusalem should surrender. All would not be lost, for one day God's discipline would end and the exiles would return and rebuild Jerusalem. During the siege of Jerusalem the Babylonians pulled back from a region, and Jeremiah went there to recover some property in his hometown. He was arrested, charged with desertion, and thrown in jail. After his release he continued to publicly call for surrender. He claimed an interpretive morality, insisting all these events were God's design and purpose. He was arrested again. In the end he was right, and after eighteen months of siege, Jerusalem was defeated and its upper-class people carried into exile.

Judah was embedded in time and space. Whatever the truth of Jeremiah's claims about God's manipulating nations, national leaders make their political and military decisions about breaking alliances and conquering small states on the basis of their calculation of their national interests in the power structure of their region. Miscalculations about vital and survival interests are costly, and Judah's miscalculation was fatal. Jeremiah also believed in a providential payback, in a moral order or providence operating in the affairs of nations beyond the calculations of power politics. In what the Greeks called Nemesis, Jeremiah saw that Babylon's arrogance would lead to resentment and opposition by others, who would combine to take their vengeance on the declining empire as God's revenge.

Beyond that, almost hidden midway through the book, Jeremiah saw a new future, a way out of Israel's problem of not being able to keep the law. There is coming a day, Jeremiah wrote, when God's law would be written not in books of law codes but in the minds and hearts of his people. God will become personalized rather than institutionalized, a religion of individuals not nations (Jer 31:33–34).

During the exile Daniel and three of his friends served in public administration for the Babylonian Empire. There is no hint that such service was inappropriate so long as certain Jewish regulations were maintained, such as the regulations on food. Daniel rose to top positions through exceptional management skills. When the Persian Empire conquered the Babylonians in a Middle Eastern power transition, Daniel was retained as a provincial officer. His success and perhaps his being a holdover from the defeated empire created opponents who set out to destroy his power, for his religious practices were potentially subversive to the state. Public officials, whether spies, diplomats, or legislators have ethical obligations to their public, but must recognize and observe boundaries to their commitment to the state, and negotiate the bureaucratic culture and personal competition and "turf wars" among colleagues. The Daniel story demonstrates that if a person rises rapidly to a leadership position or if that person's policy is especially popular and effective, detractors will emerge who may attempt to undermine the administrator's position. A young person on the rise like Daniel should build a network of friends along the way, to keep his friends close and his enemies closer, and never burn bridges.

Later, among Jewish exiles still living abroad, was the young Esther, married to King Xerxes and living in the Persian royal court. She neither lived nor ruled with Xerxes, and as a woman in a male culture she lived quietly and deferentially, knowing the former queen was ousted from the court for overstepping her boundaries. Esther anticipated a long life of court ritual and personal luxury.

Esther's uncle Mordecai was a minor official and wise enough to constantly seek out information about national policy and court intrigue, probably with the dual purpose of protecting Esther and finding a way to promote his own career. It was through such intelligence-gathering efforts that he became aware of a plot against the king's life and reported to the king through Esther, which would have later significance. Mordecai also discovered a plot by a high official to carry out a genocide effort against the Jews. Haman, possibly motivated by ambition, fear from these resident aliens, or revenge, vowed to rid the kingdom of these ethnic exiles. Mordecai sent word to Esther to use her position to stop the destruction of Jews. She could have remained silent and safe, hiding her ethnicity while looking the other way. Instead she decided to adopt moral responsibility.

Esther developed a plan to gain the king's attention and then work to personalize the issue and change his understanding of the stakes. Even the first step was dangerous, for coming to the king without being bidden was forbidden, but the king welcomed her. Thus began a series of dinners to gain his attention and interest in her coming request. Haman was at the dinners, and when the king finally asked what she wanted, she said to spare her and her people from the evil intent of Haman's genocide policy. The king was taken aback. He withdrew to compose his thoughts, and when he returned Haman was desperately pleading with Esther to spare his life, but in a position that was mistaken for an attempt to molest her. The king had him hanged that very night. By her brave acts Esther exemplified moral courage. Through political skill she saved her people, yet not uncommon in politics and gendered societies, the book ends with the exaltation of Mordecai.

We recognize that these persons, from Joseph and Joab to David and Esther, are complex social beings. They, like us, are personality types and are made up of a combination of factors, from ethnic identity and family heritage to dreams and determinations. They lived lives of integrity and courage layered with duplicities and shadows.

THE KINGDOM OF GOD

Two sermons and a prayer link us to the kingdom of God. The Sermon on the Mount is recorded by Matthew as part of his book filled with the teachings of Jesus. It is not clear if it was directed toward the crowd or the disciples, but it is certainly plausible to believe that some parts of the sermon—such as the salt and light portion—seem more relevant to the latter, while the seven antitheses (you have heard . . . , but I say . . .) seem relevant to the larger group.

The Sermon on the Mount describes our personal life in the kingdom of God, but its meaning is contested. It includes such well-known verses as love your enemy, turn the other cheek, forgive, don't be angry, and others. Reckoning with the sermon is not easy. Are the teachings absolutes, Middle Eastern hyperbole, or merely attitudes? With his two-realm theology (church and state) Martin Luther believed the beatitudes are personal ethics and have nothing to do with this secular world of politics, while John Wesley's theology of grace led him to believe they deal with the process of salvation and social expression. The historian of the sermon set it in Hebrew poetry forms with rhythm, proverbs, and rural images. It has to be taken seriously but not literally, for when Jesus confronted the commercialization of sacrifice in the temple he physically drove the money changers out. He called the Pharisees hypocrites and snakes, and when there was an attempt to stone him, he hid and then slipped away (John 8:59). There seems to be limits to kingdom values for a life lived in this world of complexities between the times. We have to journey with the sermon in the midst of our multiple worlds and political tensions.

Living in the kingdom of God takes one's life beyond the ordinary. One can do more, put up with more, survive more, and be humble enough not to judge others or hold grudges. The Beatitudes assume life will include times of being poor in spirit, times of mourning, times of meekness during struggle, and times of remaining pure in heart in a world of complexity and ambiguity. Another four say that those who live in the kingdom will be merciful, will thirst to see righteousness or the right prevail, and they should seek to be peacemakers in times of conflict. How is such a life possible? Jesus is not saying how happy he is when one is poor in spirit, in mourning, or persecuted; he is saying they are blessed because they have access to the comfort and filling and father-son relationship that comes from the kingdom of God—God's active presence in the world through his Spirit.

These beatitudes are not unique, for similar affirmations are found in the Old Testament (Ps 37:11; Prov 21:21; Isa 29:19; 61:1–3, for example). It is important that Jesus did not pull these affirmations from the sayings of David or anyone else in the royal tradition, or from anyone in the priestly tradition. He did not quote Jeremiah about God and history or Moses about the law. He spoke to real people in the crowd, about their lives as they face disappointment and discouragement, or untimely deaths in a family, or events that are wrong. Those can include diplomats or program managers or undercover officers. He is talking to people like Jacob, wrestling with life.

As for diplomats, diplomacy can be discouraging. Young Foreign Service Officers have to deal with rebellions and mass graves, the tragedies of refugee camps, infant deaths from unclean water, as well as arrogance, duplicity, and mindless propaganda in negotiations, and reassignment elsewhere before things are made right. That can wear out one's spirit, make one hunger and thirst for the right, and spark less-than-pure reactions.

Present circumstances can be ordinary or fraught with danger and import. We live in four time zones at once—the present, the mosaic of moments and experiences that comprise our own lives, the larger sweep of history, and God's providential history. In the midst of the sermon, Jesus gives us a model prayer, teaching us to pray "Thy kingdom come" and "Thy will be done, on earth as it is in heaven." This prayer links his providential history with the mosaic of our days and lives. We are to pray that his eternal kingdom of grace and mercy, his eternal will for righteousness and spiritual communion, will come to us, even as we seek our daily bread and deliverance from evil.

The Gospel of John is more theological than the others, as is his record of the Farewell Sermon during the Last Supper. I am in the Father, Jesus says to his disciples, and you are in me and I am in you. Remain in me, he tells them, and I will remain in you through the Holy Spirit. If you love me and others, he said, the Holy Spirit as counselor will provide the guidance and discernment that makes moral choice possible in our daily lives and in the historical era to which we belong. There is no Deism here; the living God comes to us in our personal lives in this world. "I am the good shepherd," he said earlier in one of his seven "I am" sayings. "Remain in me and I will remain in you." More than that, he also tells his disciples, and us, that we are not his servants but his friends. God is God, but that does not mean we become his peasant servants, apart from and fearful of the master; God allows us to be his friends. We share in the life of God, and that alone makes us grateful, respectful, and willing to do all he asks. From this sermon we know we can live and work in this world because the Holy Spirit will fill believers with a personal relationship with the Lord. In more amazing words, we can have fellowship with him. We can live "in him" and will be embraced by grace, empowered then to engage the world.

EMMAUS AND TROAS

After this Farewell Sermon, Jesus was arrested, crucified, shed his blood for the remission of sin, and was buried. Three days later two men were traveling to Emmaus when Jesus met them and opened to them the prophetic Scriptures about himself. That is a story about a historical event with the living Jesus, written by contemporaries. It confirms the resurrection. Jesus lives. He lives not merely as a memory of a moral man but the one through whose death and resurrection we can enter the kingdom of God about which Jesus preached.

Christians have a special interest in history because they believe God the Creator loved the people of his wayward world enough that he entered history through Jesus to save the world, to create a new future for history in general and for Christian individuals in particular. We who accept Christ live in the two futures, with God's future impacting history's future through us as we are led by the Holy Spirit in the immediate and in our life's journey.

Consider Paul at Troas. Paul had a direct experience with the living Lord on the way to Damascus, believed in him and became a missionary of the gospel. Paul and his companions worked in cities with Jewish populations in the area of present-day Turkey and had success in Pisidian Antioch, Iconium, and Lystra, then returned home to Syrian Antioch. Later Paul led another group back to visit these churches and then traveled north, intending to go east into Bithynia. But Paul and his friends felt the Holy Spirit stop them from going that way. How they were led to change direction is not clear but the reality of the leadership was, so they traveled west to the coast, to the city of Troas. There Paul had a vision of the need in Macedonia, certainly spiritually induced. He and his party sailed from Troas in Asia to Philippi, then to Athens and Corinth. To them and us Paul brought the message of justification by faith in the death and resurrection of Jesus and the sanctification and leadership of the believer by the Holy Spirit. God does live and move and guide us in our decisions and life's impact.

THEOLOGICAL FRAMEWORK

Putting this library of writings into a consistent and persuasive belief system that is true to the Scriptures and related to this social and natural world is the role of theology. Since the coherence of the Scriptures is not self-evident, efforts to be true to the Scriptures and to the realities of this world have led to a variety of theologies.[5] We need an operating theology to help us understand what is central and peripheral, that can shape our character and can inform our relationship to the world. Some theologies begin with a core concept, such as divine sovereignty or liberation or eschatology or another. This chapter assumes that the gospel records of the life, words, death, and resurrection of Jesus, and his promise of life in Christ are the heart of the Scriptures. Surrounding that center are the apostolic writings, with other outer circles comprising the prophetic, poetic, historical, and legal writings. Any verse within a passage or any passage within a chapter can become an inspired word of God to the reader through the action of the Holy Spirit. As a theological principle, all Scripture is to be interpreted in the light of Christ, and we find the witness to Christ throughout the literature. The historical writings of Scripture that we reviewed about Joseph, Joab, Jeremiah, and Esther are instructive about the issues of ethics and politics, morality, and power which we, unlike them, can confront and analyze in a dynamic context as people who live in Christ and are counseled by the Counselor.

This chapter also uses the concept of grace not as a reductionist formula for a tight theological architecture but as the center point around which other scriptural and theological ideas revolve and relate. We use grace as the central concept for understanding life "in Christ" and have faith in its validity because of our experience with it, that is, with Christ. Because of that experience we can say with Thomas, "My Lord and my

---

5. Biblical theology has traditionally sought a single coherent message of the Scripture, while systematic theology brings the big issues of science and history to the narratives; narrative theology seeks understanding through the narrative of the scriptures rather than propositions or systematic theories.

God." We also use it because, as political scientists rather than theologians, we want to "operationalize" it with definitions that are understandable and relevant to the issues, dilemmas, and choices that inhabit the world of foreign and national security policy.

REFORMATION THEOLOGY

The Roman Catholic tradition sees God's creation of human governance as his gift to humanity, for it has a higher purpose than just order. In human nature resides the lens for understanding life. Within the universe God created resides a natural law reflecting the morality of the Creator. If that law could be discerned, humanity could create a common good in their societies. Catholic anthropology emphasized the divine ability of humanity to use reason and imagination to discern that natural law and build relations and structures conforming to it. Government was part of the natural order of creation to pursue justice and attain a common good through the discovery and promotion of that moral law. The church embodied that natural law, and enforced it on society until nations replaced the power of the papacy. The church then decided the moral law was to be enforced on society through the delegated agency of the state because it was now considered a part of creation with divinely delegated authority.

When Luther began his reform movement of justification by faith, this reform needed the protection of the sympathetic monarchs against the Catholic Church and allied states. The church would support the state when the monarch's policy gave protection to the reformed church, so religion became divorced from secular authority. From this came the Lutheran doctrine of the two swords and dual morality, one morality for Christian ethics and another morality for the nation.

Calvin's Reformed tradition holds to four key principles: (1) God's complete sovereignty, (2) *sola scriptura* or through Scripture alone does one find the foundation of belief and doctrine (though some take that concept "alone" further to claim Scriptures are inerrant and self-interpreting), (3) the reality, permanence, and prominence of sin, and (4), the mandate to shape culture into God's plan. God the creator is sovereign and in control of all. By his will he determines who will be saved, and by his will he controls history, directing it toward his ultimate ends. All authority is divine, delegated to government to rule over humanity as the means to shape society and culture toward God's will, a national society based on morality and common grace.

Calvin held to the *order of preservation*, which means government is used to restrain sinful humanity, but also to the *order of creation*, that is, the use of government to build a better world. Humankind faces the historical dynamics of idolatry, a power with people committed to resisting the work of God. Social conflict is thus built into history, and it is the role and obligation of Christians to resist evil rulers and rules, and to transform and shape society to reflect God's nature in this world. The metaphor for this duty is the cultural mandate. God put humanity in charge of the earth, to rule and care for it, and to do so by creating humane cultures of justice and mercy. This provides a theological basis for the obligation to obey, and is also a theological basis that makes participation in government a "high calling." Justice is possible because, though only the elect are accorded his saving grace, there is another kind of grace enabling all the rest of us common folk to be able to work together for the mutual good. This limited "common grace" makes us tolerably good and thus makes civilization possible.

Nicholas Wolterstorff is a major writer in this tradition. In his book *Until Justice and Peace Embrace*, Wolterstorff identifies international politics with the economics-based world systems theory. He calls for Christians to make justice and peace the theme of their work and study because the cultural mandate alone is insufficient to direct efforts to overcoming the suffering in the world.[6] Dean Curry affirms the hermeneutic principle of *sola scriptura*, that God is revealed only in the Scriptures, from which he then derives the view that "God is in control" of history, which means that "nothing happens in history apart from God's will." Curry then goes on to find four "authoritative principles" to be used in a nation's foreign policy and asserts they are "absolute" because they come from God. Those principles are liberty, equality, justice (not to be understood in "left-wing" terms but as virtue), and prudence.[7]

Such a tight theological architecture seems too detached from the bloody realities of war and genocide, and leaves little space in such an order for Hinduism, Confucianism, Islam, or other faiths with power and influence in the world, and little chance they will be erased and re-

---

6. Wolterstorff, *Until Justice and Peace Embrace*; in general see chapters 1, 5, 8, and page 172.

7. Curry, *A World without Tyranny*, 81, 83, 85–89, 96, 101.

placed by a universal Christianity. If governance is a divine delegation, one would expect a world government to be a natural consequence of the theology, as it is in papal encyclicals. But in Protestant thought, for whom the Westphalia order is a means of protection, justice is to be more bottom-up, achieved through more generous government aid and nongovernmental organizations.

This assertion that government is a divine delegation is both a Europe-centered and time-bound historical development, and theologically comes from a belief that there cannot be any area of life that is outside the rule of God. According to Scripture, the Israelites existed as a confederacy of tribes until the people demanded a king and government (1 Sam 6–9). The Romans 13 case for the origins of government as part of divine creation is nowhere found in Genesis, nor in the teachings, parables, or sermons of Jesus. Obedience to government is neither in the Ten Commandments nor in the law and curses in Deuteronomy 27. The Scriptures are concerned about people, choice, and access to the power of God, clearly stated in Deuteronomy 30:11–20. Rather than being the foundation for an entire intellectual architecture, especially given the realities of war and repression, it is more plausible to understand Romans 13 as the opinion of Paul the Roman citizen and recipient of the benefits of that citizenship (Acts 22:25). It is also pragmatic, admonishing the new church not to create a disorder that could bring down the wrath of the Roman Empire. If the writings of Peter on this subject—to submit to government and individual rulers—were followed, there could be no opposition to rulers because they are all agents of God (1 Pet 2:13–16). Then there would have been no American Revolution, no opposition to Hitler, no civil rights movement, and no opposition to Vietnam or Roe v. Wade. Instead there is the temptation for rulers to adopt the phrase British and French monarchs used to justify their rule: *Dieu et mon droit*, "God and my right."

Governments emerged as groups of the strong established their rule over the weak, or as means of protection against raiders, or when rules and offices were created to make decisions about collective dilemmas. Governments represent the creative and destructive work of humanity responding to its needs and environment. Divine delegation is one intellectual perspective that demands (assumes) moral boundaries on the power and purposes of governments and regimes, but leaves individual Christians the task of building laws and policies to meet the law of God for justice even though there is no common agreement on the definition of justice.

A grace-centered perspective does not leave humanity bereft of divine protection and care. Rather, it brings a different kind of sanctity to human relations by making the individual a partner with the presence and power of God through grace as he works his providential history and as individual Christians seek a sense of direction and meaning to that history. There is human freedom and responsibility here, more likelihood of misunderstanding and miscalculation leading to tragedy, but more chance of God-guided creativity in the interactions. Christian officials will have a sense of confidence and hope born of their close relationship and journey with God and may through that journey be able to impact relationships of stress and crisis. Such a view depends on specific concepts like soul and grace that are sufficiently defined and operationalized to be persuasive.

GRACE AND PERSONAL STAGES

As humanity emerged in self-consciousness and a social order, there also came an emerging spiritual awareness, often defined as a soul longing for and capable of questioning self-identity, meaning in life and destiny, and ability to experience the grace of God. Why do we seek meaning and moral understanding? Much of this emergence can be explained by sociological theory and cognitive structures and functions. The human's neural systems within the brain allow us to experience the world, think about it, and seek order and causation. At some point a mind emerges from the brain, an emergent property that brings an ability that is more than the neural systems, and that allows the search for meaning in the world.

Similarly, as part of this process, humans develop myths and rituals that give transcending understanding, meanings, and personal acceptance of our experiences and the mysteries of the divine world. Is this a psychological projection of an artificial religious reality, or is it a reaction to the presence of a very real religious reality? How can the spiritual interact with the physical? How can a spiritual God relate to humanity and individual freedom? The soul is an emergent property, an emergent spiritual awareness, and grace provides the capacity through the soul to participate in God, to live "in Christ." If we believe God exists, then sociological and neural explanations are not enough to explain the universal and individual search for meaning. That personal and social effort will to some degree be a process of projection, but the emergence of that capacity to experience the need for a religious rationale is also inescapably God's presence in the world through grace.

The soul is not a physical or spiritual property distinct and autonomous from our physicality. It is embedded in both our physical humanity and the presence of God. Put another way, humanity cannot be reduced to the bottom-up interplay of the chemical and biological factors. The concept of supervenience provides an explanation for a top-down causation; that is, just as the mind cannot be reduced to simply the brain but is an emergent property that can react to environmental factors and supervene on the neurological system, so moral properties may supervene on psychological or sociological properties.[8] The soul, like the mind, is an emergent property, the former open to the supervening action of the grace of God.

People are complex bio-chemical physical beings marked by continuous creation and common and sometimes uncommon processes and results. There are passages in life. Erik Erikson, Lawrence Kohlberg, and James Fowler developed models of the stages of psychological development, moral reasoning, and stages of faith.[9] There is similarity in Fowler and Kohlberg, both identifying moral development moving through five stages, with the latter ones of concern here. At stage 4 persons have moved beyond seeing themselves as the center of their universe and come to internalize the values of the larger society and social rules and obligations. They fit in, accept, and adopt the rules and values of their culture, and may seek achievement and recognition within that culture. In managerial language they are goal oriented, possess a long-range view, and take initiative. They are also, however, conservative, since they accept their world or organization as given, improvable by their efforts, but not open to change.[10] Thus there is little room or use for critical reflection on one's own identity and belief structure.

Those reaching stage 5 are able to step back and critically examine their own values and those of society. Sometimes this stage comes after a defeat or disillusionment or a realization of the inadequacy of one's

---

8. Murphy and Ellis, *On the Moral Nature of the Universe*, 23.

9. See Erikson, *Identity and the Life Cycle*; Power, Higgins, and Kohlberg, *Lawrence Kohlberg's Approach to Moral Education*; and Fowler, *Stages of Faith*.

10. For the managerial implications see Fisher and Torbert, *Personal and Organizational Transformation*.

family-based beliefs to deal with inconsistencies and paradoxes of life. In managerial terms, they can "look around the corner" and see the need for significant organizational change, move beyond standard operating procures, and take the organization into the future. They are generative, able to generate a meaningful life and productive organization through the capacity for restructuring. As individuals at this stage, people are able to see beyond their time and space, able to reinvent themselves, not in a horizontal way of acquiring new skills, but vertically in terms of a new conception of themselves and their future. Such is the goal of a liberal arts education, which seeks to lift students beyond their time and place and impact their intrinsic values. Beyond that, however, society provides little incentive for a person to go beyond vested self-interests and reach for stage 5.

Thinking and choosing are never driven completely by this higher stage, for elements of the concerns, qualities, and points of view of the former stages still linger. At this stage adults are still people of foibles and failures, can still find their goals and behaviors heavily influenced by unresolved tensions from such experiences as dysfunctional parents or a heavy dose of spiritual fear and guilt as children. People may become politicians to gain personal affirmation, or become diplomats to escape a past, or become clandestine operatives as part of a personal enjoyment of risk taking.

One may even consciously act with regression in order to "fit in" within one's social and organizational life. A moral crisis, whether purely personal or social, such as the civil rights movement and Vietnam War in the 1960s, can be the catalyst and drive to become the person represented by stage 5, just as a crisis may reinforce one's own limited views and society's self-interest. Grace is the upward call for people to move to a transcending moral imagination beyond themselves, and to embody respect and compassion for others as well as service and hope.

A Christian at stage 4 accepts the love of God and national patriotism and keeps the two in parallel congruity, while at stage 5 the Christian recognizes the potential incongruities of reconciling those two. The Christian may choose regression and a simplistic dualism. Or one may create a transcending integration out of the pressure of current events within the reality of competing theories of international politics and competing interpretations of Scripture and theologies, and the inadequacies of one's family's subculture and socially constructed belief structures. Given this complexity no common reconciliation, no one right answer, is going to be found. Each individual Christian will find his or her reconciliation. But to be an authentic person, to be a contender for a Rhodes Scholarship, to deal with the moral complexities of intelligence operations, or to be a successful political leader, attaining this stage is crucial.

What is the value of this discussion of soul, supervenience, and stages? First, transcendence. We have a soul and are not reducible to merely physicality or a self-referential and autonomous individualism. We can experience life in Christ. Second, free will. Our mind and soul are higher-level properties that can impact on the margins of the indeterminacies of our physical and cultural processes. That in turns allows us to deal with being and doing good in the face of the complexities of the forces, events, and choices that we face in our time and place. Since our understandings and choices are not determined, we have the capacity for envisioning higher purposes and for making choices that are cautious, risky, or stupid. Third, maturity. Living in Christ does not automatically make a person mature and the choices of their free will good choices. The purposes and choices in foreign policy are so high that people desiring to engage those issues need the maturity to avoid overly risky or stupid goals and choices.

GRACE AND GOODNESS

Given the reality of the soul, of supervenience, and stages of maturity, it is not too much to believe in a biblical concept of life in Christ and a resulting life of holiness. Holiness means more than mere intellectual assent to doctrine and weekly routines of worship and Christian practices, with little impact on life beyond being good and avoiding evil. The concept of holiness has several definitions, however, with varying degrees of separation from the world. Generally it is to be "like Christ," understood as being a person of love and care and self-sacrifice, generally not including his cleansing of the temple, his paying taxes from money found in a fish, and his walking on water.

For this book, holiness is both a goal and process. The goal is to be the kind of person God calls us to be, and that is both personal and communal. The personal, however, is primary, including any specific call to a ministry and any specific leadership in situations of choice or dilemma. The process is the daily seeking to be open to the grace of God and penitent for our own personal weaknesses and failures. Such a definition includes the full range of the life of Christ, including his struggle during the temptations to understand and define his approach to his ministry, his continual prayer, and his friendship with publicans and sinners.

A MODEL OF GRACE IN OUR LIVES

A complete understanding of how God works in this world and its history is beyond us. But one knowable, predictable, and permanent way God works is through grace. If we can define the concept of grace and postulate how it relates to our lives we can strengthen the channels through which it can flow. This section gives content to the concept of grace. The next section describes its potential impacts on us as individuals, and the later "Grace and Governance" section will describe political and international structures through which grace can work in the world.

As a summary definition, grace is God's active presence in the world through the Holy Spirit to energize the remnants of the image of God in our lives and evoke a response. There is nothing outside of God's presence in grace, and in the Wesleyan tradition all grace is one. It is universal. Though the phrase "the family of man" rings hollow across the years, grace is a uniting bond across time, space, and societies that affirms the unity of the human family and inspires the highest and best in service to humankind.

Grace is primarily personal, the call to each person to recognize God's presence and kingdom and to live "in him." As a call rather than an overpowering force, it leaves the individual free to respond to God's initiative and to choose or deny a life in Christ. God calls; individuals respond by opening themselves to God's love in grace or closing themselves off.

A two-sided spectrum, running from +5 to −5, can help visualize the role of grace in the process of human moral development. The top side represents one's openness to grace. From 0 to +5, one moves through five As: spiritual apathy, awareness of a vague spiritual realm, acceptance of a God, active involvement in the Christian life, and absorption in the grace and power of God. On the opposite side one can close off grace to move from agnosticism and antipathy to things religious to abandonment to one's self-absorption, with all the consequences toward others that follow.

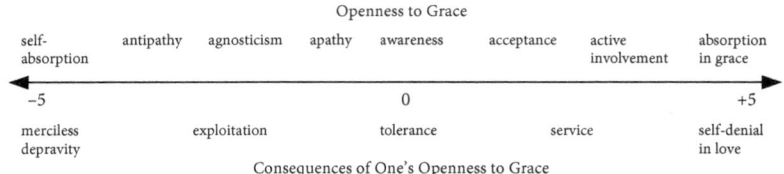

Figure 1: The Role of Grace in Human Moral Development

The bottom side reflects the consequences, from tolerance at point 0 to assumptions of parity with others, to service to others, preference, sacrifice for others, to self-denial in love for others on the plus side, to points of exploitation and merciless depravity toward others on the other minus end.

Individuals have freedom in matters of both salvation and history, and those without priests or predestination to assure their salvation look for God's grace in personal experience. Those who emphasize God's holiness believe one can live "in Christ," in a living or dynamic relationship of growth in depth in spiritual life, despite the Christian's failures, foibles, and infirmities. Church communities provide dimensions of grace not found in private faith, but faith and grace remain a personal belief, commitment, and opportunity for growth. To live in the fullness of his Spirit is to be embraced by grace. Living in grace is a privilege, but not a prescription for a life above boundaries. It calls us to the personal ethics of being honest about ourselves and caring about others, and reaching out in love and mercy to humankind, especially the poor.

The reason and context for constructing a model of grace and engagement are the historic changes taking place in global politics and economics. Wars of blood and faith are spilling the blood of Americans abroad and at home. Self-righteous detachment and "blame America first" cynicism are inadequate and unacceptable when global change has enormous consequences for values, security, and welfare. This country needs young professionals who live "in Christ" to (1) become engaged in American foreign affairs, (2) understand the complexities of the world, (3) have moral anchors, (4) assume moral responsibility, (5) have moral courage, and (6) be willing to risk walking along moral margins.

Accepting the "view from the thirty-fourth floor" may require a stage 5 synthesis that provides a mental and moral framework for engagement in a world of power and national self-interest. For those in the early years of a career, it will more likely flow from a personal sense of duty and responsibility to shape and invest one's life in response to the events of history's sweep in this generation. No Faustian bargain here, for it cannot be outside the moral bounds of Christians to respond to the evil potentialities of current events. Instead, Christians can engage in this response to the lethal danger while embraced by grace.

Choosing engagement does not mean rejection of grace. Choosing engagement means we will be engaged with shadows wherein ethical boundaries of the Sermon on the Mount have been stretched or blurred. Professional needs may deviate from the sermons of pastors, and the sense of self be stretched to accommodate the shadows. To do so may well become a continuing and self-justifying process, so we need to be clear about the dangers.

Political choices in a world of risk are rarely easy. Decisions may involve choices when the percentages of good and bad are nearly equal but have little control over the second- and third-order consequences. Leader's orders, action of colleagues, misunderstood information, frustrations of recommendations being rejected in favor of less favorable options—all these and many others will create dilemmas and lead to reactions and decisions that contradict the oft-intoned prescriptions of purity, love, humility, and self-sacrifice. Where are the margins in coercive diplomacy? What is the definition of national necessity that justifies devising and building weapons of war? Where is the protection from the seduction of reversing sides for members of Congress? How long can masks be required for a clandestine operative before the self is damaged?

The answers come through our daily and life's journey as the Holy Spirit bridges and connects our being with the Trinity. Often we find the journey and connection alive and active, which is exhilarating, both in the moment and when we recognize in it God's leadership. Sometimes along the journey we recognize that "things worked together" to reach a high point. Sometimes there is silence in the connection, perhaps even after an expected development failed to happen. Connection, journey, leadership, silence—all are part of an active fellowship with the Lord, and all of which require both the grace of God in our lives and our trust and faith in the goodness of the fellowship.

We develop a theology to understand this spiritual connecting with the physical, and we develop practices to cultivate this fellowship, grace, and trust by our personal meditations, rituals, and intentional openness. Through all of it we search for a unity among the ethical and foreign affairs worlds so that we may live in fellowship with Christ and be engaged in this world through his good grace.

EMBRACED BY GRACE

Grace is God's personal and purposeful presence in the world. We can experience his living presence through our souls, which is the emergent property that was conceived and brought forth in humanity through his grace. The scriptural metaphor is that God breathed into his human creation and we become living souls. We have the opportunity to so open our lives to God's presence or grace that we become embraced by that grace, and experience his hallowed kingdom much like a loving family is embraced by affection, protection, guidance, and satisfaction. His grace is not merely a passive feeling of goodness added to our lives. His grace is evocative, for as love it elevates our lives to see beyond ourselves and respect others, to take account of their needs or interests, and be of service to others. On the other hand it is disruptive. It causes unease and critique about thoughts, intentions, and actions that are unworthy, unethical, and unacceptable to his good pleasure. It shapes our moral character so that our freedom is normative and active. As an evocative and disruptive force it cultivates a moral sense of what to avoid and a moral imagination of what should be done to build graced values in our world. Grace provides motivation and ethical boundaries in this Westphalian world.

This represents a Wesleyan approach to grace and ethics that marries the Protestant ethic of grace with the Catholic ethic of holiness, fusing justification and sanctification. Its emphasis is more on virtue and its connotations of aspiration toward and cultivation of spiritual values than on the molding of character, which carries overtones of resistance and steadfastness against the ever-present bent to sinning.[11]

To live "in Christ" is not a position but a relationship made possible, personal, and prescriptive through the Holy Spirit. This is the center of our theology for engagement. Around it we can build our beliefs and shape our character. Kantian moral absolutes give normative guidance but crumble in the dilemmas and paradoxes of international politics.

---

11. See Bassett and Greathouse, *Exploring Christian Holiness*, 2:203–4; and Cahill, "Christian Character," 6.

Advocates of "virtue ethics" emphasize the development of virtue ethics through their practice. They result from being defined and habituated by a church community, but there is no common definition of the various virtues. This Wesleyan position emphasizes the virtue that flows from the grace of God in our lives. We have the Counselor.

Grace is actively personal. God through his Spirit can lead individuals by moral imagination, which transcends ethical rules and commands, and makes us aware of a responsibility to the larger human family, however limited by circumstances. Grace inspires people to shape their decisions around ethics that treat people fairly, rebukes the forces of indignity, rescues the victims, and resists and reforms those social structures and values that promote the values of the world's pharaohs and pharisees. Grace is the dynamism of the ultimate meaning of life in personal and social reality; as such, it becomes the moral power for those in national service.

Moreover, that personal leadership can be very specific. It may call a person to something unwanted or may consent to our ideas and plans. It may be the call to do the extraordinary or the personally dangerous, with no guarantees of success. Those criteria do not validate or invalidate God's leadership. Imagine the conversation among the disciples inside the boat when Peter stepped out to walk on water. They likely said one of the following: "don't be stupid, because you will sink," or "we didn't vote to authorize you to step out," or "our community decides what we believe, so don't act like you are better than us," or "it's a delusion that you have convinced yourself it's the voice of the Lord." When the Lord calls, you step out, and when he cautions, you step back, regardless of others.

We live by the voice of the Lord—that still, small voice that we come to recognize as his promised Counselor in the circumstances and needs of our lives as we journey with him and the Scriptures through our careers. It is the primary subjective way that God through the Holy Spirit speaks, for it "most engages the faculties of free, intelligent beings involved in the work of God as his collaborators and friends."[12] We rely on it to escape biblical deism, the belief that God gave us the Bible and then went away, leaving us with no individualized relationship to its library of writings. That voice, that expression of grace, individualizes the Scriptures to us as we seek guidance while using our best reasoning and judgment.

---

12. Willard, *Hearing God*, 100.

This is not a call to an individualistic spirituality or purely private judgment. We need the church as an anchor and a tradition, a place of friends and resources for learning, a plausibility structure in a secular world. Christians are not individual islands at sea in the tides of history, but faith is personal. Our lives are doctrinal but also existential, public and private, growing and maturing, reaching up for that high calling of Christ Jesus, reaching in for growth in grace, and reaching out in our place in history. Preachers and teachers come and go, with views and opinions that may seem too narrow or too flexible, so there must also be a degree of detachment from the community even as one is deeply engaged in its mission and activities. Without that, we trade in the Counselor for groupthink.

In return for being personal, each individual's faith must be responsible. It is far too easy to claim God's leadership, confusing self-interest with divine leadership under the pressure of circumstances or psychological defense mechanisms. True it is that the easy reference to God becomes a kind of "God talk" and is far too common on issues far too minor but beneficial to one's own self-interest to be credible. Experiencing God's leadership takes deep spiritual communion in which reason is not a criteria but neither should it be easily dismissed.

Grace is a power of healing and restoration. People are complex, with strengths and weaknesses, fears and motivations. They embody contradictions and have different facets of personality. Grace is not a reductionist force, but it can be a uniting force, even a healing force as it brings a normative congruence into lives and changes attitudes and behaviors. Grace energizes the remnants of the *imago Dei*. Cleansing from sin as a concept may be more hope than reality, yet there can be an inescapable sense of judgment and a significant elimination of particular weaknesses or impulses, coming as a renewal or crisis or deep penitence, leaving the Christian freer and feeling cleaner than before.

Grace sustains. It sustains in times of pressure, for grace can be translated Emmanuel—God with us. The fact of this personal relationship means one is never alone while dealing with orders from superiors, misunderstandings among colleagues, and frustrations with failure. This grace does not lead to the default of withdrawal. It sustains when all choices are close, difficult, and stab the conscience, or when one is convinced that a policy train wreck is rapidly approaching and no one listens. It also sustains in the midst of an overwhelming crisis when it becomes clear that scriptural promises of protection in the Psalms will fail to protect us.

Grace brings perseverance and hope in the larger sweep of history and providence. We are not orphans, and the present does not define the future; God's loving activities in the world will ultimately prevail. Hope then strengthens resolve, keeps present arrangements open and provisional, reminds us not to absolutize the present, and provides a standing ground outside the system for evaluating and critiquing the system.[13] Hope, like faith, is the evidence of things not seen but made real to us by our experience with the living Lord and our knowledge that God is at work in the world. Hope calls us to use our reason to tackle the problems of nations. Leaders deal in hope, and so do diplomats and scholars of foreign policy.

Grace makes us truly human. God's grace makes us fully human as it leads us to be agents of moral values in the social world. Grace is a dynamic and should not be wasted or stifled by confining it to one's personal spiritual happiness. Embracement without engagement is overly individualistic. In fact, it is "in moral action where we find the center of the human person, the core of our humanity."[14]

Christians are in this world with its times, places, and spaces, and live in the dialectic between the ideal and the real, the present and God's future, and the physical and the spiritual. One should be reluctant to claim too much specificity in what constitutes a Christian foreign policy in a world of power and change. Rather, one must be open to the leadership of the Holy Spirit and to the values represented by grace in our lives. Living "in Christ" does not end our finitude and our involvement in this world of power and choice. Instead, it operates in one's self-awareness and the struggle between what we are and what we ought to be. It creates a moral framework for our lives in this world and the foundation for a moral imagination. This grace is available to all, a single source of power that operates in us and within the world at large.

The previous chapter, "War and Renewal," considered theories of international politics devoid of any spiritual context. Can the model of grace in this chapter be plausibly related to the practice of foreign policy and international politics? The next section considers a model of theology

---

13. Brueggemann, *Hope within History*, 80–81.
14. Weigel, *Witness to Hope*, 176.

and governance, followed by a section applying the model to two specific historical events.

GRACE AND GOVERNANCE

In an article entitled "Theology after Hiroshima," Richard Bauckham argued that theology had to change in the nuclear age because we now know that humankind can do what we thought only God could do: destroy the world. We have to put new emphasis on human choice.[15] The passing of the Cold War and its danger of a nuclear winter have not erased that basic insight. We cannot risk the future to statements like "God created the nations and uses them to work out His purposes in history."[16] Grace means we are not puppets and statesmanship is neither a fiction nor our efforts a sham. Grace and choice come together to struggle against determinism and fate.

At the end of World War II when Hans Morgenthau wrote about the persistence of the power struggle, Arnold Toynbee wrote an article called "The Meaning of History for the Soul," in which he said the world needed a cumulative increase in the means of grace.[17] The church has always considered its sacraments as means of grace, but are there other means? Does grace enter and flow in world affairs through political means? Are there realms of statecraft that increase the means of grace in the world and our struggle with the issues of history? How does grace work, and are there means of channeling it into our historical processes?

Grace is God's spiritual presence with us, and around that belief are the dynamics of openness or closure and the opportunities of leadership, support, and hope. Around that very personal model of grace we can also build social structures as means of grace. How, then, does grace work in the world? Political processes and structures can operate in ways that open people up to the flow of grace in the world or become dynamics of closure.

Political reality itself can cloud the reality of God's presence. Such horrors as ethnic cleansing, genocide, starvation, and ideological construction of demeaning images are events through which a person recognizes the value of the principles of dignity, morality, service, and hope. That recogni-

---

15. Richard Bauckham, "Theology after Hiroshima."
16. Curry, *A World without Tyranny*, 75.
17. Toynbee, "The Meaning of History for the Soul," 221–29.

tion can develop slowly or come suddenly through a flash of insight where people or even the whole nation are confronted with the existence of an evil like genocide or poverty or sex slavery. Through such a contrast between what is and what ought to be, the Holy Spirit brings a creative prophetic insight to those who then can work for rebuke and rescue.

Second, the dynamics of openness can also come through laws that embody the values of dignity and justice, cooperation and community. Such laws repel dehumanization and establish a normative framework that reinforces moral values, and they confront people with moral choices. The feminists have the basic idea: new social values can be a dynamic to reorient public opinion and reshape social structures and sustain hope.

Grace can also impact persons through organizational culture. Political and bureaucratic cultures can be parochial, based on the values of zealotry, utilitarian treatment of others, and deceptive strategies of decision making. In practice they strangle the flow of grace as members become socialized into that culture. An organizational culture that is open, that promotes discussion and cooperation, can be the means by which people open themselves to insights about dignity, moral choice, and hope, which can impact basic policy and/or crisis decision making.

Additionally, grace can be expanded in a situation through social interaction—diplomacy at all its levels. Some diplomacy relates to partnership politics such as creating and working on common projects with a moral quality to them—promoting human rights, programs of social development. Other diplomacy takes place in a context of disputes and crisis, when issues of ambition, power, deception, and violence dominate. A set of conflict resolution procedures and processes have been developed to move situations away from actions that feed the dynamics of conflict. Hardening positions, however, or increasing threats or deciding to gamble may be necessary in the context, but they also restrict any flow of grace in the situation. If the work of grace is to call persons to transcendent insights, to the value of people as individuals as well as a group, to moral choices, to a sense of hope for a better future, then real statesmanship must find creative grace-laden diplomatic initiatives to disrupt the dynamics of conflict.

This model of grace does not go as far as does Wesleyan scholar Theodore Weber, who believes government can become a means of salvation.[18] Instead, this model holds that government can be a means of grace but does not claim that people are political by nature of their creation, or that government is a divine agency. Government is an organization created by people but which can be used, consciously or unconsciously, as means to increase the flow of grace in the world.

TWO TEST CASES

Consider the outbreak of World War I and the Cuban Missile Crisis as to whether political processes and structures could be conceived as dynamics of openness and closure to the presence and power of grade.

World War I. The strategic aspects of World War I were discussed in chapter 1, and while those aspects explain the structural context for the outbreak of war, they do not explain the reason war came. World War I is both fascinating and tragic because while there is agreement among historians on the many necessary causes, there is no agreement on the sufficient cause. Can closure dynamics help explain what happened? There was a full set of such dynamics in the period preceding the outbreak of the war. There were strong forces of militarism and nationalism after 1870 flowing from the Prussian culture that created Germany.

The kaiser was a "God-fearing Lutheran Prince, conscious that he enjoyed special favor in heaven."[19] Several European nations felt superior to others (especially the Russians), and an emphasis on national honor took precedence over political solutions. The emperor of Austria-Hungary was intent on absorbing Serbia as part of a plan to bring "Middle Europe" into the Hapsburg Empire. Russia had long feared the existence of a German policy of influencing Turkey and its control of the Dardanelles. There was belief among the heads of state (at least in Germany and France) that war was inevitable, but also a reassurance from the past that none of the earlier crises had led to war. None really wanted war and therefore expected the combination of public bluster and private good sense to bring the leaders back from the brink.[20]

There was a bureaucratic culture that focused on the immediate tasks rather than either the consequences or the moral issues. The German's Schlieffen Plan, for example, was rigid because it depended on

18. Weber, *Politics in the Order of Salvation*, 391–420.
19. Thomson, *The Twelve Days*, 29.
20. Lafore, *The Long Fuse*, 210–11; Remak, *The Origins of World War I*, 145.

preemptory mobilization and railroad schedules and was inherently escalatory because its design was not coupled with political objectives and planning. Those forces, coupled with the presence of a court faction who had wanted to make war on Serbia for a long time, operated to generate the crisis. Their actions undercut crisis management and inhibited a diplomatic solution, a stubborn movement along the steps to war that closed leaders off from the dynamics of grace to energize their perceptions and insights and moral choice.

On July 27 the German kaiser, having been told that Serbia had agreed to nearly all the demands, and fearing British entry into the crisis and a resulting three-front war, proposed a Halt in Belgrade (limited war with partial occupation), but German Chancellor Bethmann disagreed with it and did not send the proposal to the emperor.[21] He still believed Austria could attack Serbia without serious interference. The next day Austria-Hungary declared war on Serbia and bombed Belgrade. The tsar and the kaiser had both tried to work together to control the escalation of the crisis and keep it confined to Serbia, but the kaiser felt duped when the tsar wrote that he had approved partial mobilization five days earlier.[22]

There was still time to avoid catastrophe. The tsar was listening to the various efforts to restrain the war. On July 29, the evening when his order for full mobilization was to go out, he changed his mind and canceled the order. The generals and foreign minister were furious and demanded mobilization. "Think of the responsibility you are asking me to take!" said the tsar. "Think of the thousands and thousands of men who will be sent to their death!" Under the pressure of the crisis and the time necessities of mobilization, he relented and gave the order. Chief of Staff Sasonov went to the other room to telephone the order, and ended with, "Now you can smash your telephone. Give your orders, General—and then disappear for the rest of the day."[23]

On August 1 the kaiser, recognizing the imminent three-front war, ordered Moltke to stop the invasion of Belgium. Moltke, an organization man whose life was invested in the Schlieffen Plan, resisted that effort for bureaucratic reasons. "Those arrangements took a whole year of intricate

---

21. Thomson, *The Twelve Days*, 104.
22. Remak, *The Origins of World War I*, 115.
23. Ibid., 119.

labor to complete and once settled, it cannot be altered."[24] The dynamics of bureaucratic culture, fear, and self-absorption closed leaders off to the work of grace, narrowing the scope of moral choice and allowing fear to prevail over hope.

We can hear echoes of Stephen in Acts 7:51: "You stiff-necked people.... You always resist the Holy Spirit."

The Missile Crisis. The 1962 missile crisis was a similar close encounter with war between the nuclear superpowers. The contextual conditions and political dynamics were like those of 1914. The Cold War was still intense and militarized, with moralistic self-images and distorted images of the other nation. The Bay of Pigs endeavor failed badly, and Kennedy's leadership was in question. On Tuesday morning when President Kennedy was first informed of the missiles, his initial reaction was "We are probably going to have to bomb them."[25] That assessment was strongly supported and promoted by close advisors—McGeorge Bundy, Douglas Dillon, Paul Nitze, John McCone, John McCloy, Maxwell Taylor, Dean Acheson, and the Joint Chiefs of Staff. There were seriously distorted images—General Curtis LeMay assured the president that we could launch a major attack on Cuba and Russia would do nothing. Dean Acheson argued that we had to attack because the United States was dealing with a "madman" and argued forcefully for a showdown. There were bureaucratic dynamics as the CIA, unknown to Kennedy, continuing to support covert sabotage operations in Cuba in the midst of the Crisis.

During the initial five days of discussion Robert Kennedy (RFK) argued against a surprise air strike on moral grounds. It was a violation of American ideals, a betrayal of the ideals we fought for in World War II, and too similar to the sneak attack on Pearl Harbor.[26]

Dean Acheson thought RFK was an inexperienced fool, obsessed with morality. Douglas Dillon had contempt for RFK and Ted Sorenson because they were young and new, whereas men in his generation had thought the "unthinkable" before. Dean Rusk thought the moral argument was overly emotional, but RFK persisted. Maxwell Taylor dismissed the argument and was not afraid of nuclear missile strikes.[27]

---

24. Tuchman, *The Guns of August*, 99–100.
25. Reeves, *President Kennedy*, 370.
26. Allison, *Essence of Decision*, 197.
27. Rusk, *As I Saw It*, 231; Taylor, *Swords and Plowshares*, 268.

The group was still divided on Thursday. On Friday, October 19, the strike group went around the committee and met separately with the president to push for an immediate air strike. The president declined and had the committee go through the arguments again. During the meeting something happened to Douglas Dillon. He stared at Bobby for a long time. "He was finally impressed by what he thought the President's brother was trying to say. He was thinking: 'He's right; we fought World War II for ideals and we should not change now.' Waves of bombers appearing over the horizon at dawn began to register with him, too, as somehow wrong—if not morally wrong, historically self-destructive."[28] So Dillon switched sides and opened up the possibility for a consensus on an alternative. U. Alexis Johnson later said in an oral interview, "Bobby Kennedy's good sense and his moral character were perhaps decisive."[29]

There would be another long week of arguments among themselves and exchanges with the Soviet premier, hours and hours of discussion, advantages and disadvantages of diplomacy analyzed, two conflicting letters from Khrushchev, the shooting down of a U2 and how to respond to that, what to do if there were a limited nuclear exchange, "wordsmithing" public statements and the crucial return letter, the stress in the Robert Kennedy and Anatoly Dobrynin meeting when Kennedy said this was the "last chance" and Dobrynin said, "The Politburo is too committed to back down now," and Khrushchev's finally believing the U.S. would attack. In all of this there was collective discussion in the White House and very personal decision making in the Kremlin.

Are there dynamics of grace here? The triumph of hope and insistence on moral choice were clearly dynamics of openness in the White House. What makes someone respond to the importance of human dignity and moral choice? Grace, which empowers one to see beyond the bureaucratic, parochial, and fatalistic perspectives, made the marginal but decisive difference. Decisional structures are not abstract; they are shaped by the human and moral qualities at play, and they in turn foster those moral qualities. The two different decision structures and organizational cultures in 1914 and 1962 produced two different outcomes; in Washington the organizational culture opened up space for grace.

---

28. Reeves, *President Kennedy*, 386.
29. Schlesinger, *Robert F. Kennedy and His Times*, 549.

Yet grace is not enough. There had to be wise crisis management calculations. There had to be a president who, unlike the tsar, would not give in to pressure from the military. There had to be a General Maxwell Taylor who would, unlike Moltke, act in obedience to a presidential decision with which he disagreed. A thoroughly disgusted Dean Acheson would have to support a decision with which he disagreed, and, unlike Bethmann, seek to persuade French President Charles de Gaulle of its wisdom. Why did these men, as well as CIA Director John McCone, who could have secretly undercut the process, go along? The United States had an organizational culture that was open enough to allow grace to operate in the lives of these men.

Do these examples prove the existence and operation of grace? No, but they do provide examples of events that conform to the nature of grace and so give circumstantial credence to its impact when people and conditions are right. With the freedom to make moral choices in the hope for a more humane and meaningful world, a theology of grace provides a foundation for understanding and acting in the world of foreign policy. As we approach a global power transition in the near future, we must do all we can to leverage good judgment and graceful purposes and policies. This model of the interaction of grace and foreign affairs provides such a foundation.

FROM GRACE TO ETHICS

Grace is God's openness to our living "in Christ" and to leading us in the contingencies of our time and experiences. Our openness to grace brings us guidance, support, and hope. In possession of such virtues we can operate in the world with a moral imagination. The policies, processes, and organizations of foreign policy can be means of grace, through which Christians operate to build a more humane world as they rebuke the forces of darkness, rescue victims, resist forces of irrationality and repression, and reform our world.

Ethics define our approach and boundaries to issues of physical and historical forces, with meaning, vision, and choice. Ethics and ethical action or applied ethics give substance to our moral imagination as we live between history and meaning, between fate and choice.

Deontological ethics are satisfying but difficult to make work beyond a circle of reality. Utilitarianism is easy to make work, but the cost is too high in terms of moral meaning. In the choices and consequences that come through the dialectics of our lives one finds the meaning of history to be ambiguous at best. In this world of power and parochialism, however, the hope that supervenience makes possible is a motivation to act and decide toward a better world.

Modern society is complex and complicated, and a series of ethical systems operate within it. There are personal, organizational, and operational ethics. Personal ethics center around respect for one's self and others, and are exemplified by being honest, caring, faithful, responsible, and dependable. There are organizational and corporate ethics revolving around the goal of maximizing profit and exemplified by four categories including an organization's members and leaders, social and stock-holder responsibilities, products and customers, and acquisition and distribution.

Public administrative ethics differs from those business ethics. Public officials are responsible for more, for society as a whole and to all of its citizens who are afforded certain constitutional rights and safeguards from predatory business, and to the moral values of freedom, justice, equality, and the future. Ethics in the realm of foreign policy differ still. While nations cooperate, their more fundamental ethical commitment is the moral value of success since national security policy has much higher stakes and values than, for example, agricultural policy or the National Park Service. We know about conquered states, dominated states, and failed states. Those are not options; success in protecting the nation is the fundamental goal of foreign and national security policies.

Foreign policy takes place in a much more gray area than public administration. As individuals and a nation we must be smart, accept the role of force, mixed motives, and double agents in foreign policy, and be committed to the success of the national interest. However, a political ethic of success cannot be defined in ways to prevent any moral boundaries.

I want to suggest five personal affirmative ethical principles and five political and policy boundaries.

First, though global politics go on under the sign of the verdict of the Bible, grace is universal and unites humanity. Life is not dualistic; morality is built into reality. Policy and administration must always remember that people are unique spiritual humans, that the fact and fate of humanity matters. What is done in foreign affairs should also serve the greater good of humankind. An embrace by grace should lead to efforts to rebuke the forces of indignity, rescue the victims, reform structures of pharaohism.

At the same time, knowing the hallowedness of life and privilege of life in Christ brings a sense of awe and purpose. Lives can connect to both the sweep of history and God's own providential history through efforts to work for the greater good of all humankind.

Second, grace should evoke an inspiration to serve others. Increased grace should increase preference and sacrifice for others, a principle that escaped Joseph. The foreign affairs community is a distinct world of service to the people of this country and to people of other countries. The view that the government is the problem and we have no obligation or responsibility to American democracy is counterproductive in this era of historical change and danger. The commandment to love one another is defined in the larger national and global world of foreign affairs by the ethic of service. Blessed are those who hunger and thirst for the right to prevail, and work to make it so.

Third, grace as the dynamic presence of the kingdom of God in our lives should bring a creative hope to our work, supporting our struggles and dialogue with events to prevent historical fate. We live in a web of possibilities, in a process of continuing creation, and the movement of grace makes moral imagination and freedom of choice possible. David and Joab may claim there were no other means of crowning David king except through the "dirty hands" of war and duplicity. Granted the necessity of walking along the moral margins, and granted the lethal dangers of being wrong about policy, efforts should nevertheless be sought with less tragic second- and third-order consequences. Efforts at renewal and humane reform should characterize the work of those embraced by grace.

Fourth, grace should bring a foundation of moral courage. We are fortunate to actually be able to experience the divine, to have personal leadership from the Holy Spirit–Counselor. Moral courage must face the political opposition and professional risk endemic to promoting public policy. There are no guarantees of success, but when one is certain of being led by the Lord, declining one's moral responsibility or succumbing to the pressure of others to conform is an affront to those like Jeremiah and Esther who stood up against the risks, even though the outcomes of their particular situations were different.

Fifth, we should let grace bring seriousness to the opportunities and choices in the early years of careers. Careers in public service in this context of grace should be marked by policy value and personal advancement over safety and mediocrity. David and Joab were in their mid-twenties when they embarked on the quest for the promised crown. Esther was likely in her late twenties when she undertook the action that represented the high point of her life. Zedekiah, the king in Jerusalem who chose the advice of his court counselors over the advice of Jeremiah, was in his mid-twenties when he broke with Babylon. He chose badly.

The first political boundary to the central ethic of success is a commitment to regime values, that is, the processes and ethics of democracy. Though the central ethic of foreign affairs is success, the basic values of the country are not expendable. Those values must be protected, and illegality and other forms of subversion of our democracy avoided. Where that line is currently is disputed and will ultimately depend on decisions of the Supreme Court. Nevertheless, regime values are the moral purposes for which a nation defends and promotes itself and cannot be lost.

A second political boundary to the quest for success comprises the professional ethics of administrators and officials to the public rather than the private good, such as Esther rather than Joseph. It involves accountability to the public and obligation to "speak truth to power." In the negative it means to avoid organizational and policy parochialism and the discrimination and favoritism that define corruption. It is the hunger and commitment to righteousness applied to policy and process.

The third policy boundary to the central quest for success is solidarity ethics or the principle of universalization. The national security interests of a global power with a volunteer military must have the active support of allies, so the United States must take care that its actions and policies are sufficiently limited and moral to retain the political and moral support of allies and reluctant nations willing to cooperate with us. Meekness cannot be applied to foreign policy, but it can be a metaphor meaning to avoid hubris and arrogance, and avoid acting unilaterally on operations with significant moral overtones.

The ethic of human value or dignity provides a fourth boundary. The Farewell Sermon is about an ethic of service to others, the ethic rejected by Joseph with demeaning consequences. The ethic of a floor of minimal dignity to citizens and adversaries in the modern world is enshrined in the prohibitions against discrimination in domestic politics and torture and into noncombatant immunity in the laws of war. It is a crucial boundary that prevents the slippage into social Darwinism and fascism. The exact definition of that boundary has again been contested in the War on

Terror, but in the negative it means to avoid the evils of torture and mass suffering of both combatants and civilians.

Fifth, there must be an ethic of rationality. Joseph got this one. He made a forecast of a major future challenge, then clearly analyzed it and developed a policy to be a solution. His "political" use of that policy was not inherent in the solution and does not negate the value of rationality. His political use of rationality violated the boundary of dignity and national values. That does not mean he should have made reason subordinate to religion, but that rationality and dignity are boundaries to each other as well as to the primary value of success.

Those boundaries are not fixed. Our lives are dialogical; we live in the interplay or dialogue between our best sense of political and kingdom ethics and the long-term fate and short-term conditions of history, between national choice of policy and personal choice about it, and between our personal goals, organizational responsibility, and personal danger.

What then is left?

We participate in the life of the Trinity through grace, living "in Christ" and guided by his Counselor. Around that center core we add persuasive theological concepts to shape our personal and public moral sense. As Christians we have the opportunity to use politics to build structural means of grace, to find providential meaning in the sweep of history, to analyze, organize, build what is necessary for the crisis of our time, and in the midst of all that to live a penitent life within the grace of God.

3

Diplomacy: The Professional Front Line

> When the international order is in flux, the past and present are no longer a clear guide to the future.... States formerly devoted to the defense and preservation of the status quo must become assertively demanding.... The transition to such an assertive diplomatic strategy is often difficult for a state that has prospered in the now collapsing status quo.[1]

THE GLOBAL ORDER BUILT on U.S. hegemony is collapsing, which comes as a shock. The sudden implosion of the Soviet Union ended the fifty-year Cold War and left the United States and its global reach intact. The anticipated "peace dividend" did not happen, nor did the new order of global peace and prosperity through widespread international cooperation and the goodness and wisdom of the United States as the world's leader. Instead, long-repressed ethnic animosities and cultural rejections tore apart nations much more fragile than we assumed. The United States itself suffered a new Pearl Harbor attack on the twin towers in New York, and the vaunted supremacy of the military might of the United States and its strategy of "shock and awe" failed in Iraq and Afghanistan. The financial storm of 2008 ravaged U.S. prosperity built on deregulation and easy credit, limiting the options for U.S. policy in the world. The fact that the U.S. was blindsided by all these events made the situation even worse.

There are some projections of the future that one can make with confidence. Will Iran build its own nuclear weapons? Without a doubt. Will the rise of China be peaceful? Not likely. Will the world's population continue to grow faster than jobs? Yes, and several governments may well crumble under the social strains. Will religious zealots mobilize vast parts

---

1. Freeman, *Arts of Power*, 74.

of the world against the U.S. and its secular civilization? The answer to that question may well be the "tipping point" in determining the substance, stakes, and style of American foreign policy for the next fifty years. The quality of life in the United States and the survival of its influence in international relations will be at risk if the world moves against the West. Will it all be determined by war? The best answer is that we must be determined that it does not. Underlying that determination is the hope that the art of diplomacy can shape attitudes and promote cooperation to make a better world.

DIPLOMACY

If war is the continuation of politics by other means, then it is one thing if war comes because there are vital interests at stake higher than peace, but another thing if war comes as a failure of the other means, particularly diplomacy. Diplomacy is the front line of responding to the challenges of this era, the reshaping of global politics. "For all our military strength," one retired Foreign Service Officer said," the demands on our diplomatic skills will be the greatest in our history. The stakes are high, and the margins for error of our foreign policies are steadily narrowing."[2]

History is in transition. America's war in Iraq and its economic trauma have deeply wounded it as the leading nation of the world, making the relative rise of other nations much easier. Reaching a point of serious decline has risen in probability. If this country is not going to passively accept "whatever," it will need an assertive and demanding diplomacy. Those two adjectives are not found in the Beatitudes. Where and how can a Christian be involved in such diplomacy?

Foreign policy is about goals, and diplomacy serves those goals that revolve around preserving and promoting the nation's national interest. The national interest is the long-term and continuing purpose of the state in protecting itself, its people, and their ideals, within a particular historical and global context. In the nineteenth century the national interest was sought through isolationism. During the Cold War it was nearly identical to national security defined in military terms, protecting the physical nation from nations with the intentions and capability to do harm to the United States. Twentieth-century threats came from the combination of strategic capability and adversarial intention.

2. Freeman, "Can American Leadership Be Restored?" 45.

Today the numbers of issues that affect the United States directly and indirectly are numerous. There is still too much poverty in the world, too many refugees, and too few clinics and hospitals. New issues that do not include human intention now threaten the nation, from global economic meltdown to global warming, the spread of AIDS, and a growing scarcity of resources such as water. Priorities and prudence are necessary to prevent the concept of the national interest from being so broadly defined as to exhaust this country's foreign policy resources and will.

To keep the national interest manageable, it should be confined to concerns based on the human factors—the purposes of the other nations. America's liberal values mean it cannot be unconcerned about evil and suffering elsewhere, for it cannot survive with its humane values in a sea of suffering. Capabilities, at the same time, relate to opportunities as well as forces, meaning those with hostile intentions toward the U.S. may find opportunities to expand their capabilities by mobilizing insurgencies in failed states and capturing the hopes of the suffering. The goals of foreign policy have to include the moral values and cooperative processes of international politics, the creation of a humane world. The programs devised to create that more humane world can function as means of grace in the world for both those involved in the programs and those benefiting from them.

While the term "national interest" may be contested, it continues to imply two elements. The first is the physical protection of the nation's territory, economic well-being, and political independence. The second is the protection and promotion of its values, meaning the continuing global leadership of the Western world and global respect for its commitments to political and economic liberalism. Those commitments include democracy, development, defense of human rights, and equality of treatment, including the treatment of women. Foreign policy is about goals, which are not disembodied abstractions but are fully human and humane, political and programmatic, self-interested but cooperative.

In this era of change, risk, and probable projections, and with the absolute necessity of preventing the tipping point, diplomacy is always a double gamble, because it deals with events that are complex and unpredictable, and takes place at the forward edge of the inscrutable future. Predictive certainty is a dangerous daydream in an uncertain world—as in the coming of World War I—while caution and flexibility in the face of uncertainty can lead to success, as in the thirteen days of the Cuban

Missile Crisis, or to a "pit" as in the U.S. paralysis to the Serbian ethnic cleansing in Bosnia and Kosovo. Few response decisions in foreign policy are heavily weighed in favor of one option over another by a margin of 90/10; many are 55/45 or closer, for even if the choices seem clearer than that and achieve the short-term goals, the follow-on consequences are rarely clear at the time of decision. Later consequences can make the situation wonderfully better and history marginally worse, or make the situation marginally better with history terribly worse.

Diplomacy in turn is the use of persuasion and programs to reach those goals. Diplomatic policies and processes are used for multiple purposes: (1) to define and defend the broader Western values and the more specific American interests in other countries, (2) to analyze other countries' capabilities, intentions, and degree of threat, (3) to manage the transition from a unipolar to multipolar world, (4) to build cooperation among nations in pursuit of peace and community, and (5) to carry out programs that relieve suffering and build infrastructures for democracy, development, and human defense.

Diplomacy is both confrontational and cooperative, always working to shape the forces in play, whether by making this nation's image, policy and resolve clear, creating a structure of restraint through the elements of coercive diplomacy, or developing international agreements that replace rivalry with predictive cooperation. Diplomacy engages other nations in what is hoped will be partnership politics, but it also makes clear this nation's views and intentions to those nations rejecting partnership.

Agreement is not always the goal of diplomacy. Global structural changes can create security issues for which there can be no accommodation; images may be so distorted and firmly held that diplomacy is mere show and designed for domestic consumption. High-level diplomacy carries high stakes, is held tightly by the highest officials, and is covered (as best they can) by media. Lower level issues are less crucial and more routine, and of less interest to the media. Yet those issues may be just as intentionally designed to compete and undercut an adversary in the shadows while conducting open negotiation with professionals of good intentions and good faith.

Decisions by low-level officials in unexpected opportunities, such as the forced landing of a spy plane said to be violating national air space, if handled badly, can have more impact on images than negotiations. One assumes such an action would not be taken without higher approval, yet not all nations are centralized, not all military forces are under unified military command. Diplomacy is often a gamble that a nation will follow through on an agreement; diplomacy is sometimes intentionally ambiguous to get an agreement with the hope of gaining advantage later.

Partnerships with other nations are important in a changing world, for they can provide information that helps decision makers "read" another nation, obviously vital in minimizing the margins of misunderstanding and unpredictability among those less inclined to be partners. Diplomacy is about words, but words are not abstract and self-evident. Words communicate information, but also social and mental values. Not everyone who speaks English thinks in English, and a cultural understanding of the words of another culture helps penetrate beneath the surface of a society. Words can have very discrete meanings as well as a thousand ways to say yes or no without actually saying so. Words of agreement meant merely to say "I understand" can be taken to mean "I agree," leaving one side believing agreement has been reached when there was no such intention.

At all levels of diplomacy there are wide margins for misinterpretations, clumsy proposals and rejections, and officials with narrow views and no working moral compass. Roger Morris drafted the National Security Studies Memorandum on what became the Nixon presidency's policy toward Africa, and he later wrote that in retrospect it was "a disaster, naïve in concept, practically impossible for the government to execute, and thus a ready cover for pursuing the most reactionary and short-sighted U.S. interests in the region."[3] Add national or global stress, and reactions of leaders become unpredictable, and existing agreements lose their moderating power, rendering international statecraft "diplomacy in the dark."[4]

Diplomacy requires the ethic of rationality, but diplomacy also has attributes of a gamble; diplomacy is about wisdom in a context of uncertainty. As Secretary of State Warren Christopher wrote about the risks involved if the Dayton negotiations failed, "Had it been wise to take the chance? I decided it was too early to engage in postmortem thinking. We had launched the process, and it simply had to work." The issues were complex, two hundred and fifty thousand people had been killed and another two million made refugees, so the bitterness and distrust ran deep. To complicate the situation further, there was the gamble with the public,

---

3. Roger Morris, *Uncertain Greatness*, 111.
4. Hoffmann, *Duties beyond Borders*, 21.

for some White House domestic advisors hoped the agreement would fail because polls showed the public did not want the U.S. to have to enforce a shaky peace.[5]

Diplomacy can be conceived narrowly as negotiations, but it can also cover a wide range of foreign policy activities and purposes, especially for a great power like the United States. This chapter will use the broader meaning since all of the activities we consider will be done through the Department of State. Variety of activities means variety of people. Young people can look at engagement in diplomatic activities as a job, or a professional career, or a path to making an impact and difference, or a career of personal fulfillment. The professional career is the world of the Foreign Service, which is small and closed. The term job here is not necessarily a pejorative term. A diplomatic job can embody responsibilities and functions done for personal satisfaction—living abroad, having the panache of working out of an embassy, and meeting the needs of both the United States and the host governments. As a job it may be merely a short-term experience between other jobs or a résumé builder for gaining access to global organizations. In these times of change it needs to go beyond a job and be a career-long time of determined and assertive service to the nation and the needs of people elsewhere.

In the first quarter of the twenty-first century the American nation will need people in diplomacy with a determination to make a difference in defending and promoting the interests of the nation in an increasingly dangerous international system. Diplomacy as routine has to give way to diplomacy as determination. The ethics of bureaucratic culture and professionalism, the ethics of personal advancement and diplomatic service will all be in play.

Given its stature—and the modern world in which events in one part of the globe can no longer be isolated and ignored by the other—the U.S. does not limit its diplomacy to its own national needs but also focuses on growing stress and conflict between other nations. The State Department seeks involvement in conflict resolution and peacemaking projects. True, its priorities relate to its larger national interests, but not always. Also, given modern Western values, diplomacy extends far beyond negotiations and now includes contractors to help other nations on

---

5. Christopher, *Chances of a Lifetime*, 260, 267.

issues from economic development to drug trafficking, from health issues to agriculture.

Diplomacy is about peace, being a peacemaker. "Blessed are the peacemakers," said Jesus. A work of grace is healing and reconciliation, and that can be done with minimal results or more extensive results. There is the peace of non-war as the United States seeks to end conflict and war between states or insurgents, called peacemaking. Often Christians dismiss non-war as a goal, thinking shalom is the only goal worthy of their efforts. Yet non-war means people are not dying, making a space for grace and being a goal worthy of a Christian's calling. Non-war is fragile, so the United States is deeply involved in the diplomacy of peace-building, with efforts at reconciliation between people, resettlement of displaced persons, reconstructing the capacity to trust and a moral sense, and re-valuing persons. Those are good goals, and difficult to achieve, but again worthy of our efforts. Christians have a special task of finding a way to make the power of pain into a broadening of the moral imagination of a failed or devastated state.

GRACE AND DIPLOMACY

Diplomacy involves a target nation and wider audience. The diplomacy between two nations in deep disagreement or conflict takes place at the highest levels. The wider audience of other nations reacts to those two nations and their issue, and it is the task of U.S. embassy personnel to explain U.S. policy and persuade those other nations, allies and not, that the policy is legitimate and not contrary to their interests. The explanation may be weak in the view of some while others may be automatically opposed. Lies and double standards by Foreign Service Officers destroy mutuality. Assuming the United States has not adopted anything close to Nazi policies, assuming its policy protects its rightful interests without arrogant disregard for, exploitation of, or blindness to the rightful interests of others, then diplomacy assumes and seeks to link to the goodness or better side of human nature and common interests. This is not a process of "dirty hands" but in fact becomes an ethical process.

As diplomacy promotes openness and common and transcending (such as human rights) values, it can become a means of grace, that is, a means that reduces dehumanizing forces, makes moral choices explicit, and promotes hope, all of which can move people and situations beyond social

Darwinism to at least tolerance if not mutual good regard. Diplomacy requires people of maturity, open to more than venal self-interest.

Diplomacy is about uncertainty; grace is about assurance. Diplomacy is about persuasion; grace is about optimism. Too often the preferred way of dealing with uncertainty is dualistic thinking, processing reality into polar opposites and simplifying ambiguity and paradox by projecting onto rivals the worst motives and predictions of behavior. Uncertainty is unsettling. At the personal level grace is a release from paranoia as theology. While security issues can act as closure dynamics, individuals who have reached stage 5 of Kohlberg's levels of maturity are able to take a broader view of others as well as themselves, and grace works to reveal larger meanings and opportunities. The humanizing grace of God that exists throughout the world provides a basis for bonding and opportunities for continuing creation, while personal confidence can flow from one's openness to grace. Grace does not preclude steadfastness or assertiveness in tough negotiations, particularly on issues of moral importance involving power and human conditions, but it should engender patient perseverance in seemingly intractable negotiations and creativity in personal and team searches for breakthrough ideas.

How is that possible in a world of power? Given both the national security concern with threats and the foreign policy goals of a humane world, diplomacy can be a process of coercion, or exploration, or bargaining, or construction. The first, coercive diplomacy, tries to force concessions by the other party. It is a zero-sum game, a win/lose outcome with little margin for seeing larger opportunities, no space for grace. The interests are irreconcilable, and the means used in such diplomacy could be brutal threats, actual economic or political sanctions, even military displays, and always include distortions of issues and portrayals of the other party. War is averted through submission. The outcomes include pride and humiliation, attitudes of superiority and animosity.

Diplomacy as exploration takes place in situations of low intensity as a U.S. diplomat works with officials from another nation to solve their basic policy issues. Sometimes the context is reconstructing a failed state, other times a new pro-American leadership regime attempting to find its way before opposition forces can coalesce against it, and other times a change in policy that represents a new beginning in relationships. Whatever the situation the diplomat seeks new possibilities, new options, clear analysis of choices and clear understanding of the impact of the new ideas on the web of interconnectedness internally and externally. The diplomat's own creativity will help shape the future of that country.

Bargaining diplomacy is done through offers and steadfastness, rewards and denials, demands and concessions, and making choices. It seeks to find a multiple-sum result, a compromise somewhere between the interests of the parties. Maximum positions are relaxed to a point that achieves the minimal interests, plus as much more of the goals being sought as possible, thus avoiding conflict or war and achieving relative satisfaction. While the grace of God may be present or result, closure dynamics may also remain as the nations continue in a hurting stalemate and an enduring rivalry after the negotiations.

Diplomacy as construction seeks to enlarge the benefits to each party. In situations where goals are not incompatible, diplomats should seek to find what is behind the interests of the parties and find ways to satisfy those implicit needs. They seek not just a settlement of an issue but the meeting of basic political needs and the creation or deepening of a cooperative relationship.

In the 1978 Camp David negotiations the demands of Egypt and Israel appeared irreconcilable. Egypt demanded the return of all of Sinai while Israel refused. Probing revealed the deeper needs; Egypt considered Sinai sovereign territory which it could not negotiate away, while Israel laid no claims to the land but insisted on control of the land as the only means of security against future invasions. In light of their different values, an agreement was reached that returned Sinai to the nation of Egypt, but it would be demilitarized and under international monitoring. If such a political process is attempted, there is space for grace to influence participants.

No lower-level diplomat operates on his or her own; department instructions and policy always confine individuals in negotiations. While there are policy-based limits, they are movable, to some extent expandable, and it is up to the diplomat to explore those limits and push them out. Instructions are subject to reality. Communication is a two-way process within a delegation and between them and the department. The struggle among American policy makers over how to view a rival and its positions, over what to demand and to concede, can be as delicate or strained as between the negotiating teams. An individual who constantly seeks to be open to the presence of a grace that sustains an elevated view of a common humanity, who seeks through that grace to gain new insights and ideas, can be a diplomat comfortable with uncertainty and ambiguity. Diplomatic outcomes are not determined; grace reaches across time and should be a force for personalizing relations across societies, bringing hope that uncertainty will not collapse into destruction but will empower those open to grace to find acceptable if not positive agreements.

John Foster Dulles spent a career in foreign affairs within the context of religious principles. His early experiences, particularly as a low-ranking advisor to the Americans at the post World War I Versailles peace conference led him to understand the necessity for an ethical component in policies dealing with world politics. When he became a central figure in the crafting of the Japanese Peace Treaty after World War II he tried to implement those views, for if ever there was "the occasion to try to make a peace which would invoke the principles of the moral law," it was there. To that end he worked to insure that the treaty invoked

> the spirit of forgiveness to overcome the spirit of vengefulness; the spirit of magnanimity to overcome the spirit of hatred; the spirit of humanity and fair play to overcome the spirit of competitive greed; the spirit of fellowship to overcome the spirit of arrogance and discrimination; the spirit of trust to overcome the spirit of fear.[6]

Dulles's subsequent career as secretary of state seemed to reverse those ethical principles, but even if that is true, the values he sought did create a world of friendship that has lasted over a half century.

THE FOREIGN SERVICE

The United States Foreign Service is the nation's professional diplomatic corps, each Foreign Service Officer (FSO) commissioned by the president, by and with the advice and consent of the Senate. FSOs enter through a professional exam and so are protected from political patronage. Diplomats have the equivalent rank of their military counterparts, and their rank and pay are invested in them as persons rather than in the specific job they have in one country or another.

Still, like attorneys, they are professionals who are accorded little regard until needed. Unlike architects or dentists or accountants who have specific and visible accomplishments, diplomats are thinkers, persuaders, and advisors in a field with few if any visible and lasting accomplishments or public notice (unless things go wrong). Other departments have always

---

6. John Foster Dulles, "How My Faith Helped in a Decisive Hour."

wanted their own foreign operatives and resisted the Department of State being made the single Foreign Service corps. Also, like attorneys, they are professionals, sworn to uphold the U.S. Constitution and the peace and security of the nation despite some misgivings, just as attorneys defend some clients out of a commitment to the rule of law.

Diplomacy through its professional FSOs is this nation's front line in the changing world. Yet this is a shocking number: the United States has more musicians in its military bands than it has FSOs around the globe, and there is a shortage of mid-level and senior-level FSOs caused by earlier hiring freezes. War is the failure of diplomacy, but the State Department has annual budgets far below that of the Defense Department. Diplomacy is slow, and "political." Weapons are visible, their impact immediate and dramatic. As Secretary of Defense Robert Gates noted, the entire diplomatic corps of about 6,500 people is less than the staffing of a single aircraft carrier group. Furthermore, the Foreign Service has no built-in support group. For example, the F-22 aircraft is produced by companies in 44 states, meaning it has the support of 88 senators.[7]

Diplomacy, for the political, economic, and public information FSOs, is the process of reporting "what is going on," and determining the set of arguments and personal relationships that best achieve U.S. goals. It maintains if not improves relations, and reduces the level of distrust and criticism of the United States. That process may be noble, or satisfying, or conflicting. Many times the process is very satisfying as one works with a host nation's leaders to solve their foreign relations problems or promote economic development or fight human trafficking, or multiple other worthy causes. Many times the process is noble as it relieves suffering of refugees or promotes peacemaking between contending foreign leaders or creates a better world for people there and here. Many times the multiple (if not ponderous) staff meetings, the reports, the discussions with media and politicians, and the myriad other activities seem morally tone deaf. At other times not everything is so noble as individuals deal with the trade-offs that come from complicated issues and sets of conflicting U.S. needs and policies.

Diplomacy is the nation's front line, yet there are structural issues. Diplomatic personnel can find career options at four levels: a routine job with travel privileges, an exercise of one's personal best in the manage-

---

7. Quoted by Kristof in "Make Diplomacy, Not War."

ment of complexity and crisis, a means for constructing a better world, and a thing of beauty as the lines of effort come together. The Foreign Service was a noble career after World War I. It was then marginalized in World War II by a wartime president and criticized when not mocked by members of Congress for being too soft on leaders making trouble for the United States. No new officers were brought into the Service during World War II to prevent the label of draft-dodger being applied, leading to a shortage of personnel and therefore plans and programs after the war. FSOs were not defended by their own secretary of state during congressional attacks in the 1950s, demoralizing the corps. The State Department did not even escape Billy Graham, who publicly criticized it in his revivals in the early 1950s, an action he later considered "foolish and presumptuous."[8]

FSOs work as professionals despite congressional budget cuts. Congressman Otto Passman (D-LA) made his reputation cutting State's budget. When the Soviet empire collapsed in 1991 the State Department needed to open nine new embassies, but Secretary of State James Baker was unwilling to ask Congress for the additional funds, so personnel were pulled from existing embassies to start up and operate the new ones. Even more personal, the limited budgetary allowance to each embassy goes to the ambassador. FSOs wanting or needing to host an event for their circle of notables and influentials, despite the value of those events, have to host them out of their own personal funds.

The Service does not escape generational change, important for keeping it vibrant and creative. A new generation of young people entered the Foreign Service in the 1960s, bringing with them a new culture. They were the generation of the civil rights movement, more aware of modern technology, critical of post-war mythology, and much more willing to fight for their ideas.[9] Many of them became known as the Young Turks, and their success came with the passage of the Foreign Service Act of 1980, which specified the merit qualifications for recruitment and advancement, including affirmative action, raised salaries to be comparable with the Civil Service, and introduced performance pay as a tangible reward for exceptional service.

New recruits to the Foreign Service at the opening of the twenty-first century brought another new culture. Young FSOs from Generation

---

8. Gibbs and Duffy, *The Preacher and the Presidents*, 40.
9. Bean, "Down in Generation Gap," 77–81.

X are highly computer literate but lack people skills; they are effective in a team setting but are pessimistic about authority. There is also a concern that the Foreign Service will not be a lifelong commitment or the single focus of their life, with young people entering it as much to see the world and live an interesting life from their personal perspective as they will be to serve. Many graduates take the attitude, "I'm young and I'm single, so why not give it a try?" These young people are worth the risk for the department because "a lot of people who say they'll try it for a couple of years end up staying."[10]

Despite the generational difference, the nation will need people like Kiki Munshi, who retired from the Foreign Service after twenty-two years, only to return to become involved in some of the new tasks for foreign policy, leading a Provincial Reconstruction Team at a forward operating base in Iraq. "I felt a sense of moral obligation to try to help rebuild Iraq," she said.[11]

Another structural issue relates to the culture of American diplomacy. Charles Lerche wrote about two styles of diplomacy. With lawyers occupying the top echelons of diplomacy, Lerche wrote, U.S. diplomacy is like poker, individual discrete issues in which one wins or loses, while the Soviet Union's diplomacy was like chess, in which individual events form a longer strategy of success.[12] Henry Kissinger wrote about three types of diplomatic leadership and consequences: communist ideological diplomacy from a culture of historical determinism that cannot admit leaders can be swayed by argument; Third-World charismatic-revolutionary diplomacy that is personal and domestic-oriented and tends to be reckless; and Western bureaucratic-pragmatic diplomacy that is slow and gets caught up in bureaucratic dilemmas.[13] Raymond Cohen wrote about differences between liberal and communal diplomacy, that is, diplomacy with communal societies like Muslim Pakistan that are relationship-oriented rather than deal-oriented societies. In Western societies events and time are linear, leading to an end point, a decision; while in communal

10. Stevenson-Yang, "Anatomy of an Officer Corps," 32.
11. Quoted in Tyson, "Applying Diplomacy to Conflict," A19.
12. Lerche, *The Cold War . . . And After*, 11–15.
13. Kissinger, "Domestic Structure and Foreign Policy," 18–28.

societies politics are personal, decisions are reached through consensus, requiring time and saving face.[14]

Religion-based diplomacy—is it another type of ideological diplomacy with fixed and basically irreconcilable conflict in vision and goals? Is religion the explanatory and motivating factor in diplomacy based on more traditional political and economic inequalities, or is religion merely a mediating factor between a conflict and choices, allowing perspective but also freedom in choice?[15]

Time and historical evidence will tell, but one example may be the unwillingness of communist leaders to place their nations in danger. Stalin's "socialism in one country" trumped Trotsky's commitment to sacrificing the Soviet Union for promoting world revolution. Their values and theory of history constructed and shaped their view of the world, but the national interest moderated their actions. Will that be true of Iran?

The United States will require a Foreign Service able to overcome these structural issues and so meet the new challenges with successful responses, helping to bring into being a more humane world, a safer and a renewed America.

THE SERVICE AT WORK

What do FSOs do? They report and lobby the department and the host country on what is reasonable and wise, a routine endeavor at times, yet often performed during a time of crisis, and other times includes being caught between the politics of the host country and those of the U.S. government. For example, during the Dominican Republic crisis in 1963, Congress was about to pass legislation that would make relations worse by reducing the quota of America's sugar purchases, falling particularly heavy on the dollar income of the Dominican Republic. Not only would the new democratic government in the Dominican Republic feel betrayed, it might severely damage the new Alliance for Progress by withdrawing from it, and the civilian government itself might be jeopardized. Ambassador John Bartlow Martin sent a long and strong cable to the department about the consequences, then assembled his staff and told them to "slow down the Dominican reaction before it got completely out of control." He divided the department up and made assignments on

---

14. Raymond Cohen, "Negotiating across Cultures," 469–82.
15. See Hasenclever and Rittberger, "Does Religion Make a Difference?" 109–15.

whom to contact to get and gauge reaction to lobby the American government. As Martin recalled:

> The next day we kept sending cables—what our sources said, what the press said, the talk on the street, over-all wrap-ups, everything. We simply kept piling the cables in, making them for immediate action, and transmittal to the White House.[16]

The embassy diplomats hoped Congress would stalemate, thereby extending the existing law. Elections were coming up, however, and the law passed. During all that time the ambassador and FSOs worked constantly with Dominican authorities and influentials to reassure them that something could be worked out and to prevent a military coup. Then President Kennedy stepped in to make up the dollar difference, and an amendment to a wholly different bill gave the president discretionary authority to increase the quota, resolving the crisis. The relief was interrupted when the embassy's CIA officer informed the diplomats that the Castro regime in Cuba, having lost an issue that could undermine the democratic and pro-American Dominican government, was organizing a protest that could threaten the embassy and might spark a military coup. The protest took place, but the police line held and the sugar crisis ended.[17]

"Do you want war or peace?" the ambassador asked the newly posted FSO to the nation of Laos, a country sandwiched between Vietnam and Thailand and now itself torn by war between nationalist and communist forces. John Gunther Dean had worked with the military in Vietnam where the war was still raging and wanted to work for peace in his new assignment in Laos in 1972, so said "I'll take peace." From there he worked with the contending factions in Laos, and also the contending factions within the Embassy and back in Washington. As part of the web of conflict in Southeast Asia some U.S. officials favored pressing for a military solution, while others favored Dean's small efforts. The ambassador left for reassignment elsewhere, which left Dean in charge as acting ambassador, giving him the space to take new initiatives to broker a deal. In the midst of his efforts a Laotian general took over a radio station and announced his attempt to overthrow the government. His forces took over an airport from which they intended to bomb loyal forces. Many embassy people were there to watch developments, as were Laotian forces waiting

16. Martin, *Overtaken by Events*, 164–65.
17. Ibid., 161–77.

to see which side would prevail. Dean drove out onto the runway to block any planes from taking off. The general tried, could not get by the car, and crashed at the side of the tarmac. Soon everybody left. From that point on the diplomacy of bargaining made progress and an agreement on a coalition government was reached, ending the fighting. It was purely a non-war agreement, and later failed when all of Southeast Asia fell in 1975, but Dean considered his efforts worthwhile. It was an imperfect peace but also the least bad option.[18]

FSOs can advise partner leaders on domestic as well as international issues. In another region of the world a nation was implementing a new election system in the 1980s to move toward a democratic monarchy. It appeared the new system would allow an anti-American group to win enough votes to displace the existing governing group, a significant setback for the United States in a sensitive region. The U.S. embassy's political officer understood the sociological basis of voting behavior, had studied the politics of the nation well, and understood its politics. He advised the leaders to target a specific area of the country that had not been politically active but whose interest was congruent with the government's policies. American-style campaign strategy worked, and the governing group won the election, avoiding the emergence of an anti-American government in a sensitive region.[19]

FSOs explain U.S. policy. Howard Simpson was a public affairs officer in the embassy in Paris in the 1960s and spent countless hours over long lunches with members of the French press corps, working to cement relations and gain the confidence of influential newsmen, insuring U.S. policy received a fair presentation in their press. As Simpson recalled, "Selling an idea or explaining a specific U.S. policy in the face of a French journalist's Cartesian logic when the policy itself was vague, inconsistent, or practically nonexistent was extremely difficult. Arguing our role in Vietnam with veteran French newsmen who had spent some of their working life in Indochina and were considered area experts often proved impossible."[20]

FSOs seek out and build strong personal relationships with key influentials, which can be more useful than tough negotiators in protecting our interests and deflecting outrage, especially in nations like Pakistan

18. Dean, *Danger Zones*, 70–81.
19. Related to the author by the political officer.
20. Simpson, *Bush Hat, Black Tie*, 93.

where politics is very personal. Reaching out with even modest favors or special lunches or speeding up a visa or two results in personal trust and complementary favors—like insight or advanced notice of developments, both of which take reporting beyond the basic knowledge to real intelligence. Those same favors can extend to introductions and avenues of access to opinion makers and other notables so important to conveying the clarity and intensity of the United States and its policies to key influentials. In even broader terms, building a network among politicians, journalists, academics, and social leaders is a "vital part of America's accumulated national security capital."[21]

Diplomacy can be largely routine but also take place in a movement toward crisis. Disputes move along a bell-curve cycle of increasing intensity, which may stall and become a circle of enduring rivalry or militarized dispute at a higher level, or not stall and increase in intensity until the nations are at war. Then there is a downward curve from a minimum of a cease fire to the maximum of good relations. Diplomacy operates in all segments and on both sides of the bell curve, seeking to slow the rise up the curve or stall it as soon as possible, either as an enduring rivalry or a stalled militarized interstate dispute. On the other side the goal is to push toward the lowest point on the descent down the curve, trying to reach good relations.

The crisis may be an ongoing state of affairs. For an FSO in the embassy at Islamabad, the routine takes place in the midst of multiple tensions. The nuclearized enduring rivalry between Pakistan and India often jumps up the curve to threats and shootings in Kashmir. Both countries are allies of the United States, and the diplomats work within and between the two countries, trying to diffuse fears, animosities, and enflamed images, and to find opportunities to move the two countries closer together and further along the down-side of the conflict curve. Pakistan is a dangerous country, requiring U.S. diplomats to travel in armored caravans. Danger also derives from the competing factions in the country that comprise multiple power blocs within the government, military, and politics. Strategically, the country is crucial for the U.S. War on Terror, which means the political officer has to work not only within the multiple power blocs but also with the additional tension of supporting Pakistan's partnership in the War on Terror and the broader American

---

21. Kiesling, *Diplomacy Lessons*, 75, 77.

goals of promoting human rights and democracy. Every year the embassy has to develop a report on Pakistan for the annual Human Rights report mandated by Congress, a report that is truthful yet does not sour relations between the embassy and the Pakistani government.

That report is just one of several irritants that feed much of the population's anger toward U.S. policy, with some opposition so intense that it presents a danger to the embassy and employees. This danger is sufficient to have warranted three evacuation orders for embassy personnel since 2000. For this reason, the political officers work on a third relationship, that between the population and the United States, speaking to a variety of audiences (many of them hostile) about the United States and its policies. Within the embassy itself the political officer works with counterparts from multiple U.S. government agencies, from the FBI and the Defense Department to the Departments of Agriculture and Commerce, seeking to ensure all of their efforts are coordinated with our foreign policy efforts in Pakistan. All of this contributes to the definition of routine diplomacy in Islamabad.

The context of routine and crisis is the line of policy a president and foreign policy team pursues to achieve their goals. That policy line may be a continuation of previous administrations, or a break with that policy and the assertion of a new one. The policy may be flexible and respond to changes, or frozen into a hard line despite developments, or in flux as disagreements over policy within the administration continues and no single line yet chosen. The policy may work or fail, may be irrelevant or make conditions worse. The task of the Department of State and individual Foreign Service Officers is to find the tools of persuasion to make the policy achieve its intended goals of protecting and promoting the national interest. If the policy is irrelevant to conditions, or failing or exacerbating conditions, professional ethics would demand that individuals, to the degree tolerated, give a more realistic view back to policymakers. The toleration of dissent diminishes rapidly the higher one ascends in the structures of foreign policy.

THE DEPARTMENT OF STATE

The Department of State is the central government agency for U.S. foreign policy, but being central does not mean it runs foreign policy. The department is an organization structured for programs and personnel to carry them out, with leaders and staff.

Three primary functions have traditionally taken place through the department. The Secretary of State is the main foreign policy advisor to the president and the Congress. The Foreign Service Officers have the other two traditional functions: those in embassies report to the Department of State on conditions in their assigned country and represent the department and the president to the leaders and people of that country. Their reports are a source of intelligence or knowledge for policy makers and crisis managers. The more successful the diplomat is at developing contacts for insights about the country, the better his or her representation of the U.S. can be, and the sooner the department can be advised of developing conflict.

Changing conditions lead to changes in the department. One transformation occurred during the turn of the last century as the U.S. expanded its power and goals in the world. After World War II the department transformed into the U.S. front line against the Soviet Union. The George W. Bush administration molded it again to make it an agent of change for other countries, which necessarily put its programs at the "critical intersections of diplomacy, democracy promotion, economic reconstruction and military security."[22]

These two FSO functions alone are no longer an adequate definition of the work of diplomats abroad. Diplomats now investigate human trafficking, track the drug trade, set up refugee camps, arrange for consultations by health care professionals from the United States, and promote U.S. business. The State Department has its own (contract) air force in Colombia for battling drug lords, coordinates efforts to build schools and bridges, and contracts with multiple groups to carry out its programs abroad.

The department, in other words, is no longer synonymous with the Foreign Service. Take refugee camps. Often situations arise in which hundreds if not thousands of people have to flee lawlessness, targeted persecution and lethal danger, and outright genocide. They take refuge across a border where they are not welcome and in inhospitable terrain where they are out of sight and contact with the population. Hundreds of people make up these camps. If the host country will not resettle them and the home country is still too dangerous, they have nowhere to go, often for

---

22. Rice, "Transformational Diplomacy."

years. It takes upwards of sixteen nongovernmental organizations to provide water and food, schooling for children, protection from bandits, and a host of other needs. The United States does not have the capacity to fund and administer such programs, so along with other nations it provides funds to a UN department, which organizes and coordinates those various organizations. A State Department civilian administrator periodically travels to the camps and oversees the operation and use of funds. This is a good and humane work.

Though embassies reflect the territorial nature of foreign policy, much of the work of the department is transnational, so its structure is complex. The Political Section of the Department is organized around regions and individual nations. Each regional bureau is headed by a president-appointed Assistant Secretary of State; each country has a Desk Officer who maintains contact with the embassy and advises them and the Assistant Secretary. There are transnational bureaus dealing with a variety of issues from arms control to democracy and global affairs, from economic affairs to narcotics and law enforcement affairs, and more.

Within the Office of the Secretary of State (S/S) a Coordinator for Counterterrorism takes a leading role in developing coordinated strategies to defeat terrorists abroad and in securing the cooperation of international partners. The department used Foreign Service specialists such as Larry Johnson, who became an expert on terrorism while at the CIA and then transferred to the Department of State and its Office of Counterterrorism. While not a FSO, Johnson's expertise proved invaluable to the department for building counterterrorism assistance programs, and he also helped write the short-lived annual Report on Terrorism.

Failed states and post-conflict states can be national security threats, for in such areas rogue militias and crime organizations threaten vulnerable populations, provide space and conditions to generate terrorism, traffic in persons, and lead to humanitarian catastrophes—all threatening to destabilize an entire region. The Office of the Coordinator for Reconstruction and Stabilization focuses diplomatic energy on preventing when possible the conflicts that tear a nation apart. Beyond peace, the Office manages stabilization and reconstruction operations in countries emerging from conflict or civil strife to lay the foundation for the well-being of the victims. Given the dangers of failing states, the Bureau of Intelligence and Research and Policy Planning staff developed a Watch list—a system for identifying countries that are vulnerable to state failure and need assistance with conflict prevention and mitigation. The Watch list is prepared from various classified and unclassified sources and for the State Department's Foreign Emergency Support Team, which is the only interagency, on-call, short-notice team poised to respond to terrorist incidents worldwide. This important goal of peace and development is motivated by self-interest, but does not preclude concern and care for others.

State does not work alone in operations abroad, which impact both policies and the embassies. The Department of Agriculture oversees a major food program, while Commerce promotes trade with other nations. Defense sells arms to other countries, trains their forces, partners in joint military exercises, and sets up policy within its six regional commands. The CIA is there to conduct clandestine intelligence operations. The difficulty arises out of this decentralization of foreign policy; each department advises the president through the White House's National Security Council (NSC), but State has no legal authority over any of them and their programs. Basic policy may be decided at the NSC, but the devil is always in the details, with plenty of latitude in understanding of that policy, allowing individual departments to interpret the policy in view of their goals and cultures.

Coordinating these efforts is a major continuing issue. After the Bay of Pigs disaster President Kennedy asked General Maxwell Taylor to recommend an institutional mechanism to improve the ability of the secretary of state to coordinate the departments within existing law.[23] His plan still exists in the form of a central interdepartmental group at the undersecretary level to work out differences, and six similar groups at the regional level. Still, with dispersed authority, decisions can only be based on consensus, often reached through hours and hours of discussions and vagueness in language. The current structure has sought to increase State's influence in the groups by designating the State Department official as the chairman of the groups, yet their effectiveness will always depend on the personalities involved.

ORGANIZATIONAL CULTURE

Foreign Service Officers are bureaucrats in one sense yet take on other roles as well. The Foreign Service traditionally drew its members from the Ivy League universities, reflecting both the "high politics" nature of

---

23. Taylor, *Responsibility and Response*, 65–80.

diplomacy and the belief that diplomacy required a unique expertise. That elitist and "cookie pushers" nature of the Foreign Service, if ever true, is long since gone. The department actively recruits a wide variety of persons for both the FSO and civil service ranks.

The 1968 book *Fires in the In-Basket: The ABC's of the State Department*, by Leacacos, reflects the culture of immediacy, the assumptions of the reality of surprise, the futility of planning, the primacy of the political officers, and the need for generalists rather than specialists in the Foreign Service. Most of the operations of the department are routine, but not all. An immediate, urgent response may be called for at any time, and the department must avert, stop, or resolve the issue by buying time, through the use of waffling, ambiguity, and vague responses, according to Leacacos, to move issues "from the front burner to the back burner, to the steam table, to the cooling shelf, where eventually they may be handled without second-degree burns and with equity and possibly even reason." To do that, the key ingredient is multifaceted versatility in all aspects of the political, military, economic, and psychological factors that enter the equation. That versatility has to be developed as a "combination of experience, training, and native talent."[24]

To develop that versatility, the department rotates FSOs to new assignments every three years. The department wants them to understand the country of their assignment but not be there so long that they become an advocate of that country rather than a policy advocate of the United States. Expertise is never deeply achieved. On the other hand, the ability to understand and function in many different kinds of countries and regions develops a nimbleness and skillfulness that makes FSOs valuable as they rise in their career. Ideally, they develop a geopolitical perspective from their rotations. Recently the department has allowed diplomats to "major" in a region, rotating between countries within a region for several assignments.

Planning and management were outside the traditional culture of the department. In the late 1960s President Johnson tried to impose the Planning, Programming, Budgeting System (PPBS) that worked so well in the Pentagon across the Potomac River. U. Alexis Johnson, ambassador to Japan, spoke for the diplomats when he said:

---

24. Leacacos, *Fires in the In-Basket*, 67, 73.

The overwhelming mass of foreign-policy problems and decisions, and those that determine the fundamentals of our relations with other countries, are political in the broadest and best sense of the term and do not lend themselves to any budgetary approach.[25]

The PPBS effort failed completely. Deputy Under Secretary for Management William B. Macomber was sympathetic to some of the criticisms of the Young Turks and installed a new Policy Analysis and Resource Allocation system in the early 1970s.[26] In 1994, however, Congress legislated that all executive branch departments must prepare annual performance and accountability reports, specifying their mission and core values, specific goals, and results. The Under Secretary for Management took on new priority, and each section of the department met with the Deputy Secretary of State for annual discussions of their goals and performance results.

Secretary of State Colin Powell came to office by way of the military, which emphasizes people and morale. Very few former secretaries considered the organization important, which usually rates only one sentence in their memoirs, and that sentence refers to who they put in charge of management. Powell was different, taking a personal interest in the people, and they responded. During a military career an officer will have two years of leadership training; in the Department of State training averages two weeks. Powell instituted mandatory leadership training for mid-level officers and a mandatory Senior Executive Threshold Seminar for newly appointed senior FSO and civil service people, and upgraded the building. The sterile linoleum-floored and gray-painted walls of the 1960s government building took on a much more friendly tone with new colors, carpet, pictures, and an upgraded food court.

While the rest of the world was caught up in the computer and information technology revolutions, State was not. Explained to some degree by diplomats who value the personal nature of their job and by congressional budget cuts, the department had outdated computers and no e-mail capability during this period. Secretary of State Colin Powell would have none of that. Powell's prestige carried weight in Congress and he made a "resources for reform" deal with Congress. New funds were

---

25. U. A. Johnson, "Memorandum on Planning-Programming-Budgeting (PPBS)," 427.

26. See "Secretary Rogers Announces Management Reform," 103; and Macomber, "Change at Foggy Bottom," 206–13.

provided for a major recruitment drive for a new generation of FSOs and for modern technology.

By 2003 the department was operating at a high level of expertise. In diplomacy, diplomats receive personal satisfaction and the leaders receive accolades. However, diplomats also receive blame if defective ideas go badly. It is a profession many times unappreciated by leaders, whose experience is in winning political campaigns, leaving them convinced their ideas are right and preferable. Those features sometimes create binds on a professional. For example, in 2003 former Congressman Newt Gingrich wrote an article in *Foreign Policy* magazine calling for a transformation of the State Department until it rejected the world-order values of the United Nations and became a presidential tool for active confrontation with nations in his vision of U.S. leadership against tyranny.[27] Professionalism would be replaced by campaign management.

That bureaucratic culture and the fact that most diplomats are overseas, dealing with "foreigners," clashes with the partisan "politics" between the legislative and executive branches. In the post–World War II years, the "loss of China" was blamed on the "China hands" in the State Department by a small band of dogmatic Senators. They were left unprotected by the White House and by their own State Department leaders who might have defended them and their professional standards. This conspicuous failure of the department to protect its own led to a torpid culture for the rest of that decade and into the next. Dean Rusk was one of the few who survived the purge of the Far Eastern region of the department, making the Foreign Service more of a gentleman's club of people avoiding disagreement and decision. Rusk himself would later lament the unwillingness of FSOs to make decisions, and President John F. Kennedy called the State Department a "bowl of jelly."[28] The Foreign Service of the United States had become merely the Foreign Service of the Department of State, the primary operating arm of the department, but not fully in control of the department.

---

27. Gingrich, "Rogue State Department," 42–48.

28. Schlesinger, *A Thousand Days*, 406. The rest of the chapter of which this quote is a part continues Schlesinger's indictment of the intellectual exhaustion, enforced conformity, and punishment of independence by senior members of the Foreign Service, which rendered the Department unable to take the kind of leadership President Kennedy wanted for it.

The State Department, like all other governmental departments, is a compromise between the twin dangers of a professional bureaucracy and a political one. The secretary of state, the undersecretaries, and the assistance secretaries in charge of the structural elements are political appointees with Senate confirmation. Members of the Foreign Service may be selected for those positions, or outsiders may be assigned. Paul Nitze, one outsider, was a Wall Street entrepreneur selected for study groups after World War II. Nitze received assignment to the department's new Policy Planning Staff and then was used by every president from Truman to Reagan for a variety of assignments.

Personnel termed "in and outers" serve in one party's administration, are out when the opposing party takes the presidency, and return when their party regains power. This process becomes the training ground for a set of future foreign policy leaders, grounded in policy orientation and experience. To reach the highest levels almost necessarily requires the political appointee to be a confirmed and active member of one party. Nitze maintained a distance from party loyalty and was often used by both parties because of his talents, but he never reached the top ranks and ultimately found himself fired from the government four times, and he resigned three times over policy disputes as well.[29] For FSOs to reach these top ranks they must reinvent themselves and move up the career ladder, from an operational officer to an administrative and policy officer, by demonstrating skill, teamwork, leadership, and loyalty to the department.

THE PERSONAL FACE OF DIPLOMACY

Diplomacy is personal, and so is one's career. There are five career tracks in the Foreign Service. One cannot switch between them, though an officer may be doing so in small embassies. The political officers have traditionally been the most prestigious since they deal with the leaders and "influentials" in the host country, while those on the management track were the lowest because they enforced budgetary constraints. That has changed. As the scope of activities has expanded through NGOs and contractors, the importance of effective management has shot up. The Economic Officer connects with national and local business leaders and sends assessments about the economy back to the department. The

---

29. Nitze, *Tension between Opposites*, 4.

Public Diplomacy Officer runs multiple programs of information and interchange. The Consular Officer deals with passports and visas.

A conventional career will be spent in far-away places, some with malaria and polluted drinking water, others much more luxurious. Posts normally come by way of request, competing with others who may want the same post, with the decision being made elsewhere. Promotions can be regular, leading to Chief of a section, or individualized, reflecting either intention or fortune. Other times an unexpected call comes for an immediate transfer to a country where U.S. foreign policy is under stress. The culmination of a career is to be an ambassador. While some wealthy contributors are rewarded with ambassadorial appointments, most are appointed early in a presidential administration. Later-year appointments are predominately given to career FSOs. In 2008 thirty-seven persons were nominated for an ambassadorship to a specific country, thirty-three of which were FSOs (89%).[30]

All FSOs spend some time assigned to Washington, DC. Assignments range from serving as a Desk Officer or an assistant to an Assistant Secretary to positions at the Operations Center, the advance team for the secretary of state, or other. Many officers consider jobs as assistants to an Assistant Secretary bad postings because they feel lost in the bureaucracy. However, one FSO expressed professional satisfaction after being assigned to the Assistant Secretary for the Far East, Dean Rusk. That was just prior to the North Korean invasion. Suddenly he found himself as a de facto chief executive officer not making policy but quickly moving onto a different plane. "Instead of wading listlessly in a bureaucratic backwater as I had feared when I left Yokohama, I was working all-out on the leading foreign policy problems of the United States, with regular access to the senior officials of State and Defense and not infrequently with the President."[31]

Commitment to the mission of an organization is crucial for advancement. One of the weaknesses of the China Hands was their tendency to be clannish even within the department's organizational culture. For the most part "they identified with one another rather than 'the Service.'"[32]

That cuts both ways. An organization supports those who are most in support of the organization's mission (not necessarily the policy but the

---

30. The number is taken from the 2008 nomination hearings of the Senate Foreign Relations Committee.
31. L. K. Johnson, *The Right Hand of Power*, 94.
32. Lauren, *The China Hands' Legacy*, 104.

mission). Additionally, a clan reeks of superiority and lacks supporters, so when they got in trouble, they had few who would stand behind them in overt support. It helps to have friends, and a powerful ally or two.

TWO EXAMPLES

U. Alexis Johnson was a Methodist layman who rose to the top career position in the State Department, the under secretary for political affairs, because he found his calling in diplomatic service. He survived an assassination attempt in 1965, was ambassador to two countries, chief delegate to the Strategic Arms Limitation Talks in 1973, and ended his career as Ambassador at Large.[33]

His career began in 1935 with a posting to Japan to learn that language. Japan had taken over Korea in earlier decades and in 1937 attached and occupied parts of China. Johnson was sent to Korea as vice-consul to help American business around the new bureaucratic roadblocks designed to force them out of the country, and two years later was sent to China. Two years later Japan attacked Pearl Harbor, and Johnson and other Western diplomats were placed under house arrest. He was allowed to return to the United States where the department quickly sent him to Brazil. Impoverished Japanese farmers had migrated to South America before the war, and Johnson was to determine whether they were part of Japan's war effort. They were not. In 1944 he was posted to an army training school to help them understand the Japanese nation for the coming American occupation. From there he went to the Philippines in preparation for later duty in occupied Japan.

Then the Korean War erupted. Johnson's career intersected with history as his language skills made him valuable, and the Korean War provided what he called "an updraft" to his career. He later became ambassador to Czechoslovakia and Thailand. Understanding the intricacies of Asia propelled him to the 1954 Geneva Conference on Indochina, then deputy under secretary of state, where he was a member of the top decision-making team during the 1962 Cuba Missile Crisis, then ambassador to Japan, and then under secretary of state during the Vietnam years.

The early 1990s witnessed what Secretary of State Warren Christopher called the problem from hell. The breakup of Yugoslavia after the collapse of the Soviet Union led to four years of a one-sided war that left

---

33. The following is taken from Johnson's memoirs, *The Right Hand of Power*.

250,000 people killed, two million refugees, and atrocities not seen since the Nazis. A campaign that gave the world the term "ethnic cleansing" was conducted against Muslim areas in Bosnia. Sarajevo, a city that had gone from being the site that sparked World War I to the beautiful city that hosted the 1984 Winter Olympics, was under constant siege, shells from the surrounding mountains exploding on homes and market places. Srebrenica became a city of infamy when over 7,000 Muslim men were separated from their families and massacred.

Richard Holbrooke was a young Foreign Service Officer during the Vietnam War. He served as a civilian representative for the Agency for International Development working on economic development and enacting local political reforms. From there Holbrooke became a staff assistant to the ambassador in Saigon. He returned to Washington, DC, to be an assistant to the under secretary of state and was part of the American delegation to the Vietnam peace talks in Paris. In 1977 he became Assistant Secretary of State for East Asian and Pacific Affairs, a political appointee position that meant he had to leave after the election of 1980. In 1981 he joined a Wall Street bank for a decade. After the election of 1992 he was back in public diplomacy when President Clinton appointed him ambassador to Germany and later Assistant Secretary of State for European Affairs. In that position he worked endlessly to stop the war in Bosnia, finally prevailing as the architect of the Dayton Peace Accords in a thirteen-day marathon of diplomatic negotiation.[34]

The Dayton Peace Accords are probably the closest diplomacy comes to being (at the time) a thing of beauty, bringing multiple elements creatively together through frustrating and exhausting negotiations to end the war, with its refugees and death, representing foreign policy as an art full of hopes and fear. Achieving that treaty involved both partnership with and, at the same time, opposition to the leaders of all three factions in that war, and created a structure of peace that still exists. It ended "the problem from hell" and restored a minimum of humanity to the area, upon which a new and better future can be built. Nothing is guaranteed, but there is hope outside the circles of thugs and apostles of hate. Such is diplomacy.

In 1999 Holbrooke became the U.S. ambassador to the United Nations and prevailed in his effort to get the United Nations Security

---

34. See Holbrook, *To End a War*.

Council to debate and pass a resolution on HIV/AIDS, the first time that body had treated public health as a matter of global security. A decade later Holbrooke was appointed as President Obama's special ambassador to deal with the issues of Afghanistan and Pakistan. It will be a second attempt to make something of beauty out of fear, animosity, and conflict.

Holbrooke's career represents an FSO career ladder, a life lived in the midst of war and peace, a life of achievements and value, a life of power, persuasion and hope. It was a repudiation of the Foreign Service as a fun job and reflects the other three sides of diplomacy: a professional career, a career of impact and influence, and a personally rewarding life. It also reflects the growing breadth of diplomacy, from economic development to refugees and global health. He was clearly an extraordinary person, but why should ordinary be anyone's goal in a field and time as this?

SUCCESS STRATEGIES

What, then, are success strategies for a career in the Foreign Service? What needs to be developed? Start with yourself: write out a personal mission statement and career roadmap. What level do you aspire to? Identify the posts and positions you want within ten years to get to your goal, the gaps between your ideal self and real self, and the competencies you will need for your career success. Recognize that character and reputation count—once gone, they are extremely difficult to earn back. Develop time management, networking, and team building skills. One needs friends and allies for personal balance, as a circle of support in tough times, and as contacts for your career ladder, so don't burn bridges.

Working with the military can become a very important asset. You may be a person of peace, but you have to demonstrate to the men and women of the military that you are just as tough as they are, and just as committed to service to the nation and its values as they are. You have to get up earlier, work harder, put yourself in danger, and never waver. You will develop a respect for them, and they for you, and they will listen to you.[35] In Washington a CIA analyst was assigned to a group in the Pentagon, but was silently dismissed as an outsider. Phil Roundtree had been a conscious objector who served in Vietnam, flying in medical helicopters to rescue the wounded and was himself wounded in one of the missions. So he placed his purple heart on the wall next to his desk,

---

35. Dean, *Danger Zones*, 54, 70.

and he was embraced as one of them.[36] On the surface, unfair. In the real world of service and sacrifice, when foreign policy is both coercion and diplomacy, the relationship between diplomat and soldier in a context of war or continuing terrorist attacks is crucial and has to be based on mutual respect so each will listen to the other and not dismiss the other with artificial characterizations.

Specialized knowledge is a necessary asset, whether in language or trade or political affairs or other areas. The Foreign Service Institute provides a wide array of classes, and leadership and crisis management courses will be helpful. Communication between peers and layers is critical to your image as well as the substance. Writing and oral briefing skills have to be a priority to relay reality, and form a foundation for leadership skills. Leadership requires consensus building, and that is facilitated by communicating a vision that inspires and focuses colleagues. Management skills are increasingly becoming a top priority skill as the department expands its operations. It's not enough to know the six seas that surround Turkey;[37] one must also be able to manage an office and a program for any upward mobility.

Finally, be smart and look ahead. Anticipate what Johnson called potential "updrafts" for career advancement. It may be an issue, a region, or a superior. An assistant to an under secretary or an ambassador with a specialized portfolio may be no more than a chief of staff, but admission into the circle of top officials acquaints them with you, and a reputation for a quality job will circulate among them and be a foundation for a later call into the top ranks. Also, take a "long view" approach, a career necessity in any organization with changing leadership and shifts in policy.

Along the journey of a career, what do people of conscience do when they disagree with a president's line of policy, seeing it fail with no softening of the hard line within the administration, or seeing it naive and detrimental to the very nation they are trying to serve, or seeing its impact and consequences as clearly immoral? First, at a passive level, recognize that FSOs have different opinions and not all of them at the same time agree with U.S. policies across the board. People join the Foreign Service to help make policies better, and sometimes that is a long-term process

---

36. Told to the author by Phil Roundtree.

37. The six seas are the Aegean, Black, Crete, Marmara, Mediterranean, and Thracian.

during which some years are better than others. The terms of presidential administrations are limited, and so "this too shall pass."

Such passivity may seem totally unacceptable, so there is a second option for a more active level, recognizing that policies are long-term processes, with chances for influence from the inside. If things are going badly because there is no policy—or policy paralysis—involvement in processes may allow incremental changes at the margins. Policy is political, and policy lobbying is part of the process. If policies can't be influenced in the short term, perhaps they can in the long term, and the more excellent the work in your own portfolio, the more likely your views will get a hearing.

Third, FSOs are professional diplomats, not elected officials. Basic policy is made at the political-appointee level—the Deputy Assistant Secretary and above. The problem is that the professional diplomats have to carry it out, have to explain it and defend it to an antagonistic public in other countries. While the job may have times of nobility and personal satisfaction, other times it represents personal conflict over pursuing two noble but conflicting goals in which one has to give way with the attendant secondary consequences.

After the collapse of the Soviet empire and the attacks of 9/11, the Middle East, Pakistan, and Afghanistan became new centers of U.S. policy and military activity. The United States needed air bases in Central Asia to project its power, and one nation that met this national security need was Uzbekistan. That country, however, was ignoble with terrible repression of political and social life, coupled with a declining economy and top-level corruption. The United States needed to funnel funds to the country by misrepresenting the state of the economy, and avoid raising the issue of human rights, leaving the people to their fate. United States diplomats found themselves caught between the needs of the United States and the needs of the Uzbekistan people.[38]

The United States was not causing the repressions—it would have happened regardless—but the U.S. was supporting and rewarding the repressive government for other reasons. If the diplomat finds himself or herself unable to remain silent, the difference between inside and outside becomes important: inside the embassy and department the ethical frustration and dire policy warning can be voiced, but not outside. Howard

---

38. See Murray, *Dirty Diplomacy*.

Simpson had served in Vietnam twice with the United States Information Agency (USIA), as advisor to the prime minister of South Vietnam and to the political warfare section of its army, and he witnessed its coups and countercoups and corruption. Later, in his assignment to France, he was the in-house Vietnam expert and was asked to brief the country team. "I had resolved to tell the truth about my experiences," he wrote, so the American officers would get a bit of reality, and he revealed a Vietnam "that didn't match their steady diet of positive, bureaucratic thinking." Several years later, during the eleven-day Christmas bombing, he felt the United States had gone too far and sent a cable to his immediate supervisor and the USIA director. He detailed his experiences in Vietnam and said, "I cannot, in good conscience, support present policy of B52 raids over heavily populated areas of North Vietnam." To his surprise, the bombings did restart peace talks, and knowing the "vindictive atmosphere in the Nixon White House," he considered it a miracle his career survived. In fact, his next post was as consul general in Marseilles. "I had to admit," Simpson said, "to a certain pride in a Foreign Service that could accept dissent while moving the dissenter onward and upward."[39]

Diplomats may well be right, and their dire warnings, initially ignored, prove accurate. What then? Usually they will have been moved out of their assignment to silence them, and if so, and if they were right after all, the department has instituted a new award for "constructive dissent." The ominous warnings of Michael Zorick, who warned about the counterproductive dangers of U.S. covert action in Somalia, were ignored and he was reassigned. In 2007 he and another political officer who had done the same in another situation, received a public award from the American Foreign Service Association at a State Department ceremony.[40]

Firmly supporting the administration's policy is expected, yet the FSO "on the ground" in a country sometimes needs to go beyond reporting. If certain that the policy direction is unwise, *they* may try to influence the future direction of that policy, lobbying for a new approach or a change in policy. "Diplomats are sometimes like lawyers, frequently defending positions they may not believe in. The similarity doesn't go far, though, because in diplomacy, you have the opportunity to offer constructive alternatives. In the event the differences with your government

---

39. Simpson, *Bush Hat, Black Tie*, 117–18, 181.
40. Lee, "Diplomatic Critics of Policy Honored," 1.

are too great, you may resign. But when one shares strategic goals, tactical differences in approach is not a reason to resign."[41]

Career FSO David Newsom was promoted to Assistant Secretary of State for Africa in 1969, and by accepting the position he knew he would be placed in the not-uncommon situation of being asked "to craft and support policies with which I was not totally in agreement." He felt that if he could maintain reasonably effective communication with all conflicting elements at home and Africa, and find opportunities within the limits of presidential policy to advance what he thought ought to be done, he could maintain the office in good conscience. As a result, his term was what he called "an interesting test of how one can, in the complex machinery of the U.S. government, modify and shape policies." He also found another not uncommon situation, that the "American ship of state is not as maneuverable as incoming administrations would like."[42]

If, however, the policies appear just too misguided and destructive for you to give even tacit support, resignation is a way out and can be done quietly or publicly. George Kenney, who resigned in protest over U.S. policy (or lack of a policy) in Bosnia in 1992, is one example. He was passionately against the killings of Bosnians and tried to work in the formal channels of the department to change policy, even "on the margins." Ultimately Kenney believed the political appointees at the upper levels gave precedence to political loyalties rather than to policy, stating: "I did not in my own soul feel comfortable supporting and rationalizing a policy paralysis that leads to wholesale slaughter and the total deprivation of human dignity for hundreds of thousands of people."[43]

What would resignation and throwing away his diplomatic career accomplish? "Resignation was a gamble, but I believed someone else would listen."[44] They did. A change in administrations that year brought Anthony Lake into high levels of the new Clinton administration. Lake had been an assistant to Henry Kissinger in the Nixon White House and resigned that position to protest the invasion of Cambodia. Now, though Kenney was gone, Lake and the administration took action to end the killings through the diplomacy of Richard Holbrooke and the Dayton Accords.

41. Wilson, *The Politics of Truth*, 73.
42. Newsom, *Witness to a Changing World*, 215.
43. Kenney, "On Dissent," 22.
44. Ibid.

The decision to resign or not to resign in the midst of disagreement over policy is not a Judas decision, it is a judgment decision. Most often policy merits are not crystal clear but reflect something more like a 60/40 ratio of positives or negatives, making a dilemma. Richard Haass, Director of Policy Planning at the State Department, found himself on the horns of that ratio, but increasingly frustrated when he found out there were no weapons of mass destruction in Iraq. Ultimately he left government, though he had worked hard to get into his positions and though it was not an easy choice. Government service, he knew, can matter, and there are few things more rewarding than contributing to history, but it was his best judgment. "When it comes to dissent, there is no right answer, much less one that's right for all situations. That's what makes it a dilemma."[45]

ENGAGING THE WORLD

Diplomacy is one means for Christians to engage the world at a level of serious impact. The means of diplomacy are not inherently incompatible with Christian virtues, and the goals of policy may serve the nation but also other peoples too, if not humanity itself. A Christian can find diplomacy to be a noble and satisfying career for serving the nation in an era of danger and risk; overseeing programs and policies that promote the values of democracy, development, and human defense are all designed to build a more humane world. Short-term policies may be uninformed and arrogant, and having to defend them may raise questions of continued career loyalty to the president and the Foreign Service. Individuals are guided by their understanding of reality and their sense of the leadership of the Holy Spirit; as individuals they must wrestle like Jacob and choose patience, lobbying, or departure. Esther stayed and with moral courage and wise planning fought against an inhumane policy. A Foreign Service without the participation of those who are deeply ethical and quietly working to use foreign policy programs as means of grace will be a decidedly impoverished diplomatic corps with a narrowed moral compass.

A MEDITATION ON REVELATION 2–3

Religion as a belief structure and culture is back into world politics, and diplomats need to know more about the religious cultures of other coun-

---

45. Hass, "The Dilemma of Dissent," 33–34.

tries. But that is not the same as one's own spiritual walk and maturity. King David, monarch, politician, and foreign policy leader that he was, is twice referred to as a man of God. Today we would refer to a man or woman of God as having a close personal relationship with God through grace, living his or her life according to God's values and leadership, and practicing regular efforts to grow in spiritual maturity. Our country needs a new generation of young people like that, who are called to public service in this nation's foreign affairs, and among them we need men and women of God. Scripture lacks examples of such diplomats or recommended methods of preserving their holiness. How can a Christian maintain and grow in spiritual maturity in a context of multiple cultures and ways of thought, the double consequences (such as economic and strategic) of peaceful competition, the unforeseen crisis, and the clear emergence of an enemy?

James warns against being double-minded, yet by its very nature diplomacy requires one to be double-minded in recognizing the double nature of another nation's public statements and private strategic goals. The double-mindedness of diplomacy is being wise, that of James is trying to hold together pure and impure thoughts.

The letters to the churches in Revelation offer a strategy for spiritual maturity: (1) keep your first love, (2) avoid becoming lukewarm, (3) reject immorality and do good deeds, and (4) live in hope. This is a strategy for dealing with such pressures as having to move in high circles of nations with vile leaders and disgusting policies, the pressure to persuade reluctant and recalcitrant leaders and peoples to prevent damage to U.S. interests, and the risks and incomplete victories that three-year rotations can bring. It might not be a fatal injustice to these letters to the churches to say they can have a double relevance to the individual Christian.

The Christian as diplomat serves this country and must remain committed to a deep love of the ideals and values defined in its founding documents—that all people are created equal, that our government is a political tool we created to provide for the common defense, promote the general welfare, and preserve the blessings of liberty. Rather than being complacent or lukewarm in a career, the FSO must continually renew the spirit of the ethics of service, seriousness, and courage among the scorn and storms of diplomatic interchange. Third, as a representative of a nation blessed with prosperity and humane values, the FSO should promote policies that do good deeds around the world to combat despair, relieve suffering, and promote reconciliation. Fourth, by word and deed a Christian diplomat should offer the grace of hope to the repressed and downtrodden, and to those who fear the forces of chaos and fatalism in history.

For the Christian as an individual engaged in the process of both a career and pressure of events, the letters advise one to be watchful and not forget your first love—First Love, not First Power or First Success. Boundaries and margins may move, but at some point you have to stop if God is to remain your first love. Second, hold fast to your faith and attend to regular means of grace to avoid becoming lukewarm, regardless of the country to which you are assigned or the situation in which you participate.

Third, continue to reject immorality as well as cynicism and instead do good deeds personally to strengthen the fruits of the Spirit in your life. Seek the will of God in times of uncertainty and risk, whether it comes from a direct inspiration of the Holy Spirit or Scripture, from a fleece like Gideon used or a criteria the Holy Spirit suggests as a way to make a decision. If there is silence, seek counsel from trusted women and men of God who may embody the word of the Lord to you. Fourth, live in an attitude of hope that keeps you committed to the task and that foresees the failure of evil designs. In the midst of a storm at sea Jesus asked his worried disciples why they were afraid. Don't assume the fatal success of the present; work the sails and rudders of diplomacy to the end of your strength and talent, knowing you are not alone in the struggle against the dangers of political depravity.

4

Intelligence: Breaking the Threat Chain

In the United States, we obey the laws of the United States. Abroad we uphold the national security of the United States.

CIA DIRECTOR WEBSTER[1]

NATIONS KEEP SECRETS. SECRETS exist despite "hot lines," embassies, UN meetings, summits, and global conferences, all designed for nations to work together for a better world. Secrets put other nations at a disadvantage in diplomacy and in danger in military affairs for nations cannot allow themselves to be caught by surprise by the injurious policies and actions of opponents. In an armed world of competitors and bitter enemies, U.S. leaders need to know those secrets; they have to use spies. Foreign policy initiatives are gambles, but the stakes of the gambles are so high that the nation has to know enough about the other nation that the gamble has a good chance of success. Diplomacy in the dark may well turn out to be the diplomacy of failure or the diplomacy of disaster. The dark side of diplomacy is spying, done to minimize darkness in policy making for both keeping the nation safe and promoting its national and common interests.

THE THREAT CHAIN

The self-satisfaction of diplomatic success is a minor basis for intelligence operations compared to the more fundamental basis, which is fear. Movements within the shadows of foreign policy and international politics include groups developing capacities to cause pain and death, not just to groups of people but also to a nation's standing, policies, and historical

---

1. Quoted in Cogan, "The In-Culture of the DO," 211.

cycle. The response to that fear is to use the art of intelligence tradecraft and the science of high technology. To cause pain and death involves a process, or chain of events, that lead to attacks that kill, harm, and destroy Americans and elements of the society. It can be called the threat chain. In response the United States needs a parallel chain to detect and evaluate it, to advise decision makers about the threat, and the political decision to defeat it which may involve clandestine and covert operations.

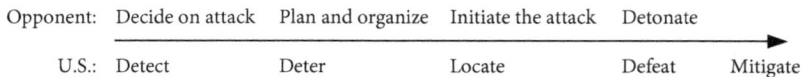

Figure 2: The Threat Chain

Covert action may disrupt or defeat a plan, or eliminate it through what is called a kill chain—locate the person initiating the attack and defeat (eliminate) him or her. The Army has Task Force ODIN (observe, detect, identify, neutralize), which uses unmanned aerial vehicles to carry out aerial reconnaissance, surveillance, and target acquisition.[2] The Central Intelligence Agency uses aerial drones for the same purposes.

To break this chain of threat, do such ends justify the means for a democracy under attack? For democratic pragmatists, the welfare of the majority justifies some abridgement of democratic processes. Democracies are fragile and survive because leaders take necessary actions and return to normal processes after the threat is past. For democratic purists, extraordinary means cannot be legitimized, for the rights of any suspect must be respected to avoid subverting democratic processes and the intrinsic value of all individuals. The dangers of generating rationales to maintain extraordinary measures are too great to risk.

In "just war" thinking the conditions provide justification for otherwise unpermitted actions, whether war or covert actions. "Lesser evil" thinking is more ambiguous, for the covert operations may well be evil. Not all evil is executed by evil people or by evil design. Justifying an act as a lesser evil is an exercise in moral risk, and doing the act is to walk along slippery moral margins. Michael Ignatieff suggests that the issue is not

---

2. See Lawlor, "Reconnaissance Task Force on Target," 59–62.

whether we can avoid evil acts altogether, but whether we can succeed in choosing lesser evils and keep them from becoming greater ones. If we so choose, they should be done in full awareness that evil is involved, done in a state of necessity, done as a last resort, and publicly justified to the United States and the international publics.[3]

Peacetime clandestine activities began with George Washington and his secret fund called the Contingency Fund for the Conduct of Foreign Intercourse. By the end of his third year as president, the fund amounted to 12 percent of the national budget and was used over the years to bribe Napoleon, fund the Lewis and Clark expedition, and enlist gangsters for intelligence, including the pirate Jean Laffite.

Covert and guerrilla operations were also part of the Revolutionary War, particularly those of General Nathanael Greene, which continued during the Indian War and World War II. The United States was largely responsible for the global values after the Second World War, represented by the United Nations and the prohibition on the use of war as a tool of statecraft. Given the dangers of the nuclear age and the unexpected imperialist policy of the Soviet Union, some means other than war had to be used to repulse their efforts. Various types of covert operations were conducted during the intense days of the early 1950s, and those evolved into the counterinsurgency and Special Forces operations in the 1960s. The Office of Strategic Services was created for World War II, and the Central Intelligence Agency emerged from it, combining both spy or clandestine operations to gain information and covert operations to disrupt threats.

Who would want to be a spy? Someone who enjoys uncovering secrets, studying technical data for clues, persuading others to reveal information not available to everyone, or working with strangers in a high-stakes effort to uncover undisclosed information. Who would want to do that? The following is not a checklist but a summary of the kinds of people who would enjoy and be successful working in the intelligence community. They are people with a particular persona, who are inquisitive, discerning about people, and articulate in expressing ideas clearly and briefly. Former CIA Director Allen Dulles listed qualities he thought junior trainees in the CIA should possess. He added ingenuity, ability to discern between fact and fiction, and knowing when to "keep your mouth

---

3. Ignatieff, *The Lesser Evil*, 18–19.

shut."[4] Those employed in this "bizarre but exhilarating job" are "people smart" and "street smart," adept at meeting people and making friends, and flexible in changing situations.

Also important for intelligence officers is an appreciation for life and work overseas, and a desire to be engaged in the historic challenges of the time. They are patriotic and find satisfaction apart from medals and ribbons, people who serve for the sake of service.

FIRST STEPS

How does one become an intelligence officer? People apply, recruiters come to campus, and sometimes your name will have been suggested to a recruiter and they come looking for you. Sometimes it is a choice made when leaving college. Sometimes it is a national emergency like Pearl Harbor or 9/11 that shifts patriotic values (or lack thereof) toward government and public service.

The application process begins with an exam testing basic knowledge, analytic skills, and language abilities (how languages are constructed and function). If you pass that gatekeeper test you move to an initial interview to test your street smarts. There are months of psychological tests and interviews to weed out the impulsive as well as to insure that an applicant has good judgment, a sense of self, and a moral compass. Then polygraph tests, physical exams, and security checks are implemented.

After testing is successfully navigated comes a year of training at the Farm. Recruits undergo three months of military training, from marching to parachute jumps. The physical stress can be too much for some; for others it's the interrogation exercise, a week-long simulation of a POW captivity with high psychological stress, to see if a recruit will cave in, rat out a classmate, or quit. Always the recruits are evaluated for strength of character, ability to work as a team, and dedication.

After the Farm the Operations Course follows. For those in the clandestine service, there are more instructions on the tradecraft, visitors with "war stories," team projects, and an actual exercise—can the recruit follow a target, carry out an operation, and write the kind of report necessary for the organizational culture? It is important not only to know if the recruit is suitable to the job but also whether he or she will be happy with the reality of the job. Robert Gates, for example, did not do well in the

---

4. A. W. Dulles, *The Craft of Intelligence*, 169.

exercises and "concluded quickly that I wasn't cut out for the clandestine service."[5] For those who do not quit, there are evaluations—pass, not pass, pass on a probationary status.

Pass. Now the recruit is recruited. The various geographical divisions bid on the students they deem the best and brightest at the Farm. Once chosen, then comes two years of language training. It can take up to four years before a recruit is ready to be an operations officer.

THE INSTITUTIONAL CONTEXT

A global nation has an insatiable demand for intelligence, that is, information that has undergone professional analysis to determine its meaning. The popular symbol for the intelligence world is the CIA, but the reality is much broader. There is an intelligence community, which was shaped by the needs and bureaucratic disputes coming out of World War II. Too much contradictory information about Japanese intentions with no means of sorting it left us vulnerable to the Pearl Harbor attack and dictated the need for a "central" intelligence agency. That need was addressed in the 1947 National Security Act, but not without deep reluctance. Neither the military services nor other civilian agencies wanted to give up their intelligence capabilities.[6] The result is an "intelligence community" of 16 different intelligence agencies.[7] The fractured "community" may insert parochial views or turf battles into an analysis, resulting in a nebulous "consensus" document.

After World War II Dean Rusk originally supported a unified intelligence service, but as secretary of state in the early 1960s he changed his mind, believing it wholesome to have separate agencies under the coordinating supervision of the CIA director. Having spent a career in government he understood that both intelligence analysts and policy

---

5. Gates, *From the Shadows*, 22. Gates went on to become Director of the CIA and later Secretary of Defense.

6. See McNeil, "The Evolution of the U.S. Intelligence Community."

7. The 16 include the CIA, the Defense Intelligence Agency, the FBI, the National Geospacial Intelligence Agency, the National Reconnaissance Organization, the National Security Agency, the Department of Justice offices of Drug Enforcement and National Security Intelligence, the Office of Intelligence and Analysis in the Department of Homeland Security, the Department of State's Bureau of Intelligence and Research, the Department of the Treasury's Office of Intelligence and Analysis, and the intelligence offices of the Army, Navy, Air Force, Marine Corps, and Coast Guard.

makers tend to interpret information to support their own views: Air Force analysts, for example, always overestimated Soviet military power that then justified greater budgets for the Air Force. "Multiple agencies can supplement and balance off each other and also highlight disagreements within the intelligence community to policy officers."[8]

The dangers and exertions of World War II required more than secrecy and deception. Survival required the extra miles of disruption, destruction, and assassinations. In such a fight, in which the survival of one nation requires the destruction of the political and military leadership and forces of an enemy, the rules of war get blurred and broken. To that end a new Office of Strategic Service (OSS) was created to carry out those covert operations against the Nazis. That organization was disbanded after the war, but the 1947 National Security Act that created the Central Intelligence Agency included the authorization for the CIA to carry out "such additional services" and "such other functions and duties related to intelligence affecting the national security as the National Security Council may from time to time direct." Those were only words, with conflict over their meaning. Some top leaders saw the CIA's mission as analysis only, and only later in the year did it take on the task of collecting information too. Some leaders like Allen Dulles believed the United States was in a political war with communism and needed to mount aggressive covert actions to hinder Soviet designs. The State Department, however, did not want to tarnish its diplomatic stature with covert action, and the military argued political warfare was not its function. So the National Security Council directive 10/2 authorized the CIA to develop a special staff for covert operations.[9]

The OSS reported to the Joint Chiefs of Staff during the war. Before it was disbanded the OSS chief Bill Donovan sent President Roosevelt a memo outlining a strong agency with independent responsibility and budget under the president. The Big Four (Army, Navy, Justice, and State) ganged up against such a threat to their own intelligence units. For President Truman, the unification of the military branches into one Department of Defense was a top priority, not the details of an intelligence agency. Out of the interdepartmental battles came the existing compromise agency and its competitors in the intelligence community.

8. Rusk, *As I Saw It*, 553.
9. The story of the enlarging responsibility of the CIA is covered nicely in Grose, *Gentleman Spy*, 279–95.

The agency is two-headed, with a Director of Intelligence (DI) and a Director of Operations (DO), the latter in charge of the "such additional services" or covert operations of the agency.

Within the Pentagon, beyond the four intelligence groups of the four services is a fifth, the Defense Intelligence Agency. The latter was an effort by former Secretary of Defense Robert McNamara to forge a unity in the department's evaluations of data. The goal was not met, and part of Defense Secretary Donald Rumsfeld's "transformation" effort was to redirect it to more operational information and to force integration by emphasizing "joint" operations between the services and the creation of a Defense Joint Intelligence Operations Center.

As at Defense, so in the rest of the community, successive directors sought to bring coherence and single focus to the community. Resistance was always strong. The 2006 Intelligence Act finally created a superstructure in the form of a Director of National Intelligence who is not also Director of the CIA. The deepest conflict is between the CIA and the Pentagon, the former specializing in strategic intelligence, the latter in tactical. As one military officer put it, "The CIA wants to know if Osama bin Laden is developing a nuclear weapon; the military wants to know where he goes out for a hamburger."[10] After the Khobar Towers bombing, then the attack on the USS *Cole* and the bombing of U.S. embassies in Kenya and Tanzania, FBI agents were sent overseas, and the Navy and Air Force counterintelligence units were sent overseas also. The potential for conflicts, duplication of efforts, and lack of training in the tradecraft was great. To coordinate all those efforts, the Directorate of Operations was reconstituted as the National Clandestine Service. It is responsible for CIA operations but now holds the additional responsibility to coordinate and set standards and training for the human intelligence activities of the big six agencies collecting intelligence: CIA, Drug Enforcement Agency, FBI, and the Army, Navy, Air Force counterintelligence organizations, and others.

Who is planning an attack, and where? Who is developing nuclear weapon technology, and who is seeking to buy it? "It is imperative that we avoid strategic surprise for our nation," says Lt. Gen. Michael Maples, director of the Defense Intelligence Agency and the Defense Joint Intelligence Operations Center. "We can't take our eyes off what is going on in other parts of the world—other military capabilities that are devel-

---

10. Quoted in Bowden, "The Point/Pentagon Spy Effort Serves a Purpose."

oping and the kinds of transnational threats that will affect our national security interests."[11]

ANALYTICAL OPERATIONS

A recruit looking for a life of James Bond-style spying will be disappointed for that is only a small fraction of intelligence gathering. The command of high technology and orbital space gives the United States vast technical means to acquire information. Through an array of satellites we are able to "see" developments through photographic images (Imint) from space, through satellites operated by the National Reconnaissance Office. We can also "hear" by listening in on electronic (telephone, faxes, e-mails) and nonelectronic (radar, telemetry) communication and gather what is called signals intelligence (Sigint). Growing sophistication in miniaturization and countermeasures has reduced that means. The emissions given off by missile and other weapons tests are captured through measurement and signatures intelligence (Masint), coordinated by the Defense Intelligence Agency, which keeps track of weapons testing or real-war launches.

The primary task of the CIA is to prevent a new Pearl Harbor by analyzing the floods of incoming information from all these sources, and then producing analytical conclusions and disseminating those. Scientists and technicians analyze the technical data, and the political analysts try to interpret what it means. The CIA Web site describes the political analysts this way:

> Political analysts support US policymakers by evaluating the goals and motivations of foreign governments and entities. They examine: their culture, values, society and ideologies; their resources and capabilities; their political and decision making processes; the strengths and weaknesses of their strategies for achieving their goals; and the implications of all of the above for US interests. Agency analysts are encouraged to maintain and broaden professional ties through academic study, contacts, and attendance at professional meetings.[12]

---

11. Quoted in Ackerman, "Defense Intelligence Assumes More Diverse Missions," 17–18.

12. See the Political Analyst position on the Central Intelligence Agency Web site Careers page: https://www.cia.gov/careers/opportunities/analytical/political-analyst.html (last updated July 22, 2009).

These are office jobs with regular hours with a culture not unlike a university or think tank. Like the rest of the government, the intelligence community "outsources" much of its work, currently up to twenty-five percent. Two recent openings by the private contracting firm SAIC reflect this development:

All-source Intelligence Analyst

>Job Description: The applicant will perform all-source intelligence analysis to support counter-terrorism/force protection analysis missions at NORAD-USNORTHCOM (NC) Intelligence Directorate (J2). Duties will include: researching, and maintaining databases, reviewing, collating and evaluating raw information, performing link analysis and timeline analysis, preparing intelligence assessments, presenting briefings, and disseminating critical information/products.

Intelligence Analyst

>Job Description: The successful candidate will work as a member of a government-contractor team conducting intelligence analysis in a functional area relevant to national security interests. As a member of this team, your responsibilities may include, but not limited to, equipment identification, facility analysis, regional infrastructure analysis, geopolitical analysis, reporting and database input, imagery-GIS integration, historical research, and intelligence fusion.[13]

These analysts at the CIA produce a variety of studies about what is happening. There is a daily briefing for the president, periodic reports, specialized studies requested by the National Security Council or staff, and estimates about what is likely to happen in a country. Mistakes and surprises can be very costly to the interests of the United States, preventing leaders from making sound judgments and taking effective actions in their reaction to events that can disrupt or threaten the good interests of America.

Some of the intelligence and analysis tries to prove a positive—to tell policy makers what is happening and what it means. It is much harder to prove a negative, to prove something does not exist, especially if the

---

13. These two job openings were found at the SAIC Web site in August 2003. For current openings see http://www.saic.com/career/.

target is using deception. In the case of Iraq, the past actions and the then-current dissembling by the Iraqi leadership made it logical to assume they were building and hiding weapons of mass destruction. To understand the true reality, that they were not building and hiding but were feeding that image for their own benefit, was a negative extremely difficult to prove, especially in the face of the assumptions of U.S. leaders and the dissembling of Iraqi leaders.

Some of the analysis warns about what is likely and thereby prevents surprises through the use of such techniques as a Threat Matrix for organizing information. To discover hidden policy and to predict action requires connecting a lot of dots, many of which may not exist. The CIA was caught by surprise in 1998 when India conducted three underground tests of nuclear devices, and also two weeks later when Pakistan responded with its own tests. Part of the reason for the surprise was that India did not use United States, Chinese, Russian, or French programs to develop its own, which would have alerted intelligence sources. They developed their program independently. Moreover, when the U.S. learned three years earlier of test preparations and strongly urged them to stop, we gave them "a road map for how to deceive us in the future."[14]

If India can do it, who else can? In Pakistan the United States was aware that A. Q. Kahn and his research group had become the father of the Pakistani bomb by developing a centrifuge technology that isolates isotopes and allows the enrichment of uranium. Pakistan was an ally of the United States, as India was not. Still, Pakistan supplied that technology through Kahn to Iran when their efforts at uranium enrichment failed, and likely supplied it to North Korea in exchange for ballistic missile technology for Pakistan. Worse, outside of official Pakistani channels, though perhaps not without their knowledge and approval since President Musharraf later pardoned him, Kahn developed his own secret and private smuggling operation to provide the technology to other nations and perhaps non-nations.[15]

Nuclear technology is not the only threatening arms trade, which demonstrates the breadth of necessary intelligence. During its war with Iraq, the leaders of Iran desperately sought weapons and parts for the sophisticated weapons that the United States had given that country when

---

14. Tenet, *At the Center of the Storm*, 45.
15. See Global Security, "A. Q. Kahn."

the shah was in power. A clandestine effort involving a network of Iranian agents stretching across the United States, Europe, and Asia sought to escape the arms embargo that followed the Iranian hostage crisis.[16] That effort continues, with Iran and other nations trying illegally to get the most advanced weapons technology possible. Success makes adversaries more dangerous, so this country has to find and break up such illegal networks of arms traders.

There are multiple pieces or elements in a threat chain, some critical, such as knowing the timing and the target. A critical element is finding the person who is the link between the commanders and the operational cell of people who will carry out the attack. For an analyst to link all those pieces or to connect the dots in order to track down critical enemies requires tips from sources. To obtain that critical tip as well as identify as many pieces of the chain as possible will require clandestine operations involving multiple sources from a variety of positions.

Connecting dots is rarely done through the insight of a single person but is the result of a process. An individual alone relying on his or her individual intuition can misinterpret an ancient text, or be too personally embedded in current events or with decision makers to have a balanced view of events. David Wurmser was a scholar linked to neo-conservative groups and published *Tyranny's Ally: America's Failure to Defeat Saddam Hussein*.[17] He was not a professional intelligence officer but was set up in an office in the Pentagon to evaluate raw intelligence files. He developed a giant spider-web chart on which he drew links between data points of information. His goal was to formulate a strategic picture as a foundation for policy change, and he found his nexus not in Pakistan or Afghanistan but in Iraq.[18] Good for policy perhaps, but wrong country. Linkage analysis and network analysis are new and emerging techniques, but to prevent such idiosyncratic pictures, analysis is done within a prescribed process within an institutional setting.[19]

Sometimes analysts can draw on a secret treasure of information. The centerpiece of intelligence during the 1962 Cuban Missile Crisis was the U-2 photographs of Soviet missile installations in Cuba. The

16. See the extensive *Los Angeles Times* investigation by Shaw and Rempel, "Billion-Dollar Iran Arms Search Spans U.S., Globe," 1, 14–15.
17. Wurmser, *Tyranny's Ally*.
18. See Gellman, *Angler*, 222–26.
19. Vos Fellman and Wright, "Modeling Terrorist Networks, 59–66.

key questions for U.S. officials included what kind of missiles they were and how long before they would be operational. These questions could be answered because Soviet Colonel Oleg Penkovsky had provided the U.S. with highly classified Soviet missile data and war plans, information necessary to evaluate the photographs in detail and know the capabilities of the missiles and how much time the president had before they would be operational. Penkovsky was from the upper bracket of Soviet society but was convinced that the democratic world seriously underestimated the peril they faced from the Soviet Union.[20] He was not recruited; he was a "walk in," a volunteer agent.

Analysts try to understand the movements in the shadows, to lower the risks of foreign policy gambles, and to anticipate the near future. While much of the information they use comes from the technology of photography, signals and signature intercepts, and other "open source" means, too often those sources are insufficient to penetrate the darkness. They need human efforts to secretly uncover the secrets of adversaries.

CLANDESTINE OPERATIONS

Despite its global interests the United States operates with relatively few people in both diplomacy and intelligence. With only 4,000 to 5,000 clandestine operatives, there are more FBI agents in New York City than clandestine offices around the globe. Clearly the nation needs more information than it alone can collect, and the same is true of its allies, many of which have long histories in a region of concern to the United States. So there is cooperation among intelligence agencies to help with specific needs at particular times.

Satellite-borne technologies are staggering. When the Soviet Union shot down the Korean Airline KL 007, the CIA listened to the conversation between the Soviet pilot and his ground control, heard the order to shoot it down, including the pilot's words, "The target is destroyed."[21] Though we can see buildings and military facilities, and hear communications and measurement sources from inside them, specific identities remain difficult. Though we can count shipping containers, we cannot identify their specific sources or contents with satellites. We can watch the movement of troops yet not know the policy purpose. We can listen

20. Helms, *A Look over My Shoulder*, 217–18.
21. Shultz, *Turmoil and Triumph*, 363–66.

in on electronic discussions, identify and listen to actual conversations with target words with embedded libraries and templates, but the means are increasingly vulnerable to effective countermeasures.

Technical means must be supplemented with a quality understanding of the "softer" intelligence on the social and cultural stresses and strains of a country, and the personalities and elite culture of its leaders, and with (as specific as possible) policy information that allows analysts to connect the dots, if not predict what is taking place or planned. Buildings that look the same can be used for many different purposes undetectable by satellite photography, and many times only human intelligence can provide the clue about where the technical instruments should target and focus.

The rise of networked terrorist organizations means money has to move around the globe. In the "old days" when threats came from a country, the flow of money was either self-contained within the country or had minimal movement, but not now. A new emphasis on intelligence is finding that flow of money and stopping it.

Little spying is actually done by U.S. personnel. Instead, case officers or Operations Officers (the official position title) cultivate friendships with people abroad who have access to certain kinds of information, called "sources." The common term "agent" does not apply to either person. These case officers are usually working out of the embassy in a "normal" job as a political or consular officer or an agricultural or commercial attaché, which they do all day. After work they seek out those potentially valuable people in various venues, mostly at social events, bars, hotel lobbies, newspaper offices, or from walking through markets, generally mingling and exchanging business cards. Later the officer will try to determine if this or that person could be a possible "asset," or is already recruited, or probably unreliable. The goal is not to recruit one source but several with access to different circles of society, weaving a network of information.

It is much like sales. The more people you meet in this way, the higher the chances of a later business meeting or a social lunch, discussing U.S. foreign policy. For an embassy's political officer, looking for insights on the country and its politics, if they have the social and political antennae set on high, these meetings are enough. If a person might know or have access to "insider," sensitive, secret, revelatory information, the officer develops a proposal they might find acceptable. At some point a version of the following conversation will occur: "You know, your insights are brilliant and absolutely on the mark. They could really help Washington understand the changing political landscape. Could you tell me . . . , or find out for me . . ." The goal is to persuade him or her to become a close friend or "consultant." Additional incentives such as money may be necessary. The political officer in an embassy appeals to a person's better side; the intelligence officer appeals to the weaker side.

Case officers are not independent. Their work is done in conjunction with a Chief of Station (COS). The officer makes a potential contact and reports it the COS, who decides if it should be pursued, the first of five steps—spot, assess, develop, recruit, and then run. At each step the operations officer reports to his or her chief, who gives guidance and instructions, which includes helping draft the proposal to be made to the potential source, the questions to be raised and the follow-up plan, and a report that protects the source and still conveys the information.

Information goes through a similar process. The officer reports the information gained and at the right time informally shares it with embassy colleagues. If it seems accurate, a report is drafted for a Field Collection Management Officer (FCMO) who manages the collection, analysis, and distribution of raw intelligence, sending it to other stations in the world that might have some perspective to share. All that information is then sent to headquarters at Langley and its professional analysts.

THE PERSONAL CONTEXT

Clandestine operations are very personal operations. CIA officers recruit and maintain (or handle or "run") networks and personal relationships with these people. United States law forbids using U.S. clergy, journalists working for U.S. news organizations, and Peace Corps workers, but non-U.S. clergy and journalists can be targets and turned into sources. Whether it is a person sitting in on the strategy sessions in a cave somewhere in Afghanistan, or a baggage worker at a significant airport, or someone from a government or security agency, these sources provide information and insights not available through technological means. Many times it is like paying a person a retainer fee, first for what seems minor, and then increasingly more important. Sometimes the source becomes a real friend who maintains contact when the officer rotates to another location. Other officers maintain a deep detachment and cynicism behind their friendly demeanor. Sources provide a continuing flow of information, or an alert or inside information when something new happens, or data when the U.S. needs specific information they need to find.

There is a personal approach to developing sources. Many times sources are typical people who cooperate because the information they provide seems relatively unimportant and they appreciate the funds or the access to medical care, admission to a U.S. university for their children, or other benefits the case officer provides, including unwholesome pursuits. Sometimes they want revenge for not getting a promotion or the stimulation of a challenge not found in their ordinary routine. Other times they are rivals of the target. Some are the undesirable members of society—drug dealers, brutal military officers, criminals. When it was revealed in 1995 that a case officer had been murdered on the orders of a senior Nicaraguan military officer who was a CIA source and recipient of payments from the agency, draconian guidelines (a term based on an ancient Greek law code) were developed to prohibit case officers from recruiting people who had a record of human rights abuses in their past. This caused the loss of important informants, but after 9/11 those guidelines were effectively ended.[22]

At times the project is much more difficult and dangerous, such as when sources are developed and placed in a country. Elizabeth Swantek was one of a group who worked for two years developing people to move into the Soviet Union. They were former Soviet citizens living in Western Europe as refugees and defectors. They were to establish and legalize themselves in the Soviet Union and serve as long-term sources.[23] Very few of those "drops" were successful since the Soviets were adept at locating and eliminating those people. That loss of life troubled some officials, but since such techniques had worked in World War II, the operations continued.[24]

Money is not the only means to induce cooperation; there is always blackmail. Whether seduced by sex or alcohol, the targets either let down their guard and talk too much or find themselves in the position of having to cooperate to prevent the exposure of their being involved with a foreign case officer. Operations officers are not allowed to have sex with

---

22. Aldrich, "Dangerous Liaisons."
23. See McIntosh, *Sisterhood of Spies*, 314.
24. Thomas, *The Very Best Men*, 70–72.

a source.²⁵ Setting up some kind of "sting" is difficult and time consuming, and it may not work or may backfire if the target goes to his or her superior and becomes a double agent. If it does work, however, the case officer now has the means to manipulate another person's life, to significantly increase their compliance and exposure to danger. These persons are usually mid-level officials without access to the highest-level secrets, but not always, and they may well pass along embellished information, or become double agents and pass on wrong information.

Secrecy surrounds the activity, but not the identity of the U.S. operative, who is obviously personally involved with sources, which makes it a clandestine operation. Working out of the U.S. embassy with a cover "day job" gives the officer diplomatic protection if he or she is identified as a "spy." But it means that, like the diplomats, they also have to move every three years to keep up their cover. Their contacts are passed off to a successor; only in this way can the United States maintain a deep and continuing source of information.

These successors are often new recruits, hoping that the source will not need a lot of "hand holding" and can help the young officer gain experience and sharpen their skills. The source may not be pleased at all, fearful that a youthful mistake will compromise his or her position at home and lead to arrest and possible execution. The chance of losing an unhappy source can push a young officer to the boundaries of professional and personal ethics, and the chief of station must be especially careful in oversight.

Officers who work out of an embassy are recognized as government officials, and many potential sources could not be seen with them. When the CIA needs longer-term assignments or deeper cover, there are other officers who work with what is called "non-official cover" (NOC). That means they work outside the protection of the embassy, often as business people or immigrants. As business people, these officers can have access to a different and wider spectrum of potential sources, and if diplomatic relationships are broken and embassy personnel forced out of the country, the NOCs may be able to remain and continue to operate.²⁶ That is a difficult and expensive effort. A new business requires business permits,

---

25. A case officer was recently fired from the CIA for accompanying sources to strip clubs and brothels and caught in an accusation of sexual assault. Warrick and Smith, "Latest CIA Scandal," 1.

26. Shulsky and Schmit, *Silent Warfare*, 12–13.

building permits for any necessary remodeling, and other necessities like insurance. There can be no contact between that person and embassy people. If those officers are discovered, they can be prosecuted in that country as spies. The revelation of Valerie Plame Wilson as such an undercover officer ruined her career, and put in danger those persons she had contact with in her assigned country.

EXAMPLES

One example of an agent in place was Charles Hostler, a USAF Lt. Col. in the intelligence division, who was loaned to the CIA in 1953 to become a graduate student at the American University in Beirut. The United States had deep concerns about the Middle East and the political volatility of Syria in particular, but contact between U.S. diplomats and Syrian officials was extremely sensitive and to be avoided. There was close surveillance on all foreigners, so even creating a CIA-sponsored businessman in Syria as a clandestine intermediary seemed unfeasible. The new Syrian president by military coup, Col. Adib Esh-Shishaki, wanted a link to the U.S. officials. As a graduate student Hostler had a plausible reason for being in the region and could pass information to influence or inform him about developments and plans. With Beirut only two hours from Damascus, CIA officials in the U.S. embassy would meet Hostler at a coffee shop or other safe place, and he would then drive to Damascus late at night and meet a contact, who would then sneak him into one of the presidential palaces. It was an important task, but it cost Hostler his marriage since he could not tell his wife about this undercover work despite her growing suspicion about his late-night travels.[27]

Another "source" was Amy Elizabeth Thorpe. During World War II she was married to a British Foreign Service Officer. At several of his postings Thorpe had liaisons with top-ranking officials, and at the request of British operatives she stole documents that were crucial keys to unlock the Nazi code machine called Enigma. Later she got a map showing the Nazi plans for dismembering Czechoslovakia and obtained the Italian naval ciphers. After her divorce and return to the United States she helped the American intelligence service by establishing a liaison with a high official in the French embassy in Washington, DC, who daily passed cables on to her. She used that liaison to leverage his help in an especially daring and danger-

---

27. Hostler, *Soldier to Ambassador*, 105–19.

ous operation to steal and copy the Vichy French naval code books, deemed essential for the Normandy invasion. "I was able to make certain men fall in love with me—or think they had, at any rate—and in exchange for my love they gave me information," she said. "Ashamed? Not in the least! My superiors told me that the results of my work saved thousands of British and American lives. Even one would have made it worthwhile."[28]

Had she no conscience? One has to be careful about easy moralistic judgments about conscience. Internet and lending predators, rapists and wife beaters, thieves and cheats—they have no conscience for they care nothing for their victims. Hostler risked his marriage, but before that he had risked his life when he parachuted behind the lines on D-Day, for which he carried a scar on his face for the rest of his life. Thorpe risked her life in her liaisons. They sacrificed for the lives of others and their country. For those engaging and combating the dangers of this world, conscience rests on a commitment to human values and the defeat of those forces that demean or destroy life and not on personal purity and "respectable" methods alone.

THE NEW GLOBAL CONTEXT

The ground upon which American intelligence operates has radically shifted in the twenty-first century. The era of knowing one's adversary, the special sites and locations of interest, the cultural outlook, the operational methods of a primary adversary—those have all been modified by the collapse of the Soviet Union and the emergence of the non-territorially-based and religion-driven global networks of terrorists. "It is," former CIA director James Woolsey said, "as if we were struggling with a large dragon for 45 years, killed it, and then found ourselves in a jungle full of poisonous snakes—and the snakes are much harder to keep track of than the dragon ever was."[29]

It is also a deadly context for any source caught or even suspected of passing information to the U.S. In the Soviet Union they were executed; in the Afghanistan and Pakistan border areas they are beheaded.[30]

---

28. Hildreth, "Code Name CYNTHIA," 23–25; McIntosh, *Sisterhood of Spies*, 25–40.

29. Woolsey testimony before the U.S. House of Representatives Committee on National Security, February 12, 1998, quoted in Imbler, "Espionage in a Age of Change," 218.

30. For a study of the linkage of beheading of unbelievers to the Koran, see Furnish, "Beheading in the Name of Islam."

Finding voluntary agents within groups like al Qaeda is different by orders of magnitude. Americans do not blend into Islamic societies. Motivated by religious passion, Cold War incentives like cash rewards usually fail to create double agents. Finding rivals may be easier. U.S. had access to those rivals from years of contact with the leaders of the Northern Alliance by U.S. officers.[31] Suitcases of cash helped persuade Afghan warlords to fight Soviet forces in the 1980s and to turn on the Taliban in 2001, and led to an informant's tip, which led directly to the death of Abu Musab al-Zarqawi, the leader of al Qaeda in 2006; but they were rivals, not insider informants.[32] While money was an inducement, their desire to oust their rivals and take power was the underlying reason they turned on the Taliban.

Access to sources is limited by the necessity for depth of language skills, personal background, personal references from movement sympathizers, and knowledge of radical Islam. Access to the top leaders of al Qaeda is even tighter, open only to those with personal and tribal loyalties. And as a loose organization of networked groups, the infrastructure is small, mobile, and decentralized. The traditional approach to three-year tours in a country will barely scratch the surface for finding sensitive information.

Language barriers are challenging since the societies of most interest to the United States speak languages very few American universities teach. Though English is the official language of Pakistan, for example, the national language is Urdu, spoken by half of the population (48%), with lesser percentages speaking other languages. Virtually no three-year diplomat or case officers speaks those national languages and therefore must rely on translators. Those translators, like the guards providing security, are private contractors.

ORGANIZATIONAL CULTURE

The point of all this clandestine effort is to develop enough information for the analysts at headquarters to make informed conclusions about developments and threats. Those conclusions are put into three forms. One is the daily briefing for the president about the most recent and overnight events. Second are special studies the president or his team request on a

---

31. Schroen, *First In*.

32. This and the next paragraph rely on Whitlock, "After a Decade at War with West," A1.

particular topic. Third are the longer-range studies of potential developments. The latter two are consensus documents, since rarely does anyone know exactly what is happening. So there is a majority opinion with some minority opinions or cautions.

That process, for all its professionalism, is confronted by three difficulties. The first is people. Several directors, enamored with technology, have minimized human intelligence and the operations side of the CIA. James Schlesinger was director only fourteen days in 1973, yet he cut seven percent of the staff. Only three years later Admiral Stansfield Turner, director under President Carter, cut over eight hundred officers in a rather heartless and cold-blooded manner.[33] In turn the Reagan administration tried to rebuild the institution. There was another reduction after the collapse of the Soviet Union, and after a politicalization of the agency in the mid-90s through new rules on who could be recruited as sources and how, nearly 40 percent of the CIA people left. Two double agents were discovered within the CIA in 1996—Aldrich Ames and Harold Nicholson—and the same year the agency was accused of selling rock cocaine to children in California. As part of the "peace dividend" from the end of the Cold War, the CIA simply stopped recruiting people while so many experienced hands were leaving, and the entire intelligence community lost billions of dollars in funding. When George Tenet became director of the CIA in 1997, he was the fifth director in seven years, and there was no coherent long-range plan or set of priorities on what to focus upon after the end of the Cold War.[34] In the late 90s U.S. leaders were aware of al Qaeda but unable to penetrate it, and thus missed any clues that might have related to the upcoming 9/11 operation.

A second difficulty is that the people in intelligence are part of a particular institutional culture. Though the institutional process may prevent idiosyncratic analysis, the process itself can produce problems. As people stay in the process for the length of a career, they develop basic assumptions about how the world works, and that can become ingrained not only in individuals but in the organizational culture as well. New developments that seem outside that perspective are not considered on their

---

33. Gates, *From the Shadows*, 42, 139.
34. Tenet, *At the Center of the Storm*, 14–16.

merits, fundamental reevaluations are not done, and the organization can miss a developing issue.[35]

Third, there is the danger of succumbing to the desire for political leaders to have intelligence analysis that supports their policy goals. Professionals have to "speak truth to power," but the report is made by the director, not the professional. The cautions of the analysts, which are in footnotes, can be minimized. The Iran-Contra Affair was run by Bill Casey, a CIA director who used "cooked" intelligence to press his policy. As Secretary of State George Shultz told him, "The CIA has a strong policy view; I always have to stop and ask myself: what is it that I am reading? What message does the agency want me to get?"[36]

If the director and the intelligence analysis do not support what the president's team wants, the CIA can be directed to study the issue again, and again, and again, until the cautions are minimized to the point of being disregarded. That was certainly the case in the run up to the war with Iraq when leaders assumed the CIA was too ingrown and not capable of seeing reality—at least the reality of the Cheney team. One neo-con and early advocate of attack on Iraq remarked that the CIA "sometimes did unprofessional work, exhibiting bias, sloppy research, faulty assumptions, internal contradictions, unclear writing, or other failings."[37] The reality was that the CIA found no evidence of weapons of mass destruction because there were none, despite the fervent belief of those who wanted the agency to find proof.

The president's team owes it to the nation, but also to the clandestine operatives who put their lives and the lives of their contacts at risk, to demand the best analysis, not the politically desirable analysis.

Given all that, there are three "s" factors that affect the individual officer that are short of ethical issues. Success—it is not easy; there are few people waiting to be asked by a foreigner to sell them sensitive information about their government. Finding assets is hard. When one is found,

---

35. See Shulsky and Schmit, *Silent Warfare*, 64–69.

36. Shultz, *Turmoil and Triumph*, 804. Interestingly Robert Gates, then Deputy Director of Intelligence, spends little space on the issue, and notes that Shultz had the political clout to stop it if he wished, and "no one thought it was that big a deal." Gates, *From the Shadows*, 399.

37. Remarks attributed to Paul Wolfowitz by a similar neo-con Douglas J. Feith, *War and Decision*, 99.

the connection is at his or her weak point, and that can lead to a great deal of unreliability in showing up and in what one provides.

Suspicion is second nature. Is the asset a double agent using you? Who is watching, bugging, laying a trap for you? There are times when an official has to make a death-defying escape after one's cover is blown. They can become obsessional. Intelligence professionals are people who have to live confidently in a world different from ours, a world of suspicion.

Silence can be something other than golden. It restricts communication with a spouse and children, it restricts one's circle of friends because there is so much that cannot be discussed. The self-confidence necessary to mix and mingle and manipulate others is not in play among circles of friends. That is true across the board for operations officers, technicians, analysts, and managers. At home the circle of friends consists of others in the intelligence community; abroad it is minimal at best.

COVERT OPERATIONS

Clandestine operations gather information about other countries; covert operations impact them. They are another tool of foreign and national security policy, but are covert because U.S. sponsorship must remain secret. Those operations range from subsidies given to rivals and opponents to organizing an overthrow of a government. Sometimes there is "an agent in place" in government influencing policy. Sometimes the means involves disinformation, sometimes sabotage; sometimes forged documents, sometimes assassination. That last action needs distinctions. An assassination by an isolated individual believing he or she can spark a movement or stop it, such as the murders of John Kennedy or Martin Luther King Jr. by lone gunmen for a political statement, is universally condemned. An assassination to preserve or promote political influence, such as the ordered murder of Congolese Prime Minister Lumumba, involves no necessity and is morally unacceptable. Necessity may change the calculation for some operatives. An assassination of the head or top leadership of a terrorist organization whose plans bring immediate threat and who cannot be captured, can be justified as an act of war and is the reason why special operations groups exist within the U.S. Army and Navy. There is the seduction of altering history on the cheap and the attraction of allowing the emergence of a newer world of beauty and friendship if a national leader or leadership team was just removed. Normally those are two daydreams. National purpose and national policy are rarely the embodiment of one person or team but have deeper and more lasting social dynamics, so those kinds of leadership assassinations are only effective if the target is irreplaceable, and few are.

Yet there are risks, uncertainties, failures, and achievements which make the boundaries unclear in this shadow world. Osama bin Laden could have been killed in Afghanistan by the Clinton administration, but they chose not to risk collateral damage to civilians. Did they step back from a moral boundary? The threat was potential, the scope unknown, and an attack a preemption that would be difficult to justify. Instead this nation suffered the death of 3,000 of its citizens in the World Trade Center attack. Bin Laden would likely have been irreplaceable and history altered with his death in the 1990s. With the scope of the threat now in evidence, the CIA went after the al Qaeda leadership. The assassination of Quad Salim al-Harathi by a Predator missile in Yemen in 2002 in retaliation for his leadership in the attack on the USS *Cole* in 2000 was probably a revenge killing, but also ended the threat of more terrorist attacks on U.S. ships and personnel from al Qaeda in Yemen.

During the intensity of the 1950s and into the 1960s Cold War, the legacy of the OSS lived on in a series of operations to achieve what is now called regime change, the most well-known being Iran in 1953, Guatemala in 1954, efforts to assassinate Fidel Castro into the early 1960s, and the coup in Chile in 1972. Other covert operations were violent "special operations" and used teams of paramilitary forces, sometimes Navy Seals, sometimes outside contractors such as in the Congo in the early 1960s. Other operations were conducted with rebel forces, as in Tibet and the infamous Bay of Pigs invasion.[38] One set of writers considered covert operations so embedded in the CIA that they called it a "cult, a secret fraternity," further stating that the CIA is not independent but "a resource that come[s] with the office of the Presidency."[39] Whatever the veracity of that line in the 1950s, little remains of it now after all the purges of the 1970s.

Intelligence needs changed as the era of Middle Eastern terrorism developed. Not only do terrorists not wear recognizable military uniforms, they have a different military culture or organization, order of battle and

38. For histories of these and other operations, see Tully, *CIA: The Inside Story*; and Wise and Ross, *The Invisible Government*.
39. Marchetti and Marks, *The CIA and the Cult of Intelligence*, 4, 20.

tactics. "It requires different tools, particularly at a lower tactical level," Maples said.[40]

In this War on Terror the United States has entered what former Vice President Cheney called "the dark side." In the midst of an unexpected ground war in Iraq, the military needed specific tactical intelligence. To that end Defense Secretary Rumsfeld enlarged and deepened his department's covert military intelligence operations. That move reflected both a lack of confidence in the CIA to provide the need for more war-fighting-relevant intelligence, and it was outside the scope of congressional oversight.

The CIA is a full partner in the war in Iraq and Afghanistan against terrorist leadership through covert operations. They are among the users of armed unmanned aircraft as a platform for air attacks in Pakistan. In the complexity of this war, officials of the Pakistani intelligence service (ISI) help the United States develop a list of terrorist targets for the Predator unmanned aircraft, while the top officials of the ISI support military insurgent groups in Pakistan, which the U.S. follows through its telecommunication intercepts (Sigint). These actions may strengthen the Pakistani government, which is a crucial ally of the United States, but the strikes could also cause a domestic backlash that could weaken or overthrow the government.[41]

Without some sort of outside oversight, secrecy can breed independence and recklessness, or give a president the freedom to undertake covert actions against political opponents. As part of the Vietnam/Watergate era Congress reasserted itself against what was called "the imperial presidency," and a particular focus was covert operations. The 1974 Hughes-Ryan Amendment to the Foreign Assistance Act established two requirements. First, the act improved presidential oversight by requiring that the president had to make a "finding" that an international threat existed and required a covert operation to block it. Second, that finding had to be reported to a total of six congressional committees. That potentially porous reporting process was modified in 1977 and 1978 when Congress reduced the requirement to two new intelligence committees in 1980. In 1976 President Ford signed Executive Order 11905 prohibiting any em-

---

40. Ackerman, "Defense Intelligence Assumes More Diverse Missions," 18.
41. Solomon, Gorman, and Rosenberg, "U.S. Plans New Drone Attacks in Pakistan."

ployee of the United States from engaging in or conspiring to engage in assassination.

After the Iran-Contra scandal President Reagan issued National Security Decision Directive 286, requiring the "findings" to be in writing and not to be retroactive. A list of accountability procedures was codified into law in 1991. They include (1) a finding must be in writing, (2) it cannot be retroactive, (3) the covert action must be necessary, (4) all government agencies involved must be specified, (5) no covert action can be intended to influence U.S. political processes or policies, public opinion, or the media, (6) no action can violate the U.S. Constitution, (7) the committees must be informed of significant changes in the covert actions, and (8) no funds can be spent for this action by any government agency until there is a written and signed finding.

Congressional legislation established procedures for oversight and accountability for covert operations, but after 9/11 new developments have called that oversight function into question. Never enamored with the CIA, Secretary of Defense Rumsfeld expanded an existing intelligence support group into a new intelligence organization within the Defense Department to allow the Pentagon to conduct its own clandestine and covert operations free from the legal restrictions on the CIA.[42] Referred to as P2OG or Proactive, Preemption Operations Group, the group operates in the "dark" zone, insulated from outside pressures and congressional oversight.

Intelligence activities run a spectrum of activities, or an escalation ladder. Loch Johnson devised a four-category and thirty-eight step model for intelligence operations in other countries.[43] They can easily be reduced to a more manageable fourteen steps, still using Johnson's four levels. Ethical issues will obviously become more pronounced and difficult as one moves up the ladder to increasingly secret and coercive operations. The purpose of these activities is to break the chain of threat, early if possible by detection, later if necessary by deterrence, and ultimately by disarming, defeating, or destroying the source and agents of the threat.

Level 1: Routine Operations

1. Normal observation and interaction activities of the embassy's political officers
2. Recording signals and measures by surveillance satellites

---

42. Arkin, "The Secret War"; Hersh, "The Coming Wars."
43. L. K. Johnson, "Ethics of Covert Operations," 266–99.

Level 2: On-the-Ground Clandestine Activities

3. Recruiting agents
4. Funding democratic forces
5. Spreading disinformation
6. Providing arms and training to foreign military forces

Level 3: High-Risk Covert Operations

7. Planting a listening device that requires an embassy break-in
8. Large-scale funding of allied forces, whether governmental or insurgent
9. Interdicting, disrupting, preventing attacks

Level 4: War-Like Operations

10. Kidnapping, interrogation, imprisonment
11. Creating major and widespread economic dislocations
12. Secret military actions such as retortions and retaliations to send a cease and desist notice
13. Assassinating leaders, destroying sites
14. Overthrowing a government

It is easy to develop a vertical escalation like this, but it needs to be complemented with a horizontal sense of time of impact, especially for operations in Level 4. Interdicting and ending a specific threat like a bombing, done at level 3, is crucial and has immediate salutary impact. Actions in Level 4 are generally targeted at longer-range impact. Even overthrowing a government may only be effective for a couple years or decades, and so only buy time. Time can be a precious commodity if used well and as part of an overall strategy. In other words, level 4 must be closely connected to a sophisticated diplomatic strategy to achieve decisive and long-term change.

COUNTERINTELLIGENCE

As a world power with competitors, adversaries, and enemies, the United States is a target of intelligence operations by the intelligence agencies of other nations, officers who try and do turn Americans, especially within the intelligence community. After the fall of the Soviet Union, the operations of the KGB were taken over by its successor, the FSB. That agency continued to handle Aldrich Ames, ran FBI special agent Earl Pitts (arrested for espionage in 1996), ran CIA officer Harold James Nicholson between 1994 and 1996 (who planted a listening device in a State Department conference room in 1999), and ran FBI special agent Robert Hansen until his arrest in 2001. In other words, if we can do it, so can they—the multiple allies and adversaries of the United States. This is a topic worthy of more consideration than is possible in this chapter.

ETHICAL DILEMMAS

Ethical dilemmas abound as one moves from ends pursued by open diplomacy to the secret and shadowy means of the intelligence world. A former director of human resources at the CIA put it like this: "We are a secret organization in a democracy, and we often work in gray areas. We are an organization chartered by our government to break the laws of other governments. This puts a heavy obligation on us to be honest and ethical in all our dealings with one another, with the consumer of our services, and with the people of the United States."[44] This is about a decent person, a Christian, operating on the dark side, or in gray areas and shadows, even, perhaps, in areas of moral murkiness.

Where one begins exploring the ethical issues may determine their conclusion. Americans are born into a democratic value system of liberty, equality, honesty, openness, representation, and fair dealings. Americans in the twentieth and twenty-first centuries are also automatically born into the Westphalia system and its culture of risk. Christians are born into a value system of love of neighbor and enemy, Christian community, and peacemaking as a child of God.

How are these three worlds reconciled? How does one live embraced by grace and engaged in the dark side of foreign policy? We begin with the moral center, where life is lived in personal communion with our Lord through the Holy Spirit. From there we find our careers and attendant moral boundaries or margins. Life in the clandestine and covert service of the nation is unique because officers live at the moral margins. As former CIA Director General Michael Hayden put it, Congress and the admin-

---

44. Quoted in Kessler, *Inside the CIA*, 249.

istration create the space for intelligence operations, and all that space needs to be used, even if operatives get chalk on their cleats.[45]

The boundaries come from a variety of sources. The Hague Conferences laid down a basic legal framework for the threat and use of force between nations, which recognized that when one nation withholds secret information from other nations that threaten their security, that nation for its own protection can take steps to uncover those secrets. The rules adopted by the conferences recognize the fact that the highest priority for nations in risky or ambiguous situations is national defense, which in turn makes intelligence critically important. It represents a shared-expectations theory and holds that social institutions develop their own moral boundaries in which spying is necessary and legal.

American intelligence officers are bound by the boundaries of professional ethics. Just as the professional ethics of "an officer and a gentleman" prevent war-fighters from becoming mere thugs, so the professional ethics of the clandestine and covert operation officers prevent them from becoming mere crooks and thieves. Those ethics include service for the national defense, moral purpose of the action and a career devoted to that moral purpose, direction from a superior, legitimate target, complete honesty with the superior, and compliance with constitutional requirements. Within that ethical world are American regime values that make the secret worlds of the intelligence community accountable to the president and the Congress. "The nation must to a degree take it on faith," said former CIA Director Richard Helms, "that we too are honorable men devoted to her service. We are alleged to be out-of-control and irresponsible in action. We are neither. For intelligence is the servant of the U.S. Government, not its master."[46] That is a fine testimonial, but Americans need some basis for assurance.

Levels 3 and 4 of the model of intelligence operations described above lie beyond the shared-expectations ethic of the first two levels and require some specific ethical constraints. Three ethical boundaries seem important. First, there needs to be the moral purpose of self-defense in the face of a severe or supreme threat. Second, a decision to engage in the upper levels of action must be a shared decision of the two branches of government and not short-circuit the established principles and processes

---

45. Hayden, "CIA Director's Address at Duquesne University Commencement."
46. Quoted by Hayden, "The Influence of Richard Helms," 61.

of American constitutional democracy, the ethics of regime values. This is difficult because while passing judgment on an intelligence operation cannot be divorced from the circumstances, the totality of those circumstances can never be shared with the public. Still, political legitimacy is conferred by the fact of congressional authorization through the creation of the Central Intelligence Agency and the others. That authorization is the reasoned political response to a national danger by a second branch of government.

A third ethical boundary problem is that terrorists are not recognized military forces as defined by the Hague Conferences, so are not covered by international law. The U.S. courts have moved in the direction of extending the rules of war to terrorists, however, as an affirmation of American constitutional values. This position is a matter of continuing debate and is in legal flux.[47]

The ends of foreign policy are the crucial ethical issue in diplomacy, but in intelligence it is the means that raise ethical issues, particularly the issue of "dirty hands." Two practical ethical issues are important: the means used and the resulting consequences. The general excuse for clandestine and covert operations is their necessity. Pornography might be regarded as unethical but it is discretionary, not necessary. Leading a lover into levels of activity that imply a serious relationship without being serious is ethically odious but again is discretionary. Clandestine operations differ because they are taken out of necessity and both sides know what is being done and why.

Consider these hypothetical examples. The United States desperately needs access to information from within Hamas to deter or defeat any future attacks on Americans. The CIA recruits a young person with a PhD in Middle Eastern studies and who grew up in Lebanon. He takes a job with a United Nations humanitarian agency that will give him regular access to Palestinian refugee camps to both acquire information and recruit possible sources. At issue are the unknown impacts on the moral image of the UN agency if the recruit is discovered, whether refugees should reasonably assume privacy in the camp, the naiveté or assumption of the Palestinians in assuming the agency is probably penetrated, the information that could be discovered and prevent surprise and suicide attacks, whether the recruit will be doing less than a full-time job, and the risks

47. See Gellman, *Angler*, 160–84, 354–58.

that might befall other workers in the agency. Is it morally acceptable to use a UN humanitarian agency for such intelligence activity?

The CIA has a very valuable source within al Qaeda in Germany, who has passed information that has prevented attacks in Germany and Europe and led to the arrest of an al Qaeda operative in Spain. In a meeting the source asks the CIA to provide him a prostitute, since that would be safer to his cover than visiting red-light districts. Should the CIA do so? At issue is the involvement of the CIA in such activity and the use of U.S. funds for prostitution in another country with different laws, whether the prostitute has chosen her profession so it is a case of consenting adults, and whether the urgent necessity make a morally wrong activity in this case morally acceptable.

The CIA is often criticized for not penetrating terrorist organizations. The CIA has an agent in place in an Indonesian terrorist group that has exploded several bombs in hotels and a U.S. embassy. To gain access to the inner councils of the group she must commit a terrorist act herself to prove her loyalty to the group. Should the CIA give its approval for the agent to carry out a bombing of a police official who has arrested two of the group's members? At issue is whether the police official can be warned, the ratio of how many lives could be saved because of the killing of this one official, whether the killing of an innocent person can ever be justified, and what moral obligation the CIA has to an agent who is then killed for proving she is not a true and loyal terrorist and probably an agent.

Finally, would it be morally acceptable to make secret deals with U.S. software firms, cryptography manufacturers, and broadband providers to install secret "back door" technologies in their products that would provide the National Security Agency the ability to eavesdrop and decipher communications to and from terrorists? At issue is whether the U.S. should use all necessary means, whether the privacy of innocent Americans can be maintained, whether this program could keep up with the dynamic and evolving technology, whether the United States should bribe or coerce a firm, and the fallout on U.S. public opinion when discovered.

These four hypothetical cases come from James Olson in his book *Fair Play*. Olson suggests many such hypothetical cases and then asks a series of intelligence officers, academics, novelists, and students for their opinions. The number of commentators differs in the various cases. In the first case four of the commentators said yes, one said no, and two said it depends. In the second case all the commentators said yes. In the third case no one said yes, four said no and no one said it depends. In the fourth case there were three who said yes, two said no, and one said it depends.[48]

Moral dilemmas abound if one takes seriously the need for intelligence operations to discover and break the chains of threat. The foundational premise of this chapter is that Christians cannot depend on these operations for their own safety and well-being and then call them inherently unethical. Individual means may be unethical, but not the necessity for some intelligence operations. A common rationale for dirty-hands operations is "if I don't do it then someone else will." The rationale has gravitas because it is unethical to depend on someone else to do what is necessary for your well-being while criticizing them and washing your hands of being responsible for doing what is necessary for the well-being of others. It is the responsibility of being a citizen, which is inescapable, except for those Christian communities and feminists who believe citizenship and patriotism are too flawed to be acceptable.

This is the dilemma of choosing a lesser evil to avoid a great evil. The ethics of purity represented by deontological boundaries rejects the claims of necessity. Opponents of a lesser-evil posture can claim the boundaries will keep moving until they are nonexistent, but that gives no credit to the character of the individual. Virtue ethics represent an escape from deontological demands, but the definitions of the virtues are often vague. The reality is that the individual in his and her personal life in Christ, complemented by a life in a Christian fellowship, and while journeying with the Scripture, must find peace with himself or herself and with God, and then make the ultimate decisions about any personal limits on the ladder of operations. For those who want to tell other people how to live—the deontologists, legalists, and literalists—that is not enough and too individualistic. Some participants living in the light and embraced by grace may find the operations too murky, and some may not. It is for us, living in the light and seeking to "see the right as God gives to see the right," as Lincoln put it, to make those decisions.

There is a moral divide that comes into play as the stakes rise and the consequent actions become more severe. As Christians living on the edge of normal moral boundaries, the point of that divide will be personal and may differ from where others may locate that point. To even consider a

48. Olson, *Fair Play*, 87–89, 101–3, 105–9, 199–203.

career in the intelligence world the individual will have already accepted the use of deception, subterfuge, and bribery as ethically tolerable activities in light of the dangers to this country, whether potential or immediate. Some of the operations are voluntary, that is, once the proposal is made and the target accepts it, deception is over and there is mutual accord. At a different level where the target's information is high value, deception will need to be maintained. Seduction may be the only route to cooperation, or some type of coercion may be necessary. At some point officers or their agent may have to choose whether to participate in illegal or disreputable behavior or not, or in personally repulsive behavior. At that point the officer has the option accorded to all officers in the intelligence community to drop out of the operation. If not, and if the officer is not a callous personality, there will be guilt.

For covert operations the means become much more questionable. In a situation where ethically tolerable acts become more questionable and can become intolerable, there is also the fact that the stakes of a situation can go from minor to severe. Threat seems tolerable, but the chain of threat can become the "chain of pain" or the "kill chain," or move to a "massacre chain" or a "cripple the giant chain." As the stakes become more severe the acts may move toward a point of being intolerable. The principle is, the more just the cause, the more latitude to ignore or set aside moral borders to action. A moral divide reflects a point at which the stakes do not justify intolerable acts, and so they become atrocities. When that point is crossed the lesser-evil rationale is inoperable.

Or is it? What is justified by a "supreme emergency," an imminent threat with catastrophic consequences? An attack on the World Trade Center? A crippling of the U.S. energy network or its information networks for banks or military command? Action has to be taken or there will be massive death and destruction. How is *massive* defined? Does preventing another imminent Twin Towers qualify as catastrophic? The difficulty of definitions precludes much precision in locating the moral divide.

Intertwined throughout all of these issues is personal character. This government has to rely on the integrity of its officers, which is why the equivalent of conscientious objection is available. So, in the end, it becomes a personal decision, an exercise of human freedom and moral choice and personal character. Yet secrecy sometimes requires the officer "on the ground" be kept in the dark or even deceived about the full meaning of his or her actions. The John Le Carré novel *The Spy Who Came In from the Cold* explores issues of shadows, deception, and being used as a pawn. Any officer in such a situation faces limits on the full play of his or personal morality and choice.

Will one decision that stabs the conscience make a later decision easier, with less discomfort to one's conscience? J. F. Drexel Godfrey fears the corrosive impact on the intelligence officers of a career of deception, manipulation, and subverting the integrity of others.[49] That was echoed by a former chief of the European Division when he said, "You have an organization of professional liars . . . and it's a system that can be taken advantage of."[50]

Tony Pfaff reminds us that we do not know in advance where those secrets are or whether they are essential to national security; therefore intelligence professionals tend to cast a wide net. Deception can needlessly poison relationships; determining appropriate actions and targets is a matter of good judgment.[51]

In the end the trustworthiness of human intelligence rests on the character of the officers. They have to be honorable people with moral boundaries that hold regardless. Larry Devlin was the chief of station in the Congo in the 1960s, a newly independent nation full of chaos and intrigue, led by a prime minister who was quickly turning the country into a Soviet base of operations in Africa. Orders came from headquarters for him to carry out the assassination of Prime Minister Patrice Lumumba. As he relates his struggle, "I could never assassinate Lumumba. It would have been murder. While I could have justified the assassination of Hitler to myself, Lumumba's case was not the same. It would have been murder."[52] In the midst of the Congolese civil war Lumumba was captured by Congolese insurgents and killed.

GRACE AND OPERATIONS

Grace is easy to explain in a chapter on theology, but not so easy in a chapter on diplomatic conflict and deception. Is it enough to assume that grace will cover actions that individuals make and that stab the

49. Godfrey, "Ethics and Intelligence."
50. Warrick and Smith, "Latest CIA Scandal."
51. Pfaff, "Bungee Jumping off the Moral Highground," 77.
52. Devlin, *Chief of Station, Congo*, 96.

conscience? To try to live around the +4 or +5 of the grace scale while involved in operations found at the lower end of the consequences of that scale can be tense and tenuous. Clandestine and covert operations require intense efforts, not unlike those of business people in a declining or failing business, be it car parts, cattle ranching, or computer software. Alike they require constant planning, calculating, and full attention if not absorption, leaving little time not preoccupied with the issues. A Christian in such circumstances of absorption must commit and rest, that is, remain committed to living in fellowship with the Lord and rest in the confidence that the embrace of grace will remain throughout the crisis and after.

Christians engaged in the world of intelligence operations must recognize the importance of both attitude and boundaries. The attitude that one takes toward operations and agents can be humane or cynical, the latter destructive of the humanizing effect of grace as well as its energizing power of hope and critique. One ought to have one's moral boundaries clarified long before operations begin. Even then a boundary may seem movable, and one is confronted with the decision to step over or step back. To step over and spill the blood of one in a situation of war to prevent wide-scale death of others may seem the lesser of the two evils, however, and we must choose between them. The ethical formulas of dual morality or just war principles provide their advocates with some measure of justification, but neither seem adequate to either a holistic sense of morality and reality or to the shadowy ambiguities of intelligence operations. If one decides to step over, then one must be prepared to accept the legal consequences if law comes into play, or to experience remorse and penitence if legal but still ethically questionable. Or, if an act of war, one may find the peace of necessity and the peace of rest.

To step back may be the only way to preserve peace with God and oneself, though it may halt any career advancement. To step back may also preserve one's career if legal accountability follows upon those who stepped over.

We live in multiple time zones. We live in the present, the snapshots of our lives with its routine and in its crises, its joys and tragedies. We live in a second time zone, this one of one's personal life span where those snapshots become a mosaic of the extended meaning of one's own life. The third time zone is the sweep of history and background events that we do not control, to any measurable degree. We are born and live in specific times and conditions, in this current case an era of war, power transition, and economic stress. We did not choose our time, and there is little justice in when we get to live. We must understand the dangers of our time, its issues and ambiguities, the presence and limits of opportunities, and a conception of one's self in this wider world, and we must anchor our lives in Christ within our times and circumstances.

We live simultaneously in God's time too—his presence and grace and his larger purposes and mysteries as he works in our world. We may come to see a larger pattern of meaning or only mystery. When the waters don't part for us in our time of history, we look for the fingerprints of God on whatever piece of wood floats by. We live in the trust that God's providential time is not confined to the grand sweep of history but also intersects with our lives, in the immediate and in the structure and portrait of our life's mosaic.

The power of grace to help us commit, trust, and rest brings a new kind of wisdom to us in the midst of these issues and choices. The "capacity to transcend one's self, the ability to view the overarching sweep of cyclical time, leads to a profound realization of the mystery of God's involvement in time."[53]

Grace is God's gift to us. We are a part of God's presence in this world, and as such we move into it to confront the issues. We enter God's time zone while remaining in the zones of history and our life's mosaic where we do the necessary moral work of this world.

To be a Christian is to believe, to be, and to do. To be embraced by grace does not guarantee operational success. To be involved in foreign affairs means we have assessed our time and place, and we have determined to serve the greater good of our nation and the broader world by walking along the margins of morality.

Given the reality of international affairs, foreign policy will always involve intelligence operations. The nation needs people who will risk their own moral margins to reduce the diplomat's margin of ignorance and so avoid the risks of "diplomacy in the dark," and to disrupt an adversary's kill chain.

A MEDITATION ON PSALM 137

The writer of Psalm 140 lived in fear of the men of violence who devise evil plans and stir up war every day. Such plans characterize life around

---

53. Brown, *Character in Crisis*, 144.

the world today, some of it directed at Americans, and the consequences can be physically and morally destructive. For example, Psalm 137 begins, "By the rivers of Babylon we sat and wept." A people in exile, tormented by their conquerors, they lived in thoughts of revenge, vengeance, and murder of infants by "smashing them against the rocks" (Ps 137:8–9). Terrorist attacks can bring similar thoughts of revenge, for on 9/11 we were violated with extensive destruction that cannot be undone. There is evil in the world, and there are anti-American predators. At another level, that of our careers, we will have enemies and opponents. In Psalm 138 David prays for help against his adversaries, and in Psalm 141 he prays the Lord will not allow his heart to be drawn to evil. In Psalm 139, the writer sees beyond Babylon and the snares that can warp his heart, as must we. "Search me O God," he prays, know my heart, and lead me (Ps 139:23–24). In the midst of enemies and the search for response we open ourselves to God's searching, knowing that we are embraced by his presence or grace ("you hem me in," Ps 139:5) and always desiring to know his thoughts.

How can we relate those verses to clandestine operations, in the fight against the plans and plots, as well as threats to our own careers in diplomacy, intelligence, or politics? First, against evil we need to *fight right*—in the name of higher values such as the international laws of war. A commitment to the ethics of regime values and solidarity ethics can prevent operatives from becoming thugs who mirror the terrorists. Second, against our enemies we need to *fight smart*—not with evil actions for revenge but with the professionalism of the intelligence officer and crisis manager. Third, *fight in grace*: the calculations necessary for successful clandestine operations must be done within a determined openness to the presence of God and the willingness to either step over or step back. The calculations for advancing one's career or overcoming a superior's "difficult personality" or holding firm against a furious opponent of one's decisions must also be made in reaching up to God and in openness to God's grace to rise above the inevitable personal hostility, and to avoid becoming fixated on adversaries and warping of relationships and peace with one's self.

To walk along the moral margins even to the point of getting chalk on your cleats requires one to maintain a constant attitude of meditation toward the care of your soul, not for a dual morality but for the fullness of a Christian life in the existential reality of a world of David and Joab and Esther—and our own. Similarly, against your career opponents who seek to frustrate your plans, undercut your status, or destroy your career, you need to pray for help, patience, protection, and perhaps preemption (Ps 140:6–11). In the midst of the stress that comes from battling enemies in the shadows and opponents within the layers of wheels in the organization, avoid theodicy (why me? why did God allow this?). Recognize that there are no guarantees in a life in which everyone has freedom of thought, freedom of action, and freedom of intrigue. Replace theodicy with trust in God's providential history for you, and with confession and supplication; limit the unavoidable animosity and replace hatred with wisdom (Ps 143:3–11). In that spirit be creative and trustworthy, never give in, and never drop out.

Revenge should not warp one's heart, but what about rue and regret later for intelligence activities, decisions, or actions, or in retirement for a career lived on the margins? Perhaps. If new information comes to light that invalidates the context as it was understood, casting the decision in new negative light, then perhaps there will be regret. Short of that, no. Do faculty members regret giving a student the grade earned even though it damaged that student's grade point average and perhaps prevented that student's qualification for a scholarship or law school admission? Sorrow for the student perhaps, but not regret. Should it have been done differently? No, for changing the context does not invalidate decisions made in another context. Would one regret falsely posing as a sympathetic friend to a student thought to be involved in a radical group intending to destroy a university research center, alerting the authorities, and then watching as the student and her group are arrested and expelled from the university? No. One does what is necessary in a context for professionalism, safety, and the public good, and changing the context does not invalidate the action.

If one lives embraced by grace at the time, with courage and right attitudes and purposes, one can rely on grace later to keep from becoming bedeviled by doubt and guilt for decisions and actions in the engagement against the powers of threat and destruction.

5

Defense: Minds at War

> In the early days of nuclear weapons, there was a great deal of literature coming out of think tanks, universities and other institutions about when and how to use atomic bombs. That just isn't happening in this new kind of warfare [cyber-attacks].[1]

WEAPONS CARRY CONSEQUENCES—DEATH AND destruction, wins and losses, rise and decline. The twentieth century began with one of the worst wars in history, and its follow-on world war was even worse. After mid-century and the arrival of the nuclear age, war became limited to regions, fought on the periphery but with consequences for the United States and its allies as well as their main competitors in the Soviet Union and China. Near the end of the century, with the Soviet Union expired and the periphery released, violence flared in the world with internal wars of ancient animosities.

The near-parity of the U.S. and Soviet blocs in the 1960s should have led to a central war, which would have been a nuclear World War III, a decisive power transition if not a global holocaust. The central war among the great powers occurred, not through a hot war but through a Cold War with a definite winner and loser. Escaping a nuclear World War III was a great achievement of humanity and reason, diplomacy, and deterrence. The "greatest generation" won the Second World War, and its successor generation won the third—no small feat. The global problem now is the potential for World War IV.

I am defining World War IV as such a change in the status of the United States in the international system within the next thirty years that it ceases to be a leading global power. Such a loss can come several ways,

---

1. Magnuson, "Cyber-Attack," 22.

the quickest and most dramatic being a military defeat so severe it destroys the U.S. force structure and economy. That is not likely, but World War IV could happen without the clash of forces. A technological development on the order of nuclear weapons by another nation could put U.S. forces at such a high level of risk that they cannot be deployed. It could also happen through a realignment of world powers with the nonpeaceful rise of China or a realignment of civilizations against the U.S. and its allies that slowly strangles U.S. power. The United States could emerge from a series of regional wars so cynical, demoralized, and divided, so insistent on a "never again" policy, that it sidelines itself. Finally, but not the least possible or probable, it could collapse through economic depression, or a serious erosion of its social capital, or such a loss of its industrial base that it cannot sustain a global and leading-edge military force.

STRATEGIC DOCTRINES

Wars are intellectual in the sense of understanding the nature of the threat to America's defense, then designing and developing weapon systems appropriate for the time and threat, and then devising a strategy for their use. Strategic doctrine is not the battlefield doctrine but the broader doctrine of how to think about the use of force in the historic circumstances of the times. The United States needs minds at war, with the first priority to deter war and the second to prevail if war comes.

In very broad and simplified terms there have been three defense eras and three strategic doctrines. The first was the era of the young republic. Small and weak, secure from the west, the three main threats to the United States first were internal from a standing army, second from a possible attack from across the seas, and third from entanglement in the ongoing power transition struggle between England and France. The founders of the nation recognized this era clearly, so the Constitution they wrote provides for maintaining a navy but only for raising and supporting an army when needed. Externally the strategic doctrine of these early years was to avoid any policies that required an army and to limit military activity to coastal fortifications and small naval forces. Congress authorized the construction of six frigates, though only three were actually built, the 44-gun *United States* and the *Constitution* and the 38-gun *Constellation*. This defensive mentality was inadequate for the War of 1812, particularly when the United States tried to invade and capture Canada.

The War of 1812, the Mexican War of 1840, and the permanent Indian frontier required a continuing need for an army, so an army war college was established at West Point and all military leaders attended there together. That was timely, for the wars of Napoleon in Europe reflected a new European era when armies were not upper-class nobles and knights waging chess-like defensive skirmishes (think Yorktown), but a nation's mobilized population, utilizing new military technologies that gave the advantage to offensive forces. Napoleon smashed other armies and subdued Europe for a time. Otto von Clausewitz's book *On War* drew central lessons from Napoleon. Wars can escalate to a degree of total war, or what Clausewitz calls pure war, with such destruction that the original purpose of the war gets lost. To prevent that all-out escalation, wars must be considered not ends in themselves but "the continuation of politics by other means." Thus civilian political leaders must have ultimate control of strategy. Napoleon's approach to war was offensive, and Clausewitz understood the need for a strategy that destroys the other nation's army in a climactic battle—the Napoleonic battle at Austerlitz being the model.

None of this typified strategy under Winfield Scott, who, during the Mexican War, was careful to avoid killing of civilians and determined to capture Mexico City to win and end the war rather than fight pitched and bloody battles. At West Point instructors did not use Clausewitz but used a reinterpretation of Napoleon by Antoine Henri, Baron de Jomini, who considered Napoleon's battles too chaotic and demonic. Jomini was a traditionalist who abhorred indiscriminate violence and emphasized the offense by means of siege.[2]

When civil war broke out in the United States all the military commanders had studied at West Point and all seemed to all learn the same tactics. Northern troops spent time building fortifications, the southern troops tried to sneak around northern positions and threaten Pennsylvania and New York (Antietam and Gettysburg, both failures). Near the bottom of the West Point class was Grant, who adopted a true Napoleonic strategy (more out of personal understanding than military theory) and relentlessly fought the Southern army to finally smash it out of existence (Appomattox). The North won the war in part because of the navy's ability to prevent outside trade and aid, but also because the North had far more men and wealth to give to the war, and learned how

---

2. Weigley, *The American Way of War*, 82–85.

to mobilize them into a mass fighting force for the war effort. Grant used them mercilessly to finally annihilate the Southern army while General Sherman made war on the land, livestock, infrastructure, and people. This period of defense and borrowed strategy soon came to an end.

The second intellectual period of American military strategy commenced with the creation in 1884 of the Naval War College, the world's first such school to focus on strategy as well as seamanship. It was augmented by the National Defense Act of 1916, which enlarged and professionalized the army into a modern military that would avoid the gallant but uncoordinated and mismanaged Cuban campaign of 1890. The United States was industrializing and prospering, and with increased capabilities come increased intentions; more means lead to higher goals. The United States was on its S curve at the end of the nineteenth century and beginning of the twentieth. Secure from any probable land invasion, it focused on the seas, but for purposes far beyond coastal defense.

At West Point the prize teacher was Captain Alfred Thayer Mahan, and his writings and teachings outlined a coherent national strategy. As a maritime nation, he taught, the United States needed to protect its merchant marine as it transported goods around the world and to preserve access to ports and markets through a global naval force. Modern naval warfare needed a battle fleet that could destroy the adversary's fleet; that was the first and primary goal of strategy. To service and move that naval presence, the U.S. would need locations around the world for resupply and an inter-ocean canal somewhere in Central America. The United States defeated the rival Spanish naval power in the Spanish-American War and gained recognition as a rising power and gained bases in Guam and Puerto Rico. Later the U.S. helped insurgent forces create the nation of Panama, which in turn suggested we build the Panama Canal.

When the United States entered World War I it had the five basic elements of a national strategy that had evolved by the end of the nineteenth century. Those elements were (1) a strong navy and battle fleet, (2) a small regular army that embodied military knowledge and a general staff, (3) a large manpower base that could be mobilized, (4) a strong civilian industrial economy, and (5) a clear geo-strategic perspective and doctrine for national defense and foreign policy at the turn of the century.

The terrible experience of the ground war in World War I led to a determined effort to find a strategy that would lead to such a quick victory that such ground warfare would not be necessary again. Four military leaders from four different countries came to the same strategy—Brigadier General Giulio Douhet ("the Mahan of air power") of Italy, Herman Göring in Germany, Major General Hugh Trenchard in England, and Brigadier General Billy Mitchell in the United States. They advocated using airpower to take control of the skies and then attack civilian centers, causing such trauma that the public would demand an immediate end to the war.[3] All through World War II nations attacked each other's cities, which did not lead to calls for surrender but to continue fighting. The atomic bombing of two Japanese cities ended that war, although it was a close call, the emperor having to put down a military coup intended to keep the war going.

The development of the intercontinental ballistic missile (ICBM) armed with atomic weapons revolutionized war. The B-29s that carried the atomic bombs to Japan penetrated Japanese home space because the Japanese were accustomed to one or two planes flying reconnaissance and ignored them; real attacks came in swarms. The ICBM gave the power to fly over any defenses and attack cities with the most deadly weapons; swarms of bombers were no longer necessary. The Air Force doctrine to strike early to destroy enemy defenses and achieve air superiority was more dangerous now. Whole cities were at risk from single missiles. This meant there would be pressures to strike before the other did, to launch a preemptive strike—much like World War I when military mobilization forced military decisions that undercut diplomacy—for in any severe crisis the nation that waits too long would die. Napoleonic strategy of annihilation had reached its peak; without some constraints, nuclear war would become Clausewitz's feared total or pure war.

The military was caught in its mindset, best represented by the Eisenhower doctrine of massive retaliation. In a diplomatic crisis the United States would launch a massive nuclear attack "on places of its own choosing," meaning Moscow. That doctrine was spelled out in the single integrated operational plan (SIOP-62), which contemplated that a U.S. response to a Soviet invasion of Western Europe would use 1,459 bombs packing 2,164 megatons of nuclear explosive. If the U.S. struck first in a preemptive strike, the nuclear weapons would rise to 3, 423 with 7,847 megatons. It was estimated that 285 million Russians and Chinese would die, along with another 100 million in Eastern Europe and another 100

---

3. See Brodie, *Strategy in the Missile Age*, 71–106.

million in the rest of Europe, depending on the winds.[4] After the Soviet Union developed its own nuclear forces, a massive U.S. attack would be matched by a massive Soviet attack. The two sides would destroy each other. Political goals would be obliterated.

A small group of civilians in the Rand Corporation worked for several years to devise an alternative strategy and lobbied for its acceptance.[5] They became known as the defense intellectuals, and their strategy was nuclear deterrence. The leaders of that effort were Bernard Brodie, Albert Wholstetter, and Fred Ikle, and they devised the third era of national strategy. The most well known of the defense intellectuals was Herman Kahn, who took their ideas and combined them into his book *On Thermonuclear War* and later *On Escalation*. Kahn worked at the Rand Corporation, an Air Force Research and Development think tank in Santa Monica, California. The book included Brodie's concept of no-cities targeting and Wholstetter's concept of a second strike capability. He detailed policies to deter such a war—and to survive it if irrationality prevailed. Though Brodie believed nuclear weapons are necessary for deterrence, they should never actually be used. Kahn pointed out the usability paradox: the threat to use suicidal weapons will not bring deterrence unless the other side really believes they will be used. They are useless without the actual intent to use them if necessary, so there had to be a willingness to use them, but a corollary emphasis on crisis stability to reduce the pressures and risks as low as possible.[6] "Deliver us from evil," Jesus taught his disciples to pray. Which evil, nuclear war or participating in developing strategic doctrines to prevent or limit such a war? In a choice between the two, the latter seems a much lesser evil if not a positive good for Christians.

This strategy of nuclear deterrence and escalation ladders and crisis stability gave leaders conceptual tools to resist optimistic preemptive strikes or the fatalism of irrepressible ideological conflict. The strategy was based on the rationality of mathematics and economics and built on the strategy of rational choice and mutual cooperation between two competitors with a lot to lose if it failed. The empirical scenarios, matrixes, and utility scales clarified issues. It was a rationality that avoided the Meineckian assignment of absolute good and evil between the powers,

4. Abella, *Soldiers of Reason*, 158–59.
5. Kaplan, *The Wizards of Armageddon*.
6. Brodie, *Strategy in the Missile Age*; Kahn, *On Thermonuclear War*; and Kahn, *On Escalation*.

but it was also virtually devoid of humane values. It was instrumental but not morally principled. Its reliance on rational choice theory underplayed the human factor, the particular structure of beliefs and values, levels of risk taking and sensible restraint in leaders in another culture. Yet, whatever its critics, there was no ethical way out of the usability paradox in that bipolar nuclear world, and for thirty years it provided moral leaders a means to avoid a nuclear holocaust while also protecting the nation, as in the Cuban Missile Crisis.

During the same decades Mao Zedong developed a guerrilla strategy in his war to defeat the Nationalist government in China. Rather than attack the cities, Mao's strategy was to control the rural areas. From there they could strangle the cities and draw the Nationalist forces into the interior against unseen forces and no conclusive battles. That would generate such frustration that they would lash out at civilians and cause a switch in the loyalty of the people from the government to Mao. Then the guerrilla forces would form large fighting units and crush the government forces. What was true in the 1940s was true in the 1960s—a weak force could fight and defeat a modern industrialized military using space, time, and will against men, money, and material. It worked there and later in Vietnam.

The intellectual basis for the Vietnam War was Robert Osgood's book *Limited War in the Nuclear Age*. With the consequences of nuclear war too high to contemplate (except for Kahn perhaps) the stakes of future world and power transition wars would be achieved at lower levels of warfare. Using the Korean War as a model, Osgood argued for limits in goals, weapons, and territory. If those limits could hold, then the war would stalemate and diplomacy could reemerge. The United States limited its goals and means, but that was not reciprocated by North Vietnam. As in the Spanish Civil War in 1936, when one side limits their effort the other side wins. North Vietnam was not Hitler's Germany, and the U.S. had no intention of destroying the country and occupying it for decades. Its goal was limited to stopping the North, while the North's goal was to reunite the country. The asymmetrical goals and means destroyed the relevance of Osgood's ideas. Afterwards, just as the U.S. military never wanted to fight another trench warfare war, they also never wanted to fight another guerrilla war, even though the United States had just lost both its foreign policy goal and its war.

The Nixon Doctrine did not attempt to develop a counterinsurgency doctrine; rather, its approach was to limit any U.S. war involvement to those wars where the U.S. ally could win the war with some U.S. support; never again would we fight their war for them. The draft was deactivated and the military became an all-volunteer force, and much smaller. Those who joined included both young people wanting to get away from parents and their hometown for a couple years before going to college and those pushed into it by parents to force the maturation process. Others, like nurses and ministers, joined to take their profession into a second career. As the force grew smaller it became more focused on military missions. Noncombat jobs previously held by officers were outsourced to civilians.

The failure of General Westmoreland's strategy of overwhelming force against guerrilla forces in Vietnam led in time to the search for an alternative strategy. The 1992 Defense Policy Guidance document laid out a third strategic doctrine, this one of U.S. dominance. It called for a military so superior that no other developed nation would even consider an attempt to match it, and a U.S. policy to block any effort to try, whether by European allies or rogue nations. Portions of it were leaked to the press, and a later version issued by Defense Secretary Dick Cheney continued to call for permanent American dominance. It was a vision with little operational detail and no prescience of a new and different kind of adversary in the near future. That soon changed with the development of "shock and awe."

The development of precision guidance systems magnified the impact of smaller weapons, while information technologies allowed a fusion of information sources. As developed by James Wade, a shock and awe strategy would be so traumatic that it would paralyze the will and so overwhelm an opponent's understanding of events that they would be unable to offer military resistance.[7] The United States could accomplish "regime change" in rogue nations so easily and quickly that the other military services, particularly the army, could be reduced in size.

This rapid dominance through shock and awe strategy was used in the 2003 attack on Iraq, and while it reflected the policy of U.S. dominance and destroyed the Hussein regime, it utterly failed to pacify the nation. Faced with a ground war, the military turned to private military forces (PMFs) or contract soldiers to augment its ranks for nonfighting tasks.

---

7. Ullman and Wade, *Shock and Awe*, 24.

These forces were developed in the post–Cold War years, as the United States drew down the size of its military, and comprised retirees from the elite forces such as the Navy Seals, Delta Forces, and Army Rangers. They were not embedded in the regular forces but detailed in order to protect oil lines, reconstruction efforts, and officials.

FOURTH-ERA, FOURTH-GENERATION WARS

The attacks of 9/11 represented an updating of guerrilla war strategy that has come to be called fourth-generation war and led to the need for a new American strategy beyond a failed dominance strategy. The new role of passionate religion in global relations and the dislocations of globalization and ethnic/tribal nationalism are creating zealots who tear states from within and stir antagonisms without, and represent a new era of conflict with inherent moral overtones in culture and strategy.

These are not wars between nations as state entities and accountable to the Hague and Geneva laws of war, requiring uniforms, command structure, civilian immunity, and the ability to work out a negotiated settlement. Instead, they pit the United States against stateless individuals and militias who conduct unrestricted warfare unconstrained by rules. Terror attacks are used against their own civilians to keep the society unstable and unwilling to respond. They are states within states, mobilized societies with subnational loyalties, a global enterprise of political actors assisted by spontaneous followers incited and ignited by religious/ethnic values to oppose the West's culture and global presence. Women, children, and even mentally handicapped persons are used as human suicide bombers. There is no capital city, no production centers, no leadership hierarchy, no front line, but there is a network of media for consciousness raising, merchants for funding, and preachers for mobilizing.

Concurrent with those changes has been the so-called revolution in military affairs. The high priest of this "revolution" was Vice Admiral Arthur Cebrowski, who saw in modern information technology networks the ability to escape the confusion, mistakes, and misperceptions—the "fog of war"—with net-centric warfare. Now, fully wired, information dominance would give soldiers and commanders high levels of situational awareness, speed the war, fully integrate all types of forces into joint operations, and require a smaller but more agile military force. As in the invasion of Afghanistan with its difficult terrain, even soldiers on horseback could tap into this real-time information and gain the advantage. But insurgents are still more difficult to find and identify than tanks and other mechanized equipment.[8]

Robots and unmanned aerial vehicles are another new development that minimizes the human cost of war and may further revolutionize the warfare of the twenty-first century. Warbots are being developed for land, sea, and air operations, from surveillance to assassinations. America prefers to spend money rather than lives, so is moving to a techno-supremacy with net-centric warfare and robotics. In what one writer calls "The Eye of God," an unmanned aerial vehicle could search for specific individuals with enhanced computer-based recognition capability, and be preprogrammed to execute a strike on the person, all on its own.[9]

Net-centric situational awareness and robotics may revolutionize warfare, but they are exceedingly complex and vulnerable to anonymous cyber attacks from difficult-to-find IP addresses. Moreover, these new developments are not limited to the highly technological nations, for much of it is relatively cheap; insurgent groups are becoming expert in using elements of the new computer and information technology world for their own purposes, from communication to hacking into the adversary's own systems. The article "High-Tech Terror: Al-Qaeda's Use of New Technology" laid out the advanced state of technological sophistication of subgroups like insurgents.[10] The war between Israel and Hezbollah in Lebanon in 2006 was a shock; the mighty Israel military could not find and destroy its adversaries. Hezbollah—not a nation but a paramilitary organization—had access to the advanced weapons and information technology with the invisibility that comes from melding into the background. The first decade of the twenty-first century has opened a new era that is not yet fully understood. How will this nation respond when confronting adversaries armed with nuclear devices and who praise suicide bombings not as sin but as heroic martyrdom operations? Insurgent forces are acquiring potential biological/chemical weapons, advanced air defense systems, sophisticated technological ability to hack into the American net-centric war systems as well as domestic infrastructure systems, and these will present a multifaceted threat. Should the United States

8. Kaplan, *Daydream Believers*, 13–46; Singer, *Wired for War*, 179–236.
9. Forstchen, "The Eye of God—The Finger of God," 190–99.
10. Brachman, "High-Tech Terror."

prepare for traditional high-priced, big-gun, showdown wars and ignore insurgencies, or prepare for a historical shift in which the equivalent of World War IV will be fought through terrorist attacks and insurgencies with high casualties from ground operations in counterinsurgency operations, or prepare a large and multifunctional military for a full spectrum of contingencies?

Those options are limited for they do not address the rapidly emerging battlefields of cyberspace and outer space. A new unifying strategic is needed to define the dynamics and parameters of this era, and to lead strategic thinking, budgets, and operations. The former basic strategies related to physical space—land, sea, and air. Under the dynamics of these revolutionary changes of net-centric war, "Eye of God" technologies, and robotics, it may turn out that neither a traditional nor a counterinsurgency strategy comes to define the new fourth era but an even more revolutionary integrating and operating strategy built around cyberspace. Maybe.

How far into the next decades of the twenty-first century can the United States go without a new fourth-era strategy that is more than merely integration, coordination, and synchronization?[11] More than strategy is at stake, for the psychological images and the commitment to reason and Clausewitzian civilian control over strategy will be at stake. Kahn's defense policy was built on what has been called "nuclear enlightenment," necessary on both sides. Part of the U.S. strategy was to reorient Soviet military doctrine away from Marxist deterministic history of inevitable clash with capitalists. Today that posture is at risk from the "counter enlightenment" of those who see foreign policy within a Spenglerian struggle or religious holy war.[12] What is lacking for success is an intellectual construct like Mahan's and Kahn's that orients strategic doctrine.

This is not a call for a simple slogan. Whether a cyberspace strategy comes to the fore or not, the scope of the doctrine will be wide, for the elements of a new strategic vision are many, both old and new: from civilian immunity to the role of contract soldiers, from the use of net-centric warfare to the question of preemptive strikes, from so-called hybrid wars that combine high technology and street fighting to neuroscience for new ways in training soldiers and nanotechnologies for liquid armor. Many of

---

11. Those terms are from Daniel Gerstein's approach to a new strategy that relies more on reorganization and a checklist of reforms than a new fourth-era doctrine. See Gerstein, *Securing America's Future*, particularly 131–82.

12. Walker, "Nuclear Enlightenment."

the issues reach the boundaries of regime values, professional and solidarity ethics, and the boundaries of dignity and cost. We need Christian intellectuals to address these issues. The new doctrine must find tolerable resolutions to the practical and moral dilemmas and get us into the future with the nation and humane values intact.

ACADEMICS IN DEFENSE

Who will define the next era of U.S. national security policy? Congress developed the first with its naval authorizations; a naval officer developed the second; and civilian defense intellectuals developed the third. If Clausewitz is correct and civilians must control the military to insure the achievement of political goals rather than pure war, then perhaps the academic institutions of this nation may have a role to play through specialized intellectual centers.

Mobilizing minds for devising strategy requires organizational structures that allow focused thought. Universities are bastions of education, but curricular requirements diffuse focus, so specialized centers and institutes enable their members the time and dialogue opportunities to read and think, discuss and consult with experts, and shape their thought with writings. These centers can provide impact at crucial points of policy decisions, raise the recognition and prestige of a university, and shape a new generation of graduate students and young scholars. Nothing is easy, however, including structuring these centers. Funding is an underlying issue. Universities rarely have the "spare" funds to support these centers unless it is a minor element in a departmental program. Any serious center must be outside an academic department or it will suffer neglect in the ongoing balancing of departmental interests, programs, and funding. Major donors have endowed such centers to insure independence and permanence, while some centers have contracted with government agencies to conduct specialized studies. Funding and relationship issues involve academic ethics, so that a level of tension pervades the efforts.

The following is a brief and selective description of some past and current academic efforts to understand and prescribe policy ideas for American foreign policy.[13] Hans Morgenthau created a Chicago Center on Foreign Policy at the University of Chicago to support research and publish studies on American foreign policy, and one of the best known

---

13. For an early review of such centers see Lyons and Morton, *Schools for Strategy*.

books from that Center was Robert Osgood's *Limited War in the Nuclear Age*. Princeton University's Center of International Studies was founded in the 1930s by Nicholas Spykman, who made the geopolitics argument that a united Europe was the only region of the world that could defeat the United States, and therefore the U.S. had to insure it was never united, by Germany or by the Soviet Union. Later under Klaus Knorr the Center became a community of scholars. It publishes the journal *World Politics* and has produced multiple books on defense, deterrence, and national security.

Harvard University sponsored the Defense Policy Seminar, headed originally by Henry Kissinger, and the Center for International Affairs, which organized interdisciplinary studies of fundamental issues of foreign policy. Today it exists as the Weatherhead Center for International Affairs and conducts research and dialogue among scholars and practitioners. In 1989 the Olin Institute for Strategic Studies was established within the center to focus exclusively on crucial topics of national security and strategy. It offers fellowships to graduate students, supports teaching of national security affairs, and undertakes its own research projects.

The Massachusetts Institute of Technology established the Center for International Studies to focus on issues of immediate relevance to policy makers. While it specialized in weapons issues and arms control, it was also the home of Walt Rostow, who published *The Stages of Economic Growth*, led the center's study of communist societies, and became a high official in the Kennedy administration.

The Georgetown University Center for Strategic Studies was established in 1962 with Admiral Arleigh Burke as director to focus on the ideological motivation of the Soviet Union's foreign policy. Today it is known as the Center for Peace and Security Studies and hosts a Security Studies Program utilizing Georgetown's graduate faculty as well as research institutions, congressional and executive agency staff, and other professionals and academic institutions. Georgetown University is a Catholic institution that focuses on security studies, while two other Catholic universities, the University of Notre Dame and the University of San Diego, both have institutes for peace studies funded by the late Joan Kroc. The latter focuses on women in peacemaking, while the Notre Dame Institute has found a theme in strategic peacemaking and smart sanctions.

Robert Strausz-Hupé established the Foreign Policy Research Institute at the University of Pennsylvania in 1955. Strausz-Hupé supported a strong U.S. military force to oppose the Soviet Union and wrote about geopolitics and forward strategy that refused to tolerate the survival of a political system with the ruthless determination to destroy this nation. He once said that the U.S. may have no choice but to adopt a Catonic strategy, Cato being the Roman senator who argued that Carthage had to be destroyed.[14] The institute became independent in 1970 and continues to research and to publish reports and its flagship publication *Orbis*.

Several universities have operated weapons development and testing laboratories that bring into sharp relief such issues as the balance between academics (teaching and research) and public service, between science and government, between free exchange of ideas and public policy, particularly as related to the military. The Massachusetts Institute of Technology (M.I.T.) managed the Instrumentation Laboratory for the Department of Defense and the National Aeronautics and Space Administration, which in turn brought it funding and prestige. Given the context of 1968 and 1969, a student and faculty opposition movement developed, demanding the conversion of university technological resources to social objectives. Ultimately, M.I.T. divested itself of the laboratory.[15]

Throughout the unexpected long-term ground war in Iraq and Afghanistan, the military found itself operating in an Islamic culture and tribal society it did not understand. "Too many mistakes were made," Secretary of Defense Robert Gates said, "because the military did not understand the countries or culture where they were operating," and he called on universities to help the nation develop its "soft power."[16]

Accordingly, the Army created Human Terrain Teams, civilian anthropologists embedded with military units to study Iraqi society, customs, and leaders. The American Anthropology Association strongly opposed the use of their members as violations of the association's code of ethics. The association feared that information on individuals would be used by the military as part of its kill chain. Even short of that, the association is committed to the professional ethics of "do no harm" to those being studied, and the people being studied are not to be changed by the study project. Members were urged to sign a pledge statement not to cooperate, but that would not only be a statement but also could become

14. Quoted in Herzog, *The War-Peace Establishment*, 7–8.
15. For this story see Nelkin, *The University and Military Research*.
16. Gates, "Speech Delivered to the Association of American Universities, April 14, 2008."

a black list of those who did not sign, effectively ending their careers in academia.[17]

Gates also promoted the Minerva Initiative, a program to involve universities in topics of interest to the Pentagon, such as Chinese military technology and Islamic radicalism. It offers two-to three-year funding for consortium studies among universities. Critics have argued that given the indirect costs (universities traditionally take 50 percent of the funding for overhead costs), including translators, and dividing the funding by years and the number of universities, not much is left to spend on researchers.

Academics always have concerns about infringement on academic integrity, the double fear that the military will not know how to review the proposals professionally and therefore fund unworthy projects, and the fear that the freedom of the researcher could be curtailed. For those academics who believe the university should always be opposed to war, the involvement of academia in war-related studies would warp the culture of the university, shrink opportunities for criticism of a war, bring a brain drain to academe, and reduce the space for criticism.

Do not universities, public or private, have an obligation to support the needs of the nation to whatever extent they feel comfortable? One segment of the university seeks to rise above normal society, to be disinterested in the affairs of state in order to consider the great issues of life and society unencumbered by the crass realities of funding and public policy. The concept of the "ivory tower" refers to study within the sciences that claim to be neutral, and, particularly after the development of nuclear weapons, to have an ethic of responsibility for the results of their work. Ivory tower also refers to those within the humanities and social sciences who believe academics should be a witness against the use of power or violence because the community life of a campus demonstrates how life should be lived. In the 1969 effort against M.I.T., the membership of the group that organized the protest was composed of 9 from social sciences and humanities, 5 from biology, 13 from physics, 4 from chemistry, 4 from math, and 13 from various engineering departments.[18]

Other members of the academic world believe neutrality is an illusion and disinterest is a deception, for the universities are inescapably bound to the affairs and fate of public life, from prosperity and depres-

---

17. See "Anthropology Ass'n Blasts Army 'Human Terrain.'"
18. Nelkin, *The University and Military Research*, 57.

sion to war and peace. Howard Zinn, a Boston University professor of political science, argued that "the call to disinterested scholarships is one of the greatest deceptions of our time, because scholarship may be disinterested but no one else around us is disinterested."[19] A balance is necessary, with some universities responding to what Woodrow Wilson, president of Columbia University at the time, called a "university in service to the nation." That theme remains at Columbia's Woodrow Wilson School of Public and International Affairs with its "Scholars in Service to the Nation."

These centers, others at other universities, and still others independent of an academic institution have and will play important roles in the development of foreign policy and national security strategy ideas, policies, and potential appointees to high leadership positions in the organizations of foreign affairs. A Christian scholar concerned about national security affairs could find a valuable career in an academic center. In all likelihood, given the complexity of the modern security environment, a grand strategic doctrine will arise from multiple smaller studies and analyses and innovations, ultimately unified in a vision that brings harmony from the diversity as Kahn did with RAND studies. A Christian may well become a part of the development of the fourth era of U.S. national security policy through an academic center, whether linked to a university or a stand-alone.

No Christian university currently has a graduate degree in foreign policy or security studies, and except for peace studies, no Protestant university has an academic center devoted to foreign and national security affairs. George Marsden once wrote that one of the "oddest anomalies in American religion today is that there is no major evangelical research university." Public research universities are certainly competitors, but Marsden also sees a reason in the fractured world of Protestant denominations and the fundamentalists' demand for sectarian learning. He suggests that a first step to mobilizing the power of Christian universities would be to develop research centers.[20]

Can a Christian university with its value structure create a Center for American Security Affairs, or even a master's degree in international affairs or foreign policy, or must a Christian student attend a secular uni-

19. Ibid., 63.
20. Marsden, "Why No Major Evangelical University?" 294–303.

versity for a graduate degree in the field or work at a secular research center? One reason why Christian universities do not deal with these issues and one not mentioned by Marsden is the deep dilemmas of security in the nuclear age. "Forty years of experience tell me that we are caught on the horns of a dilemma and that we have no quick or easy way to escape," wrote Herbert York in his memoir *Making Weapons, Talking Peace*. York was involved in the development of nuclear weapons and arms control policy. Actually there were two dilemmas York described: First, the dilemma of how to maintain peace and freedom based on something better than the threat of mutual suicide. Second, the dilemma of steadily increasing military power and steadily decreasing national security, which has no technical solution.[21] Christians are not comfortable with dilemmas and paradoxes, and a Christian university has a focused constituency (denominational lay people, clergy, and trustees) who expect certainty even if there are no doctrinal issues. It is much easier for Christian academics to find sure footing and clear policy position in domestic politics where an established government and national identity and values create far fewer dilemmas and paradoxes than exist in the Westphalian world of international politics and foreign policy.

There are other issues too. The humanities and social science faculty at small liberal arts colleges and universities fear any program that might intrude on the sanctity of the traditional liberal arts, especially professional programs. Faculty are always concerned that a new program must have sufficient support and sophistication to insure its integrity within the field, which is difficult in the early years and precludes cobbling together a program with a variety of undergraduate faculty. Faculty at other Christian colleges and universities will also decline to recommend a low-level program to their students, and some will expect a comfortable doctrinal commitment. Funding is always an issue, especially if the trustees have too tight criteria for whom they will publicly honor with naming rights for the center or program. The other limitation on funding is that most donors want a specific policy or theology to prevail in the program, which ought to not be true in a graduate program.

Still, a Christian university ought to build such a program. Graduate programs provide the level of depth and sophistication necessary for serious careers in international affairs; graduate programs operate at a level

---

21. York, *Making Weapons, Talking Peace*, 28, 199.

of depth that shape a student's fundamental ideas in ways that undergraduate programs can never do. Given that reality, there ought to be at least one nonfundamentalist and nondoctrinaire yet seriously Christian graduate program that can appeal to serious Christian students and faculty advisors from a variety of Christian colleges and universities. With those restrictions, what are the positives for such a program? There are three, and the first is the value of having a personal Christian context affirmed in graduate study that is so shaping of a person's ideas. There is no single answer about the nature of international politics nor a single theology of international politics, and asserting so would undercut the nature and culture of graduate work. There is, however, value to students seeing graduate faculty struggle with these issues of faith, policy, dilemmas, and paradoxes. There is value in doing research papers that seek ways to understand Christian perspectives and impact on policy and operations, and thereby help students find a personal Christian-informed set of values and intellectual commitments within the field.

The second positive is ethics. While 23 percent of National Association of Schools of Public Affairs and Administration programs mandate courses in ethics, and 39 percent of Master of Public Affairs programs offer elective courses in ethics, the few ethics courses that exist in current secular universities' international affairs programs are confined to policy ethics, not personal and organizational ethics. The single exception is the University of Pittsburgh's Graduate School of Public and International Affairs, which does deal with ethical standards through its Johnson Institute for Responsible Leadership. Research demonstrates that ethics education in graduate public administration programs has a positive impact on the ethical decisions of public administrators.[22] The need for this ethical component is a natural reason for a Christian university to build a program.

A third positive reason for a graduate program is the opportunity to fill gaps and influence new developments. Another gap in curriculum relates to administrative and managerial courses relevant to international affairs, at the very time the Department of State has a rapidly growing need to deepen its managerial competencies as it expands its responsibilities. Still another curricular gap exists in e-diplomacy. Information technologies are transforming military strategy and ultimately will transform

22. Jurkiewicz and Nichols, "Ethics Education in the MPA Curriculum," 103, 111–12.

the reporting function of on-site FSOs, expand the reach of an embassy's public diplomacy efforts, facilitate maintaining connections with national and subnational groups, and create virtual embassies in appropriate circumstances. There are also no courses on diplomatic biography, a course that could teach success strategies in operations and in career movement. These are program and service opportunities for a university with strong Christian commitments.

If a university that attempts to be seriously Christian without being dogmatic, shallow, or fundamentalist cannot do this, then the world of Christian higher education sidelines itself and says that such universities have nothing unique to add to the dialogue. A donor team needs to step forward to support a nondoctrinaire, non–ivory tower Center for International Affairs or for American Foreign Policy, preferably located near Washington, DC, to be able to dialogue with professionals and other academic institutions. The future is pregnant with problems, and at least one Christian university ought to have a center promoting Christian, creative, practical, and future-oriented ideas for American foreign policy and students aspiring to important careers in international affairs. Such a center or institute, or a separate graduate school of international affairs, provides some buffer to the far different concerns of undergraduate faculty dealing with general service curriculum and nonprofessional related programs of study. Independent status is also crucial to insure continuity in budget and availability of faculty, not possible if it is subordinate to a department's curriculum, votes, or department chair, as has been discovered at several universities including Georgetown University and the University of San Diego.[23] Short of that would be to grow a master of arts program out of the undergraduate curriculum. It would be a program in international affairs with a foreign policy emphasis and that deals in a nondoctrinaire manner with Christian faith and personal ethics in the complex worlds of foreign policy and national security affairs.[24]

In the end, however, will it make a difference in theoretical understandings, strategic doctrine, policy, and/or operations? Will the insights of any academic center actually impact policy? Bruce Kuklick attempted

---

23. Based on discussions of the author with a dean of a school and three directors of institutes at three universities and from service on the Board of Advisors at the Kroc Institute of Peace and Justice at the University of San Diego.

24. For an article on the issues of setting up a new MA program see Barth, "Reflections on Building an MPA Program," 253–61.

to answer that question in his book *Blind Oracles: Intellectuals and War from Kennan to Kissenger*. He explored the interaction between university faculty and research centers on policy, and his conclusion is that "the evidence repeatedly corroborates the observation that politics trumps knowledge," that politics "dragged the erudite into the dominion of partisanship, maneuver, and advantage." One of his least favorite characters is McGeorge Bundy, an architect of the war in Vietnam, who wrote a major memoir, limiting it to a history of nuclear defense policy and including not a word about Vietnam. The fact is, Kuklick writes, politicians "outranked academics; politics seduced scholarship." Yet even as he suggests that we remain skeptical of the knowledge of the defense intellectuals, he admits that he can find no other alternatives to offer.[25]

Perhaps, but to move into this new era without an academically driven understanding of the times and the defense needs is to curry favor with disaster. From his position at Rand, for example, Albert Wohlstetter composed the seminal article "The Delicate Balance of Terror" to warn against the "willfully blind politicians leading to possible holocausts," an article that finally sparked a reexamination of defense policy.[26] Even if they grope in the dark and do not see all the movement in the shadows, those in the academic world have the best possibility of devising policy not directly linked to the self-interest of the existing groups and their organizational cultures. Finding a doctrine fit for this era, and finding means of having it impact leaders and decisions, is a valuable place for minds at war.

THE DEFENSE INDUSTRY

Masterminding the defense industry is another prerequisite for the twenty-first century. The military does not have its own production facilities. In a free enterprise economy the military contracts with private industrial firms to produce the equipment it needs. This nation mobilized its industrial base in World War I and again in World War II, and its ability to rapidly mobilize its prosperity and convert its technological and industrial competence to military production surprised friend and foe alike. The decision to assume the role of global leader after World War II required the maintenance of a full-time defense industry, and the post-

---

25. Kuklick, *Blind Oracles*, 230, 204–5, 16.
26. Abella, *Soldiers of Reason*, 117–18.

war economic boom in this country financed specialized products with little concern for cost.

Dismay over what seemed to be a "Faustian bargain" by scientists involved in the development of nuclear weapons redirected the preferred science career from physics to biology. The post-war prosperity allowed the United States to specialize in consumer goods, and Eisenhower relied on the nuclear strategy of massive retaliation to avoid the need for a large and expensive active military force. The result was that in 1958 Ford Motor Company launched its newest car, the Edsel, and the Soviet Union launched Sputnik. Would Athens fall to Sparta again, the democratic consumer society overtaken (or buried, Premier Khrushchev predicted) by the militarized socialist system? Congress responded with the National Defense Scholarship Loan program (NDSL) to fund an immediate increase in graduate students in the sciences and engineering, and a new generation of highly skilled researchers and developers was produced. Concurrently the nation established an extensive research and development infrastructure. Eisenhower's career took place in a nation without a national defense industry base or large permanent forces, and in his farewell address he warned against the "unwarranted influence" of a "military-industrial complex." For many opponents of high military spending, that phase represents a continuing monolithic juggernaut, one that should be replaced with a conversion to peace-time production.

The Kennedy administration replaced the "suicide or surrender" policy of massive retaliation with "flexible response," requiring a build-up of U.S. forces that allowed the United States to respond to any level of Soviet provocation. New orders for the military's unique and one-of-a-kind products required firms to build new production facilities that had to be funded by increased prices for the military goods. The war in Vietnam kept defense spending high, but there is spending for operations and spending for procurement, and the latter suffered. Defense spending dropped quickly after the war as President Nixon oversaw the decline of the active military from 5 to 1.5 million, and weapons buying dropped from $23.9 billion in 1969 to $15.2 billion in 1974, though overall defense budget reductions were half that.[27]

President Reagan rejected the Nixon policy of détente and inaugurated a new period of large increases in military procurement. In 1991 the

---

27. Gregory, *The Price of Peace*, 42.

Soviet Union collapsed under the weight of a deadening socialist system, and the Cold War ended. The new era of peace brought another era of defense reductions. Between 1985 and 1994 Defense Department funding for ammunition production declined by 80 percent, 70 percent of defense firms died, and the skilled and experienced workforce was decimated. Some defense firms tried to diversify, and others tried to convert their technological sophistication to peacetime activities such as rapid transit and other pursuits. Those did not work well, and defense engineers accustomed to cost overruns being covered by Congress were not attractive to civilian firms concerned with the bottom line.[28]

In the meantime the new generation of highly skilled technicians built high technology firms with no connection to the U.S. military. Defense firms were aging and would have to retool and recapitalize production facilities for a new generation of military equipment. The nation's economic structure changed and manufacturing moved overseas, a deindustrialization reflected in the numbers: manufacturing was 22 percent of the U.S. economy in 1976, but 11 percent in 2006. The generation of scientists produced by the NDSL has aged, and the loan program was converted to National Direct Student Loan Program, keeping the same initials but now funding the general student population.

In 1993 President Clinton's secretary of defense hosted a dinner for the top fifteen defense industry leaders. He told them that the defense budget faced years of slow growth, and defense firms should merge and consolidate to gain economies of scale and concentrate on military work. That dinner came to be known as "the Last Supper," as fifteen top firms in 1993 merged into five: Boeing, Lockheed Martin, Northrop Grumman, Raytheon, and General Dynamics. The Aerospace industry declined from seventy suppliers in 1980 to five in 2003, and the manufacturers of combat aircraft declined from eleven in 1950 to five in 2003. The aircraft industry cannot survive without military sales, and the shipbuilding industry is virtually dependent upon the military after a one-third drop in the number of contractors and the competition from inexpensive foreign firms.[29] Six major shipbuilders are owned by two defense firms, General Dynamics and Northrop Grumman, and five of the six build strictly for

28. Holmes and Seraphin, "Munitions Industrial Base," 39.
29. For more information see Butler, "Truth and Consequences"; Flamm, "Post–Cold War Policy and the U.S. Defense Industrial Base"; and McClure, "Is Aerospace Worth Saving?"

the military. Economies of scale were achieved but with the loss of competitive pricing.

Currently (2009) there are second thoughts about the Perry policy of consolidated firms producing defense-only products. Some companies are beginning to develop portfolios of nondefense related firms to shore up their cash flow while others acquire smaller niche suppliers and others are merging with European firms.[30] The decline of the nation's industrial base to support defense industries is a growing concern, as is the loss of critical skills, and the newer generations of young people are avoiding the STEM fields (science, technology, engineering, math) or working for commercial rather than defense firms. This constitutes a "hollowing out" of the core talent for defense contractors. The government is on the losing side of the "war for talent" with the dot com world and its rapid-paced innovation and profit bonanzas. Even the whole oversight process has been outsourced in hopes of saving funds; so, for example, the Air Force acquisitions workforce has declined from 57,000 to 15,000 in the past twenty years, yet without a savings in cost.[31]

Can an industrial and technological base for defense be maintained with superior quality control and financial stability? There are government-run facilities, but building a national arsenal loses the advantages that adhere in a flexible system that promotes creativity and innovation. Purchasing equipment from allies or non-adversaries is one option, but the outcries over outsourcing, as well as the dangers of U.S. defense forces being dependent on overseas products, are politically dangerous. The fact is, however, that the United States is already heavily dependent on allies for parts and systems, and a recent study by the Industrial College of the Armed Services concluded that the value of commonality and interoperability are sufficient to find a balance between national and foreign purchases.[32]

In addition there is currently less worry over Eisenhower's warning of the military-industrial complex than over costs. At the beginning of 2009 seventy percent of the ninety-six weapons-buying programs for the Department of Defense were over budget by $298 billion from the original estimates. Technological complexity, the thinness of the talent base, and the uncertainties about new systems and integration and supply chain

---

30. Jean, "Economies of Scale," 18–19.
31. Butler, "Truth and Consequences."
32. See Gropman, "Balancing Act."

requirements all make precise cost calculations difficult. From a military point of view the technology of a weapon system should be "locked in" long enough to be cost effective and usable over the life of a system. Yet "locked in" means missing the technological innovations taking place in the commercial world, sidelining the military "from the technology boom that is benefiting so many other sectors of the economy."[33]

Some of the increased costs come from built-in cost overruns. That is, intentional or not, there is the reality that industry and the Pentagon promise high in terms of performance and low in terms of cost. Once contracted, the pressure then is to continue to purchase despite the rise in costs. Spreading the location of subcontractors around the country then increases the number of states and congressional districts with a self-interest in the program. If a program comes into jeopardy, lobbyists in DC and the states can mobilize to defend and protect it. That is a smart way to do business because everyone benefits, except the national interest, and it takes strong efforts to actually end an overly expensive program. During the Reagan years a B-1 manager actually brought to a briefing with Secretary of Defense Caspar Weinberger a display showing how the contracts were spread all over the country. Weinberger became furious. "That's not how we do business," he said. "I don't want to see that kind of chart again."[34]

A more important factor in cost overruns, however, derives from the incredible sophistication of modern military equipment. The time frame for the military to develop a definition of its needs, then for several corporations to develop a proposal, then for the Pentagon to decide on a contractor and write the complicated contract, during which Congress must approve and appropriate funds, then to develop and test a prototype—all that requires at least a decade. In the meantime the continual technological innovation leads the military to add new options and requirements, adding time and cost. Many of the products are so unique and standards for survivability in harsh conditions so severe that new technologies have to be developed and tested during the production process to meet the standards. When initial efforts do not work, deadlines and budgets are extended out in time and cost.

33. Erwin, "Despite SecDef Pleas."
34. Quoted in Jarecki, *The American Way of War*, 208.

The defense firm operates with a factor of survival not present in the military: the bottom line—it must also serve their own corporate security—market share, profits, and corporate dividends. The costs to design a new fighter aircraft and build three to five prototypes for testing is enormous, far beyond the capabilities of any but the largest firms. Designing and producing the first stealth fighter cost Lockheed $10 million of its own funds, with no guarantee it would win a contract. Ships are a bit different, but firms spend up to a quarter million dollars just to do the engineering to make a competitive bid proposal for a ship; if it loses the bid it loses its investment.

Major firms like Boeing and General Dynamics are necessary for the size, skills, and up-front capital to build military aircraft and ships, while others like the four-person Ranger Group are start-ups by retired officers who know a need and try to get enough contracts to remain in business. Small start-up firms and women-owned firms like intelliSolutions can compete for small contracts and subcontracts, and there are hundreds of small firms supplying parts, engineering, information technology, and management. This is a revolutionary time needing new ideas; those will come from the bottom, from the minds of the young and flexible. Small-business entrepreneurs bring innovation and rapid responsiveness to governmental need. Not all those ideas will prove workable, but from the minds of the young will come the new ideas that can move America's technology forward.

Huge amounts of money are at stake for the large, medium, and small firms, as well as the job market for local towns and cities dependent on these firms. Thus lobbying is critical; cheating not unknown. The National Defense Industry Association has a code of business ethics, and the law requires individual firms to have their own. Northrop Grumman's code of ethics runs twenty-six pages, Lockheed's runs forty-four and Boeing's is seventy-four. Yet the very size and complexity of projects, variety of workers, and number of subcontractors requires constant ethical oversight. There is cheating, and there is pushing a boundary, and there are minor oversights. Regulations can seem byzantine as the corporate and regulatory cultures clash. One government auditor told the head of Lockheed's super secret project to build a stealth fighter airplane, "I don't give a damn if you turn out scrap. It's far more important that you turn out the forms we require."[35] Even if mere hyperbole, it is unfortunate.

So is the recent Department of Justice decision regarding Northrop Grumman. That firm acquired TRW, a firm that produced "heterojunctionbipolar transistors." Tests done in 1995 showed the part would fail in government satellites, but they were sold for U.S. satellites anyway, which then experienced critical failures in orbit. A researcher knew they would fail, but a corporate nondisclosure agreement prevented him from disclosing negative test results to anyone. When the Air Force asked the company whether TRW should have known they would fail, the company sanitized the report. The researcher finally acted as a whistle blower to let the Air Force know what had happened, and in 2009 Northrop Grumman was fined $325 million.[36]

The centrality of profit can also displace the ethical commitment to the customer. Strategies of competition can pit firm against firm and against the needs of national security. Protests against award decisions are becoming common, automatically invoking a process of review, stopping all work, leaving a workforce idle and program funding in jeopardy. Then a new round of lobbying is launched. Even if the protest fails, the protesting firm gets a new advantage. Losers received a detailed "outbrief" listing the reasons for the award, giving a detailed understanding that can be used in the next competition. If a contractor is working on one project while the "statement of need" for another project is being formulated by the Pentagon, the temptation is to get involved in the definition of that statement until it favors its own firm to the exclusion of others.

Individuals and corporations seek benefits, not inherently corrupt. A military officer who has worked in procurement can find high-level jobs in defense industries. They understand weapons, and they (for a few years) are friends with key people. Congress passed stringent time limits between moving from a military service where one made procurement decisions into a decision-making position in a defense industry. Even in social visits, however, an associate from the firm comes along to make a personal connection, hear the latest, and gain an advantage over other firms, and it threatens to become an incestuous relationship. The net gets wider—an award can represent thousands of jobs and income, as well as major fund-

---

35. Rich and Janos, *Skunk Works*, 80.
36. Pae, "Northrop Grumman-TRW Whistler-Blower Case Settled."

ing for university research. The net also includes members of Congress who want to serve the nation, serve their constituents, and get reelected.

The organizational cultures of the military and industrial firms are not limited to mission or profit. Each has its own budget cycle, sets of advisors, standard operating procedures, and understanding of technological possibilities. In 2007 the Navy abruptly cancelled the third Littoral Combat Ship being built by Lockheed Martin. With rising costs jeopardizing other ships, the Navy attempted to move their contract from a cost-plus to a fixed-cost-plus-incentive arrangement. The firm was advised to modernize and find new ways to build ships, while the firm, not a ship building company like General Dynamics, complained the Navy gave too little attention to the technological problems. The costs saved by canceling the third ship would pay for the cost overruns of the first two.[37]

Nothing is simple. Trade-offs are necessary in a context of uncertainty and shadows. The Air Force F-22 Raptor is the most modern aircraft in the air, so good that no competitor exists, so neither do the air battles for which it was designed, built, and purchased. The United States dominates the air, and the days of aerial combat and "aces" are over. In the late 1980s when the F-22 was being developed, the Air Force planned on 740 planes. As costs rose and the need fell, the Pentagon in 2004 revised that number down to 183. The Air Force disagreed and claimed the need for 243. To buy the additional 60 would lock in spending for years ahead; it would mean not buying something else, and aerial combat is only one mission of the Air Force. Despite heavy lobbying and employment concerns in 44 states, the Pentagon held to its number in 2009, arguing that the need has changed with insurgency wars fought on the ground and that the oncoming F-35 Strike Fighter will work in consonance with the F-22 in joint roles.[38]

How does one assess the threats in the next decade? With F-22 plants shut down and engineers gone, how long would it take to reassemble the teams and firms to respond to a threat of a new, equal, or better combat plane in an adversarial nation? When has the cost or time lag for a weapon become too far beyond expectation and production should be simply stopped? The consequences of arms are not limited just to their destructive capacities. There are also consequences if the decisions made

37. Cavas, "Showdown Ends in Cancellation," 1, 8.
38. Donley and Schwartz, "Moving Beyond the F-22," A15.

on weapons acquisition turn out to be wrong in future conflicts. Answers to these questions require the best minds to ensure that the priorities are right and that means are correctly linked to ends.

The variety of minds at war goes beyond strategists and entrepreneurs to scientists and technicians in defense, program managers, and lobbyists.

SCIENTISTS AND TECHNICIANS

Unlike the scientist who strives for objectivity, the weapons developer is a technician, a problem-solver who works for the values of the defense firm and the military. During the Cold War engineers worked on defense projects because they had a moral anchor: they believed the Soviet threat was real. Nuclear weapons were a means of preserving the peace. This generation's threat is different but no less compelling. Fourth-generation wars are the soft underbelly of American national security, for the requirements to fight such wars evolve rapidly within the war zone. Modern technology empowers the insurgents to be rapidly adaptive in offensive measures. The engineer is crucial to respond to those unexpected weapons, and the demands are higher because time is so much more important. American defense industry faces two rapidly approaching problems: One is the current race for exotic weapons by the developed nations. The other is the twofold STEM problem, the insufficiency of college and university graduates in the sciences, technology, engineering, and mathematics fields, and the large number of STEM graduates being turned out in other countries. Is making a dollar more moral than making a difference in national security? No.

The world of science and technology is a professional one, with its own code of honor. It includes such elements as the commitment to verifiable truth rather than to fixed principles, to the principle of uncertainty rather than complete knowledge, to independence in observation and thought, to honesty in tests and reports, to dissent and respect, and to serving the good of humanity. Science explores the unknown out of both curiosity and the desire to make the world more true.[39] Outside the world of science, however, people operate on different values and can use the discoveries of science not for the good of humanity but for domination of one set of people over another. "A new weapon arises because some

39. Bronowski, *Science and Human Values*, 51–76.

physical discovery or invention has been made.... It is hardly ever constructed because of a preconceived strategic vision."[40] It was recognized in the 1930s that the discovery of the ability to split the atom and establish a chain reaction could lead to an atomic bomb of incredible power. That recognition came in the context of not only the bloody world of Stalinism and fascism but also demands for Aryan science and the decree that Einstein's theories violated the fundamental principles of Marxism-Leninism. The result of the recognition and the context was anguish and soul-searching by the leading scientists. Some left Germany, some stayed because they were forced to work on the project, some stayed because they thought the war would be short and over before a bomb was ever developed, and some, like the great Werner Heisenberg, stayed, arguing it was more appropriate to stay and help pick up the pieces of his homeland after the war.[41]

Talented defense industry engineers face their own personal moral dilemmas. They live in a career made necessary by the time zone of international history. Technology jobs can be a fine career with a moral purpose of security, but the second-order consequences if and when the weapons are used create the dilemma. The engineer has no control over the means and definition of national security for which the weapons might be used by political leaders. On the other hand, the outside threat to one's vital or survival interests led some scientists to leave their scientific detachment and join the effort in the United States to beat the Germans to the atomic bomb. Even as that was taking place, Soviet spies with a different moral code were passing material on to Soviet scientists where the quest for the bomb now took precedence over Marxist-Leninist purity of thought.

The intellectual journey of Harvard's president James B. Conant reflects the movement in the United States of both scientists in particular and academe in general from detachment to active involvement in the race to build the bomb. His concern for academic freedom and for propriety and public relations made him reluctant to attack the Nazis, even to the point of sending a delegation to the five hundredth anniversary of Heidelberg University, which Oxford and Cambridge boycotted rather than lend any dignity to a Nazified spectacle choreography by Joseph Goebbels. What Conant called the "ancient ties by which the universi-

---

40. Morgenstern, *The Question of National Defense*, 166.
41. Powers, *Heisenberg's War*, 11–13, 39–43.

ties of the world are united" took precedence over the ongoing purge of Jewish and dissident scholars at German universities. The next year Archibald McLeish in his "Speech to the Scholars" said, "There are none neutral in this war," but Conant hedged for another two years, until the German panzer tanks shattered Poland and he could no longer deny "the military, and not merely ideological, nature of the German menace." Two years later he began to assume direct and vastly expanded responsibilities in the quest for America's atomic bomb.[42]

Jack Swearengen understands the Scriptures to teach obedience to authority except under extreme conditions, that all of life is religious, and that history is going somewhere. He also believed the Soviet Union was a global menace and the primary cause of arms escalation. Swearengen was a weapons developer, part of a link between government policy, the defense industry, and the military, and he used his skill in technology to respond to a declared military need. But he also had a theological understanding that rejected detachment and dualism, and believed we are living in the third element of the commonly asserted fourfold flow of the biblical narrative—creation, fall, redemption, consummation. How could working in the defense industry be redemptive? His answer was that support for arms control as an alternative to deterrence, for arms control was more congruent with the redemptive element than deterrence. The Cold War is now over and the Soviet Union is gone, and recently he shifted his emphasis to environmental sustainability, where he finds a moral purpose—meeting food, shelter, and material needs, thus making engineering a "Godly pursuit."[43]

This is Joab's world, using science and technology. Our daily professional lives and the ethical issues of the defense industry may well be given moral meaning by investing the mosaic of one's life and career as a participant in the sweep of history and in participating in the process of "deliver us from evil."

---

42. Hershberg, *James B. Conant*, 84–147.

43. Swearengen and Swearengen, "Comparative Analysis of the Nuclear Weapons Debate," 75–85; Swearengen, "Arms Control and God's Purpose in History," 25–35; and Swearengen, *Beyond Paradise*, 308.

PUBLIC ADMINISTRATION: PROGRAM MANAGER

Business firms create the products for the military and its needs for projected or actual future conflicts. Between them is the program manager (PM). The PM is part of that sector of public administration that oversees the process of extremely complex operating systems with numerous interdependent subsystems. The process begins with the requirements, objectives, and performance measures, and the strategy for sustaining the results. Then a roadmap must be created for mapping out the order, sequence, and integration of the component parts to get the product to the users on schedule and within budget. The products can be as varied as body armor for the soldier, security assistance in Afghanistan, a computer system for an intelligence gathering need on a naval vessel, or overseeing the launch of rockets carrying spy satellites.

Common to all the programs and process are concerns of performance, deadlines, and cost. Risk management is a common concern, for so much is unknown about an undeveloped weapon system or defense program and the difficulties that will arise in getting it to the field. That means determining what can go wrong, which risks are most disruptive, what will be their likely impacts, and how to deal with them. Finally, there are the people; common to all these issues are the mental creativity, agility, and toughness of the people needed to meet the challenges.

"Take off your engineering hat and put on your management hat." That remark was directed at Robert Lund on January 27, 1986, when Lund, an engineer turned vice president at Morton Thiokol, was reluctant to give final approval to the launch of the Space Shuttle Challenger because of the fears of engineers that the "O-Rings" might have been compromised by the subfreezing temperature. The code of ethics for engineers and scientists include commitment to public safety; should Lund have tried to balance the interests of safety with the other interests of NASA in getting the rocket launched, with Morton Thiokol's interest in denying any question of the quality of their product, with funding issues? What does it mean for a program manager to be a public manager? The disaster that followed made the right answer all too clear. When values conflict there has to be a hierarchy of values, and even when there are intense time pressures and high stress, public safety and the safety of individuals has to rank nearest to the top. Unlike business, the ethics of public administration focus on the public interest as a public of citizens rather than clients, and on a public responsibility that goes beyond mere legal responsibility.[44] Being a program manager whose job is to make decisions between conflicting interests does not take place outside the ethics of public administration.

One example: the intelligence community and the military depend on space-based cameras and sensors and communication vehicles. Those satellites are joint endeavors led by the Air Force Space Command for the National Reconnaissance Office and built by a lead firm and multiple subcontractors. Consider just a few of the components of a spy or communications satellite: the camera and radar systems, the solar arrays to power the satellite during the day and store energy in a battery for night or orbit changes, the battery that can take thousands of charge-and-discharge cycles, the computer and communications systems to understand and transmit the information, the stress and harsh environments of launch and space, and the ability to quickly shield itself against an attack. All of those components must be tested and meet military specifications, and done while the necessary technologies are being developed.

This is not like fielding a jet or armored vehicle, for in programs like shuttle and satellite launches there is only one chance. The PM has to insure whether the tests are being done the right way, or if efforts to reduce costs are changing tests and risks. A complete battery of tests was not done on erosion of "O-Rings" for the 1986 launch of the Challenger Space Shuttle. Are the changes the firm is requesting too risky, or is the service's insistence on the original specifications too burdensome? The PM team will have technical consultants who will argue the merits with the firm's technicians, leaving it to the team to decide. Do components meet performance requirements? Are the integration system, the self-defense mechanisms, and the engineering and manufacturing coming in under cost? After launch the user loses forever all ability to fix it or change it. Mission-assurance is crucial and requires a lot of engineering and testing. The PM is responsible for the program, and missed deadlines and budget overruns in an era of budget constraints will ultimately be overcome by restructuring the program or canceling it.

Managing programs takes a hierarchy of management teams. A program manager will be part of a team of people responsible for various aspects of a project called the Integrated Product Team, and they report to higher levels of teams with broader scopes of responsibility. The PM

44. Davis, *Thinking Like an Engineer*; and on public administration ethics versus business ethics, see Smith, "Teaching Public and Private Sector Ethics," 179–200.

team will probably meet weekly to assess progress. The contract between the military and a business firm is very detailed, very specific. The firm may want to push the boundaries to cut costs, and it especially does not want new requirements that push the workload beyond the initial assumptions. The military wants at least exactly what was agreed upon and more if they can get it. The firm will argue for changes, and the PM must have the mental clarity to assess the risks and have the mental toughness to insist the specified tests be done the right way. The company may accept a failure, but the military service cannot. Two top tips for PMs are that contracts are more than pieces of paper and, as Robert Lund found out, if you do not pay now (such as run the tests) you will pay later, and a much higher price.

Another example: consider the challenges of being a PM for the American program designed to reform and build the Afghanistan National Army and the Afghanistan National Police. This is a large-scale program that can be frustrating because it has to adjust to the ever-evolving security situation. The PM has to decide on trade-offs between programs and their margins of utility to keep the entire program within cost. These programs involve people rather than technology, and with different social and cultural traditions and patterns of leadership.[45] The PM must have empathy as well as skills, an inclination to personal partnership rather than cultural arrogance, and an ability to deal with suspicion and misunderstanding. Building a successful program from all these components and challenges would be, administratively and personally, a thing of beauty.

A PM will deal with two different kinds of cost relationships with a defense firm. With cost-plus the firm is paid its costs and then qualifies for bonuses if performance and timelines are met. If not, they lose money, and so argue that the delay was not their fault. Once again the PM must be capable of an appropriate balancing act and mental toughness. The downside is that the bonuses are such a small margin of the total contract that the firm has little incentive to do its best. It may even assign their B-level team to the project and reserve their A team for more profitable commercial projects. Here the PM must maintain sufficient pressure on the firm's own project managers to keep the project on time and within budget. A second cost relationship is fixed price. The firm is guaranteed a fixed price for the program, and any efficiencies the firm can attain to

---

45. See Cooley, Ruhm, and Marsh, "Building an Army," 14–18.

reduce costs adds to their profit line. These are the high-value projects such as classified satellites, and the military wants the firm to field its best A team to work on this project. Regulations are relaxed, giving the firm more flexibility, saving costs, improving the profit margin.

Why would anyone want to be a program manager? Challenge, impact, and satisfaction. PMs work with challenging administrative problems with highly complex yet wonderfully intriguing programs. They work on the front line of the future, when losing an edge means loss of leverage in crisis situations. Germany, for example, dismissed the development of radar, which reduced their ability to defend against Allied bombing runs to near zero. Program mangers implement decisions, making programs work, and they are judged by objective measures of cost, schedule, and performance. That is another way of saying that they are judged by their honesty and integrity.[46]

The tangible measures of success for a PM are clear. The intangibles are personal. For PMs, wanting to move up the ladder of responsibility and authority requires understanding a career roadmap. Know where you want to be in five and ten years, and work with your supervisor to identify your strengths and weaknesses and to understand possible career progression routes. They want to help. Identify the skills and competencies you will need and take on new assignments, even temporary, and especially if you are assigned the lead role. Own your mistakes and do not burn bridges. Do social networking with those above, but always stay related to those below. Join a civic group to acquire a different circle of friends and to remain connected to the broader public.

LOBBYISTS

Another hinge player in national defense is the lobbyist who represents a defense firm to military decision makers and to members of Congress. Lobbyists can be as little involved as representing a small firm seeking to persuade leaders of the value of their new product, or be an important partner in promoting a significant program for the military that never reaches a high enough priority to be included in the Defense Department's budget request to Congress, or be a foot soldier in a major and multiyear battle between two defense giants and their supporters in the Pentagon, the Congress, and home districts. Lobbying is the art of persuasion, of

---

46. Riemer, "Top Ten Rewards to Being a Program Manager," 40–41.

gathering information, evidence, and supporters, and combining them into an argument for a particular decision. It also represents minds at war. If one has decided to represent defense firms, the nature of the firm or product is not usually an ethical issue. That basic decision has been made, while recognizing that not all firms and products are equally honorable or the issue unimportant.

In the modern American military, no weapon system stands alone. Any new item must meet a military requirement, now known as a capability. Knowing the process of how that capability is defined is fundamental to any lobbying effort.[47] Any new item must be defined in an Initial Capabilities Document (ICD) to demonstrate how it meets a need or fits into the capability, and that document is disseminated widely to insure its integration. That program capability will either be or not be recognized and accepted as an approved capability program. If it is recognized as such, it may or may not be included in the Pentagon's budget request to Congress. If not included, it becomes known as an Unfunded Requirement (UFR). The role of a lobbyist is to help the appropriate Military Service understand the UFR should be revalued, or convince Congress that it should be added to the budget, an action known as a plus up. So long as it is a UFR, that is, determined by the Pentagon to be a desired item, the lobbyist has a chance; without that, no one will pay attention.

The Pentagon is a massive bureaucracy, and one has to know the process, who to approach, and the budget cycles of both the Pentagon and Congress. The people change frequently, but there are some details that reflect on lobbying strategy and ethics. First, the hierarchy. Whether one starts with the appropriate liaison person at a base or the appropriate deputy chief of staff in the Pentagon, it is proper to start at the bottom because nothing rises that has not been "staffed" at lower levels. Members of the House are easier to access, but they also will hand the material off to their staff. If you try to start at the top you will lose the goodwill of the staff officer you dismissed as unimportant and who, in reality, is the person you need as an advocate within the hierarchy.

Second, coalitions. Whether for Congress or the Pentagon, a case has more weight if it has support from other interested groups or elements of the service. Third, courtesy. When the right action person has been identified, make a courtesy call to introduce yourself and the product. Do not

---

47. Much of the following material on documents and process is taken from Kambrod, *Lobbying for Defense*.

make this a marketing meeting, but an initial meeting as a gesture of courtesy and to make plans for a meeting to discuss the project in more detail. Send a thank you note—not through e-mail but a handwritten note.

Fourth, strategy. "Often I think what lobbyists do, they might not think it's wrong, it's just kind of soul-deadening."[48] Ethical issues are obviously involved given the competition for persuasion, the role of money in leveraging persuasion, and the high stakes of money for the defense firms. The American League of Lobbyists has a model ethics code, but it is only a recommendation for adoption by lobby firms. The code covers the relevant topics with details specified in each, with topics such as honesty, legality, professionalism, conflict of interests, due diligence, confidentiality, respect for governmental institutions, and compensation.[49]

Some strategy is ethically self-enforcing. Truth telling, for example, is absolutely necessary because a lobbyist's reputation determines access and responsiveness to any staffer or politician. Half-truths and distortions carry the same risks. Shades of truth may be something else. "Lobbyists think about just how much you shade the picture without losing your own soul, short of that, losing credibility with the person you're talking to."[50] Strategy also relates to money, both funds and such events as paid lunches. The latter are forbidden unless there is a "workaround," a clever way to disguise the benefit.

Members of the House of Representatives run for reelection every two years and are in a constant search for funds. Corporations cannot legally donate funds, but do so through a Political Action Committee (PAC). These committees raise funds from employees and "bundle" them together into a single donation. Fundraisers are typical and frequent, even though "most fundraisers are about bad food and bad beer in a small room at the end of a 12-hour day."[51] Nevertheless, key subcommittee legislators receive thousands and sometimes tens of thousands of dollars from these PACs through their lobbyists.

A sincere and ethical lobbyist can bring satisfaction and value to a firm and to the military, and in return the lobbyist has the satisfaction of knowing he or she has helped their country stay on the edge of innova-

48. Quoted in Woodstock Theological Center, *The Ethics of Lobbying*, 4.
49. See American League of Lobbyists, *Code of Ethics*.
50. Woodstock Theological Center, *The Ethics of Lobbying*, 3.
51. Wienhold, "It's Not All Fun and Games," 17.

tion. When Congress or the military decides in favor of one firm, a competitor loses, as do workers and perhaps organizational stability; winning and losing is inescapably part of the business of defense firms. Lobbying for a defense industry is a business, but one with the dual rewards of profit and value to the country.

CONCLUSION

We did not ask to live in the nuclear age, especially in its current state with nuclear weapons in the possession of unstable states like Pakistan, North Korea, and inevitably in the hands of Iran. We did not agree to the collapse of the Westphalian agreement to keep religion out of international politics and foreign policy. Nevertheless, we do, and the interplay between religious zealotry and weapons of mass destruction are the brew for a dark world. In that case, is there anything distinctive that Christians can bring to the development of a new strategy? Does a theology of grace give a moral direction to this intellectual effort?

Grace and reason: Christians living in the grace of God need to bring their intellectual talents to these efforts. We need Joseph's forecast or risk analysis of emerging forces, with a policy that is rational and possible, but goes beyond Joseph and takes seriously the second-order consequences of turning this country into a garrison state. To do so Christian intellectuals will have to reject six basic assumptions, including historical fatalism, the hubris of global dominance, reliance on God's intervention to save this country, an intensely religious dualism, a reductive philosophy that violence precedes peace or the opposite, and sixth, the sociological notion that the habits of violence have mastered humanity. We are not subject to fate alone; humanity avoided World War III. Grace can operate through intellectual strategies to deter war and promote discussion rather than dualism, to make the world safe for diversity.

Grace in the service of war? No. Grace in the service of humanity and the future. War will come in the next thirty years, in hybrid forms, with all its attendant tragedy. What we need is grace in the service of reasonable attempts to define a strategy that deters massive war, that remains a human rather than demonic effort in major wars, that is proportionate yet not ineffective in fourth-generation wars, that remains linked to rather than overwhelms the political goals of the war, and that remains within a moral construct that allows solidarity with other allies.

At a more personal level, if the emerging strategy violates those attempts, grace should support the courage to disagree within an organizational culture that is highly parochial and mission-oriented, even if it brings a possible threat to one's career. Christians also need the personal grace to remember the Lord's Prayer and so understand when one's career is leading into the temptation of destroying the ethics of the time zone of their daily life. They must distinguish, as President Kennedy said at Amherst College, whether we are using power or power is using us.[52]

A MEDITATION ON ISAIAH 47

Several writers see America as a new Roman Empire or Babylonian state. The prophet Isaiah's warnings to Babylon in chapter 47 were given in the context of their role in God's purposes of punishment of Israel, but some parallels ought to be recognized and remembered in our day. Babylon had become a nation given to pleasure, Isaiah wrote, whose power allowed them to dwell securely and assume no one else mattered. They had become warped by their wisdom and knowledge and wearied by the counsel of astrologers. Trouble and evil will come, Isaiah warned, suddenly, without warning and without adequate defense.

Has American power and prosperity warped our analysis into prescribed but blind policies, devoid of any moral imagination? Has our scientific and technological knowledge warped our moral thinking? Whatever the sweep of history turns out to be, whatever the movement of the United States along its long-cycle, decisions have to be made in the short term, determined by the present needs. Perhaps this nation like all nations is but a "drop in the bucket" (Isa 40:15), but our lives are inescapably bound to it. We have to use our science and management and strategies as best we can to serve the people caught in the reality of the present and near future.

Bureaucratic cultures are prone to the dangers of arrogance, blind policies, and warped moral imaginations. We must recognize and neutralize them as we move into an era of new scientific discoveries and technologies, new dangers and new strategies, and the need for new decisions and new directions. Program managers must not grow weary in well-doing. Strategists must not lose their grasp on the reality of war on the ground in the abstraction of their efforts to find a technological

---

52. *Public Papers of the Presidents of the United States, John F. Kennedy*, 816.

"silver bullet." Academe is certainly not immune to the dangers but does offer the prophetic opportunity to step outside pleasure, to rise above entrenched interests, and to advance a critique of where we are and where we are tending, doing so outside the baser calls of "Thou art the man" of the political processes.

Minds at war is not an oxymoron for Christians; it is the avoidance of Isaiah 47. It is the place to bring together talent, values, and intellectual creativity in the service of reasoned approaches to safety in a reality in which both reason and control escape too easily.

6

Politics: The Political World of Congress

The price of politics is high, but think of all those people living normal average lives who never touch the excitement of it.

JOHN F. KENNEDY[1]

DIPLOMATS AND SPIES WORK for the executive branch, but they are accountable to the legislative branch. While only the Senate has the august responsibility to "advise and consent" on treaties and diplomatic appointments, both the Senate and the House of Representatives write legislative policy and fund their programs, as well as the Pentagon's purchases from defense firms, and that gives the House leverage on policy. Presidential administrations can silence or purge critics of its policies within the executive branch but not its critics in Congress. There they are protected by their fixed term of office. Congress is the branch through which the public can influence policy, for while governmental executives are accountable to presidential policy, members of Congress are accountable to the people of their districts. That means House members read the mail and listen to supporters and critics at functions throughout their districts.

Members of Congress work at the nexus between personal self-interest, the economic interests of their district and its people, their understanding of the needs of the nation, and the budget requests of the executive branch. Here the minds at war meet the politics of democracy. The issue of the F-22 is an example, with the executive attempting to stop a weapon that is militarily unnecessary and the Congress determined to keep building and buying more to help their districts in a time of economic distress. Defense Secretary Gates put it bluntly:

---

1. Quoted in Dallek, *An Unfinished Life*, 120.

If we can't bring ourselves to make this tough but straightforward decision—reflecting the judgment of two very different presidents, two different secretaries of defense, two chairmen of the Joint Chiefs of Staff, and the current Air Force secretary and chief of staff—where do we draw the line? If we can't get this right, what on earth can we get right?[2]

This chapter focuses on the House of Representatives for four reasons: (1) it is the location of important foreign policy and defense policy decisions, (2) it is an elective office within reasonable reach for a young person to consider, (3) it is a platform from which a policy entrepreneur can influence foreign and national security policy, and (4) it is a unique world with its own ethical values and a place for the applied ethics.

THE STRUCTURAL CONTEXT

Three realities immediately confront us. First, the United States is large, with sections differing in basic rural/urban values, static/dynamic economies, insular/cosmopolitan visions—Kansas and California. Daily newspapers are as different as the *New York Post* and the *Chicago Tribune*, television news as different as Fox, ABC, and Jon Stewart. This diversity of peoples and needs are given say and sway in the House of Representatives.

Second, the U.S. Constitution sets up a government of separate powers sharing in the decision processes. The founders did not want a government with concentrated power. The Constitution disperses political power to prevent an automatic (and potentially exploitive) majority. The founders wanted a government that is difficult to work.

Succeed they did. Social complexity augmented by institutional division stunts legislative efforts. A voting majority in Congress has to be constructed on individual issues, with coalitions put together either by party structure, lobbyists' influence, or by the persuasion of circumstances. The result: Congress is a weak partner in foreign policy, and worse, makes politics appear to be anything but noble.

Third, political parties are mechanisms to overcome those complexities and divisions. Their history is important in itself. On paper we have had a two-party system, but, in fact, until recently it has been a one-and-a-half-party system. One party has dominated the other over long periods of time, until a crisis, leading to what is called a realigning election, mean-

---

2. Quoted in Jaffe, "Gates Sharpens Rhetoric in Dispute on F-22 Funds."

ing voters have made a historic change in their voting pattern.[3] Since the 1980s no stable voting majority has been dominant.

These structures create a set of democratic values and ethics. One aspect of that set is the equality of participation. The United States was born in the belief that citizens have reason, goodness, and wisdom, and should elect their political leaders, not have them imposed by a military or aristocracy. Though the country began with a very limited notion of citizenship, the democratic values over the past two hundred years have pushed the country towards congruence between its ideals and its reality. Voting is a great ethical practice of this country, its method of self-correction, and the foundation of its moral authority.

Democratic ethics also relate to the integrity of the process. Free elections require that voters have a choice between differing opinions and sufficient true information to make a rational choice. People expect comedians to lie to them, for a laugh. They don't expect candidates to lie, because they need true information to make rational choices. People expect science fiction and horror movies to create and sell artificial worlds of fear. They don't expect candidates similarly to enflame emotions of fear to override reason. The ethics of the process is the presentation of truth. Though the reality of a large nation leads to multiple perspectives of the truth on a political issue, the ethic still holds that particular truth be presented in a reasonable manner, not as a lie or the conjuring up of a false world to achieve a national victory of a partial truth.

With only two parties, U.S. congressional candidates must put together larger pluralities than their opponents do by reaching across divisions and differences. Voters want to hear speeches that relate to them and their special concerns, while candidates want to make speeches that reduce distinctions and appeal across groups without losing the distinct groups and their special concerns. There is this paradox in the integrity of the system—the ethics of the system requires honest and clear policy positions from candidates while the system itself also requires candidates to minimize distinctions and appear congruent with each audience. Two parties and candidates mean nothing if there is little difference between them. Primaries give voters control of who become the candidates of the two parties. The United States is the only country in the world with primary elections.

---

3. There was an internal pattern within each era also, two "deviating" elections in which the voters chose the other party for no more than eight years, and then returned to its normal voting pattern in what is called a reinstating election.

On the other hand, because parties are so crucial to American democracy, reformers at the turn of the twentieth century argued they should be quasi-public organizations rather than purely private club-like organizations to insure fairness, particularly regarding racial discrimination. As a result, parties today are state organizations, organized and accountable to each state. Said another way, there are fifty Democratic parties and fifty Republican parties, which come together every four years to nominate presidential candidates (a process now largely done by the state primaries also). New political parties can be created, but they must conform to each state's regulations regarding leadership structures, openness in meetings, and qualifications to appear on a state's election ballot. State regulations also make the ability to run for office open and easy—a minimal fee and signatures.

Primaries took away the power of party leaders to choose candidates, so donors give to candidates not to parties. This is more true in primary elections, for once the candidate is selected, large fundraising dinners are given by party groups to fund campaign workers. Still, the central point is that candidates organize their own campaigns, hire their own campaign firms, raise their own funds, and form their own elector coalition.

While the reformers made the process more fair and open, they did not deal with gerrymandering, which is the process of drawing district lines in a way to protect one party and disadvantage the other. It takes its name from Massachusetts Governor Elbridge Gerry (July 17, 1744–November 23, 1814), who signed a redistricting plan in which one district was so strangely drawn that it resembled a salamander. Most states have their state legislatures draw the boundaries, so the majority party in the state legislature draws boundaries to protect themselves, both in the state legislature and in the Congress.

Incumbents should not have overwhelming advantage, and gerrymandering of district boundaries should not give overwhelming advantage to one party. In the last several decades, in congressional elections, the candidate of the majority party has had a 10 percent or more margin of victory, so incumbents are rarely defeated. These one-and-a-half party districts make gerrymandering the great ethical scandal of congressional elections. Yet frequent elections do not generate courage, moral or political. Like pastors who do not want frequent congregational votes or professors who want tenure, politicians want security for themselves and their policies and resist efforts to take the reapportionment process out of their hands.

EXAMPLE

San Francisco was Phil Burton's base and gerrymandering his skill. In the late 1940s California's politics was based on cross-filing, which allowed a person to run in both parties, a procedure beneficial to incumbents. Republicans dominated in elections even in areas like San Francisco, which was overwhelmingly Democratic. The state's Democratic Party was controlled by the State Chairman William Malone. In 1956 Burton ran for the California Assembly as a Democrat against another Democrat who lost that party's nomination but won the Republican primary. Through skillful campaigning Burton won the election, and cross-filing was soon ended. Then, reapportionment was carried out after the census of 1960. Burton was given the task of drawing lines for the congressional districts and he used his skill to increase the number of projected congressional districts in San Francisco from four to five. He drew one in such a way as to insure that it would be so solidly liberal Democratic that he would never have to worry about reelection. Burton was elected to it in 1964 and served there with passion, bluster, and accomplishment until his death in 1983.[4] With such contrived districts common, rather than having two parties, California, like most other states, can be said to have a one-and-a-half-party system.

REACHING FOR CONGRESS

Congress is the peoples' house, but the tourists who look in awe at the Capitol building and feel good about it also know a vast gap exists between being the outsider and the insider. That gap is not impassable. The person who wants to impact foreign affairs may not want to be a professional diplomat, or spy, or lobbyist. Instead, the more democratic way to achieve that impact is to be elected to Congress.

Running for Congress requires affirmative answers to two basic questions. The first is personal, are you ready to run? Multiple factors can lead to the "first stirrings" of interest, and the move beyond that is to decide to be serious and take the opportunity. While a variety of people run for office, the political track rewards those who are enterprising, competitive, willing to get the "fever in your blood," and take personal risks. If that is not you, then reinvent yourself. Move out beyond your comfort zone of obscurity, insert yourself into groups beyond your social/economic world, and learn to think strategically.

---

4. Jacobs, *A Rage for Justice.*

Are you ready? That is both a personal and situational question that involves costs, of which there are many. The first thing your opponent's campaign team will do is visit the county hall of records to see if you have been convicted of anything or had a judgment against you. Just know that is going to happen. New computer programs like Oppo-Scan searches a wide range of databases including voting records, sex-offender lists, federal grant recipients, and campaign donors. The Web site Zumende.com finds any MySpace and Facebook site an opponent may have, as well as their relatives and their backgrounds. Your past and any indiscretions will become your present.

Is your family with you in this project? You will be deeply preoccupied and gone a lot, so you need at least their tolerance. Is your family up to the opposition's advertising, distortions by opponents, particularly by the "soft money" independent groups who are not bound by the laws regulating candidates and campaign financing? There are high monetary costs for campaign expenses, but it begins with your initial investment—if you don't put in your money, why should anyone else? Can you afford the initial investment? Is your physical stamina and personal self-confidence up to the hours, stress, criticism, and piercing press questions? Do you know the political landscape and topography of your district, the community leaders, political office-holders, and their relative reputation and influence? They need to know that you are not a novice, and the best way to do that is to have worked with them in some community organization.[5]

The second question is structural: is the district ready for you? Despite the ethics of democracy, gerrymandering creates safe districts for incumbents. Look at the registration ratio—compare party registration statistics for the district. Is there enough equality among the major parties and enough voters who decline to state (are independent) that a competition is possible? Then compare the percentage of votes cast by members of your party in the last election to determine party loyalty in that district. If the loyalty is low and the decline-to-state (the independents) tally is high, the district may be competitive. If one party is dominant, the outcome is certain.

Yet there is less certainty about party loyalty in the second decade of this century. We are in the midst of near equality of party preferences nationally (though both parties are well below 50 percent) and that may well creep into states and districts. War and recession are shaking party loyalty

---

5. A very good place to start, despite its age, is Cathy Allen's "Are You Really Ready to Run?"

and may be setting up a long-term realignment of voter preferences and voting patterns. Gerrymandering in such an era loses some of its power.

A poor opponent can also negate the impact of a gerrymandered district. Too many reelections can instill a feeling of invulnerability or can make them an inept campaigner, changing the probabilities and making defeat possible. Scientific polling can reveal vulnerabilities and a campaign theme against an incumbent with rising negative numbers in the polls. Retirement also opens up an option in the primary election of the incumbent's party. Early retirements can come when a party out of power sees no hope of regaining power. In 2008, for example, thirty Republican members retired. That is a lot of openings. If you wait for that kind of opportunity, remember that others are too. There is a natural ladder from local and state legislatures to Congress, so do not wait to lay plans.

It is difficult to come out of "nowhere," overcome the probabilities set by party identification and electoral loyalty, and beat an opponent. Hope is important, but multiple factors must converge just right, which they rarely do. Rarely is not never. Recently Tom Perriello ran against a long-serving member of Congress who benefited from a gerrymandered district and always won with good margins. In 2008 Perriello, with a law degree from Yale and several years' service with the international prosecutor of the Special Court for Sierra Leone rather than long service in the district, ran and won.

Two launching pads for a run for Congress, each of which builds the indispensable factor of name recognition, are a current elected office (school board, city council) and a staff member of a state or congressional legislator. From there you get to know the district and particularly the funding sources and the political action committees that fund races in that district.[6]

One final factor: Campaigns are not fun; they are a political war, and the candidate has to be a political warrior. Remember the beatitude of politics—the meek may inherit the earth, but they'll never knock off an incumbent. At the same time, think seriously about the ethical boundaries of election campaigns. Do not convince yourself that your campaign is a sacred cause. You may well be angry at some policy, you may well feel led to make the campaign, but neither the ethics of American democracy nor the ethics of grace and holiness can countenance a political jihad.

6. These few paragraphs can only highlight some issues for the sake of the chapter. For up-to-date depth, purchase Faucheux, *Running for Office* and *Winning Elections*.

BUILDING A CAMPAIGN

A competitive district, name recognition, and access to funding are the indispensable triad, for without those, a professional campaign firm will either not be interested or not give it a priority, and a winning campaign cannot be run without professional managers. In this age in information technology, you do not run for Congress with a campaign office in your garage.

After that triad, a campaign needs a theme, a compelling rationale. Donors don't waste money by giving it to a person without passion about an issue or cause and a chance to win. Voters need to see a platform that relates to their concerns, to their hopes and fears, and know you have a chance to win.

Foreign policy is rarely a major determinate of electoral choice, especially if linked to humanitarian issues far away and unconnected to the voting public. But, as World War II was to the elections of the 1950s, the war in Iraq may well be the opportunity for veterans to run for national office. For example, in South Carolina's Second Congressional District, Democrat Rob Miller, a veteran of the Marine Corps and the battle of Fallujah, ran against incumbent Republican Joe Wilson, and though he lost, he forced Wilson into his first tough race in the overwhelmingly conservative Republican district.

However, if the Iraq war generates intense public opposition as did Vietnam, nonveterans will have the advantage. Even if Iraq fades as an issue, the rise of China, the continuing flow of jobs abroad, the rise of Atomic Ayatollahs, and the price of oil will keep foreign policy at least a backdrop for elections.

Economic or "pocketbook" issues were central in elections for the three decades after the Great Depression, and labor unions and business groups were the cores of the two parties' electoral coalitions. Civil rights issues and minority groups were added to the Democrat Party's coalition in the 1960s, while social issues (so-called family values issues) and evangelical groups became a major force in the Republican Party in the 80s and 90s. But in 2006 the war in Iraq took precedence, and voters ousted the Republican majority from control of both houses of Congress. There are surprises in politics—in 2008 economic issues came roaring back and will certainly connect with the large issues of the appropriate global role for the United States and with particular issues like defense spending, outsourcing, trade policy, and immigration. On the other hand, Joe Wilson's outburst in Congress during a speech by President Obama will certainly define the 2010 election in that Congressional district and overshadow foreign policy issues.

From all of this it is clear there is no single "public"; there are multiple publics. There are men and women, homeowners and renters, labor and management, urban and rural, rich and poor, "greatest generation" and Generation X, and more. Intensity levels vary also, some people intensely partisan for a party or issue and willing to devote long hours and large funds for their cause, others with a moderate commitment to a clear set of beliefs or to a party that wavers little over time and change, and still others weakly concerned. Moderates tend to fear the intensely partisan and are concerned about more issues than the highly partisan, single-issue voter. A campaign needs its share of the partisans but not become so identified with them that they cannot reach out to moderates.

THE CHRISTIAN VOTE

What about the "Christian vote" and its expressed commitment to a set of moral principles? First, be aware of cycles in that vote. In the 1830s liberal Christians promoted social reforms in a variety of areas from prison reform to civil rights and abolitionism. After the Civil War the more conservative-oriented Christians supported the industrial drive of the country and its values of social Darwinism, and the emergence of popularized eschatology and the "fundamentals." That movement gave way in the 1920s to adherents of the social gospel and their efforts to reform living conditions in the big cities while fundamentalists went underground after the Scopes Trial in 1926. Progressive Christianity held the moral high ground among the public for the next half century, and there were important leaders in the New Deal's reform efforts to address unemployment and poverty in the 1930s, and in the overthrow of racial segregation and discrimination in the Bible Belt in the 1960s.

The Roe v. Wade decision in 1973 sparked a revival of fundamentalism and realigned voting. The moral high ground was up for grabs. In the strong economy of the 1980s, voters could ignore issues of economic class and give preference to social issues and culture wars. Dispensationalists came to dominate the evangelical world with their view that history was getting worse and worse, so ignoring one's economic self-interest was viewed as transcending this material world for the noble issue of reversing the moral decline of the nation.[7] "Divine Guidance," one author wrote, "is the only power that can restore the soul of this nation and save it from a terrible disaster or even total destruction."[8] The emergent and agenda-setting vanguard of that movement has been known as the Religious Right, and they took their religious/political priorities into the Republican Party's coalition of business interests and recently realigned Southern voters. This new tripart coalition was solidified under Ronald Reagan, creating the successor coalition to Franklin Roosevelt's New Deal coalition.

This new politicized religious coalition conducted highly organized interventions into campaigns. They developed Christian "nonpartisan" newspapers that endorsed candidates and were given to churches for free. The basis for that endorsement was a questionnaire sent to candidates that focused on key questions. Whether a candidate was a Christian mattered not; position on issues was everything. Extensive lists of supporters carried out "carpet bombing" of Congress and White House with letters. The ethics of their campaign tactics were often overshadowed by their belief in their moral crusade.

President Reagan embraced the Christian Right and their claims of family values and high moral values. Reagan used them to pass his economic agenda, then avoided their social agenda. A series of events, from the books *Blinded by Might* and *Tempting Faith* to the sordid sexual tales of Ted Haggard, Congressman Mark Foley, and Senators Larry Craig and John Ensign, and the fall of Ralph Reed in the Jack Abramoff scandal, left many evangelicals feeling used. The movement received another hard blow in 2009 when Governor Mark Sanford (R-SC) admitted his own marital infidelity and refused to resign even though when he had been a member of Congress he had been an outspoken critic of President Bill Clinton's infidelity and called for his resignation.

More importantly, an economy nearing recession, massive home foreclosures, and $4.65 for a gallon of gas returned economic issues to the forefront of elections. The Moral Majority had already died in 1999. While Jim Dobson's Focus on the Family staff was reduced by thirty people by 2006, its

---

7. Frank, *What's the Matter with Kansas?* 168. It is not only the Right who substitutes values for economics. See chapter 11 of Bill Clinton's advisor Dick Morris's *The New Prince*, which, recognizing the shift rightward in public opinion, advocated values over economics.

8. *In the Spirit of '76*, 16.

income fell below expenses, and his magazine dropped from 2.4 million in circulation in 1994 to 1.1 million.[9] In January 2008, pollster George Barna found that four out of ten born-again evangelicals said they planned to vote for the Democratic presidential nominee.[10] In the end only 26 percent did, but it was up five percentage points from four years earlier.[11]

Christians are not a single group despite historic cycles and the high visibility of the Christian Right. For study of voting behavior, scholars of religion and politics identify six basic groupings: Evangelical Protestant, Mainline Protestants, Black Protestants, Roman Catholics, Jews, and Secularists. There are important differences between the six, and membership in one of the six serves as a major but not the sole factor in shaping political opinion.[12]

Even within the evangelicals there are differences and multiple groups. For example, the 2006 election saw cracks in the fundamentalist-evangelical coalition. Many evangelicals were moving beyond the fear platform of the first generation—such as the Moral Majority, Focus on the Family, and the Christian Coalition—and broadened their foreign policy interests from strong defense and support of the war in Iraq to issues like the genocide in Darfur, the AIDS epidemic, and global warming. This movement is sometimes called the "second generation" of the Religious Right.

When asked how well the Religious Right reflects their views, half, or 53 percent, of evangelicals said very well or somewhat well, but 35 percent said not too well or not at all.[13] Roman Catholics form the nation's largest single denomination and have more members of Congress than any other faith, and a majority of the Supreme Court. As voters, however, Catholics are about evenly split between Republicans and Democrats, and a Pew Research Center poll showed that Catholics are not a voting bloc but vote virtually identically with the rest of the country.[14]

Religious Right evangelicals do not define Christianity. There are less exclusivist groups, including "red letter Christians" who support liberal policies drawn from the words of Jesus, often identified in Bibles

9. Healy, "Is Dobson's Political Clout Fading?"
10. Hill, "Religious Right and the GOP," 35.
11. See "Voting Religiously."
12. See Fowler and Hertzke, *Religion and Politics in America*; and Smidt, "Religion and American Public Opinion," 96–117.
13. Gerson, "A New Social Gospel," 41.
14. O'Sullivan, "The Divided Faith," 30.

with red lettering. Other so-called progressives are liberal in policy and theology. Both are about a tenth of the adult population. They are found in such groups as Faith in Public Life, Alabama Arise, Faithful Arkansas, and We Believe Colorado. The work of Gary Haugen confronting sexual slavery; the ministry, purpose-driven message, and global leadership of Rick Warren in fighting poverty and AIDS in Africa; and the books of Ron Sider and Jim Wallis, and his *Sojourners* magazine, became a source of popularized ideas and news of this Christian community. But a more assertive backlash against the Christian Right emerged in blogs and Web sites such as www.JamesDobsondoesnotspeakforme.com.

The Christian vote will be a segment of an electoral coalition, but only a segment. The political advantage shifted to the Religious Right in the 1980s, and may have shifted again to a newer coalition of second generation and socially prophetic evangelicals. Party registration and social values are quite regional. In more insular districts with a singular economy and dominant social values congruent with populist evangelism, appeals to the Christian world as a whole may be effective. In other districts characterized by diversity, discovery, and dynamism (social, intellectual, and economic), a wise campaign will target particular Christian and evangelical groups and devise an "inside" coalition. That may well alienate some evangelical groups, so the coalition must be effective enough to survive the opposition and mobilization by the "outside" groups.

The election of Tom Perriello, strongly supported by a newly emergent religious left, has been viewed as reflecting a "seismic shift" in donor backing and voter preference.[15] More specifically, what about congressional elections? In congressional elections since 2002, there has been a slight decrease among those who attend church frequently and who voted Republican. The percentage of those who attend less frequently voted for the Democratic Party more frequently, rising from 53.5 percent in 2002 to 62.5 percent in 2006. The trend suggests that while the religious segment of the Republican Party remains about the same, the religious segment of the Democratic Party is growing.[16]

It is possible for Christians from both parties and political orientations to construct an electoral coalition that includes targeted segments of Christian voters. Each party has a highly partisan base of activists and poli-

---

15. Simon, "In Political Ads, Christian Left Mounts Sermonic Campaigns."
16. Silk and Green, "The GOP's Religion Problem," 2–4.

cy believers, but it is small. They provide intensity to a campaign, especially in a primary election, but not enough votes to carry the general election. They may be the foundation of a campaign strategy, or they may be targeted as extremists as a campaign reaches out to moderates in both parties. You must attract an electoral coalition of disparate groups with the right theme, and find the presentation that will "make the sale" in the minds of voters, and do so within the boundaries of personal and political ethics.

CAMPAIGN ETHICS

To win an election to Congress requires a campaign to convince people to vote for you, or at least to not vote for the other candidates. Ethics are involved in that personal process and also in preserving and promoting the values of democracy.

At the personal level there is no second place; you win or you lose. Unlike the business world, the electoral world is winner-take-all, so election campaigns are intense. Intensity pushes boundaries. The crunch comes when an intense individual confronts an intense competition. In such a heated atmosphere, a Christian will truly be engaged in applied ethics.

Honesty relates to the veracity of your self-portrayal as a candidate amidst the temptations to exaggerate and create questionable stereotypes. A campaign will test the quality of one's humility to withstand the accolades, prestige, and deference that will follow an election victory and service in Congress, for there are dangers of self-absorption, and justification for an arrogant sense of self.

Related to that humility is the third personal ethic, a decent respect for the views of others. That must remain a solid personal ethical principle. While we are to hunger and thirst for the right to prevail, all too often Christians jettison this ethic of decent respect for others when they believe they alone are standing for moral righteousness, that their positions are providential and necessary or somehow "above" those of others. That is a self-gratifying belief, and there is nothing more self-satisfying than certainty or more self-motivating than a crusade. Some crusades promote the general welfare, but there have also been crusades of fear, crusades to resist change or to return to the past. Both types risk dehumanizing others and disregarding consequences. Both personal and political ethics crumble in the heat of passion.

Finally, and most importantly, the Christian's ethics must always center on the grace of God. You must always be the Christian who happens to be a candidate or member of Congress, not a candidate or congressperson who happens to be a Christian.

The ethics of American democracy must also be considered. Though voters are equal, candidates are not. How much inequality can the process allow and yet be true to the ethics of the democratic process? One of the greatest inequalities is money, the danger that huge donations from "fat cats" would swamp the campaigns of opponents, with the danger of elections being "bought and sold." All levels of government now have public disclosure requirements, and many have established limits on the amount a person can contribute to a campaign. Financial disclosure is relatively easy because the statements deal with hard numbers, measurable amounts.

Beyond numbers, overseeing campaign ethics creates more of a challenge. The First Amendment of the Constitution insures the right of free speech, and libel laws are difficult to apply to an election campaign. The courts do not want to get involved in elections, and especially not in deciding the truthfulness of campaign rhetoric. Without rules about what can be said and a mechanism to hold candidates accountable, ethics will be self-enforced.

The American Association of Political Consultants has a code of ethics that form the outer boundaries of a campaign. Its members agree they will not use racist, sexist, or religiously intolerant appeals to voters, will not use false or misleading attacks on an opponent or member of the family, that all criticisms of an opponent will be accurate and documented, relationships with the media will be honest, and nothing will be done to corrupt or degrade the practice of political consulting.[17]

Honest and true are two ethical principles that can be vague in an election. Where is the line between emphasizing something that is true, such as a vote, and presenting it in a way that distorts the full truth of the vote? When does a partial truth become false?

Trust and specificity on issues are two important features of campaigns. Trustworthiness in personal life is a high ethical standard, but the trust that voters care about is what a person will do in office. Candid positions on issues, and trust on what a candidate will do, beat personal-

---

17. American Association of Political Consultants, *Code of Ethics*.

ity and money. An ethical campaign that conforms to the ethics of the democratic process makes an attractive candidate.

Attacks and distorted images are two other features, which run a spectrum from slander to hatred. Beginning in 1994 a meanness came to typify political style in Congress, and it can become more than just mean. Give the right issue certain subgroups from both the left and right, both subsidized by groups which claim no connection to a candidate and therefore escape all limitations and disclosure requirements, can engage in ugly campaigning and gross distortion. Just one recent example: in the 2008 election in the Fifth District in Virginia with Tom Perriello, an opposition advertisement featured a doctored photograph of a dark, sinister and bearded Perriello, designed to make Perriello look like the first cousin of Mohammad Atta.[18] Distorting opponents into enemies of the people if not country risks self-discipline. Tom DeLay (R-TX) put it like this: "I can't say the word "judge" without saying 'activist judge,' and that I think 'stupid liberal' is one word." He sometimes had what he called "an anger in my soul" that saw all liberals "as enemies trying to destroy my country. Even in an all-Republican race I can get so geared up for war that I speak of my allies as enemies."[19] Such attitudes can easily lead to the equivalent of a political assassination.[20] DeLay called Dennis Hastert (R-MI) a "model of big-heartedness" who helped him reign in his aggressiveness.[21] Such negativity in a campaign can be effective, but it also undermines a candidate's image as a clean politician and exaggerates into falsehood the consequences should his opponent win. Consequently, ethical boundaries are at risk as a candidate tries to rewrite ethics in his or her mind, for example, to justify advertising that he or she would not have countenanced earlier.

Worse, personal and political ethics both can be destroyed when smear campaigns are used to generate disgust in a calculated effort to suppress voter turnout, increasing the electoral power of a determined minority. The resulting plummeting respect people have for American politics is a terrible consequence for American democracy. People may disagree on what is right in one policy area or another, but as far back as

18. Serwer, "How Tom Perriello Showed Virgil Goode the Door."
19. DeLay, *No Retreat, No Surrender*, 102–3.
20. For examples see "Campaign Takedowns."
21. DeLay, *No Retreat, No Surrender*, 103.

the Roman Republic Cicero understood that politics is about *consensus juris*, or consensus on what is right. "Blessed are those who hunger and thirst after righteousness" or the right, Jesus said. Politics involves personal ambition and partial policy victories, campaign negativity and elector defeat, so in campaigning and legislating Christians must represent a high form of righteousness—not self-righteousness from which negativity and arrogance flow, but righteousness.

A PLATFORM FOR IMPACT

The U.S. House of Representatives is the people's house in two ways. Members of Congress operate with two potentially conflicting obligations, and therefore two sets of ethics—to serve the national interest and to serve their district's particular interests, or, to interpret the national interest from the district's perspective.

There are consequences of a representative democracy. Democratic republics are crisis-driven countries, meaning hard decisions are only made in times of crisis. People want their current problems solved, so Congress tends to make short-term policy decisions, and future problems get deferred. The people also don't like to pay for new policies, so democratic governments run deficits. The national interest for voters is not "objective truth," not something "out there." For voters, truth is personal, representing their experience, and that personal truth is the subject of political programs.

The role of Congress as a body is to avoid the relativism of these personal or partial truths and build a program that has meaning in the context of the national experience—past, present, and future. Congress passes legislation, new laws and programs of action, renewal and modification of existing laws, and final authorization of the annual national and individual budgets of the departments and agencies. Congress uses committees to gather information, oversee the operation of departments and agencies, and listen to lobbyists, academics, and citizens. These "truths" are then aggregated into a coherent policy proposal. As the media take interest and report to the public, the committee "educates the public." The process of legislation is thereby a two-way street, or a feedback loop.

To be elected to Congress is to be a part of its institutional processes and to have access to its tools and platforms, as well as colleagues, for influencing national policy. A member's time is always rushed, eaten up with meetings and policy issues. Simply doing that job is laudable, but our concern rises to another level—impacting foreign policy and national security policy. Congressional tools in foreign policy are blunt instruments, but there are avenues that can impact or change policy, from promoting a new policy like Donald Fraser and human rights, to criticizing and changing an administrative decision within a department, like the war Todd Tiahrt (R-KS) waged over the Air Force's choice of a defense firm (the firm he worked for prior to running for Congress lost the award).

Any foreign policy will have components, from military hardware to aide packages for veteran's affairs to executive structures, and one of those can become the vehicle for both change and personal achievement. Selecting one of those components for your personal interest will focus your energy, your lobbying activity on the outside public and the inside colleagues, and your topics for speeches.

Take Kirsten Gillibrand (D-NY), who won her seat in 2006 in an overwhelmingly Republican district as part of the voter reaction against the war in Iraq. She ran against a four-term Congressman who had grown rusty from lack of strong competition, and from a revelation that his wife called police to complain that the congressman was "knocking her around." Having won the seat in an unfavorable district and unique circumstance, could she keep it? She lobbied hard for an assignment to the Armed Services Committee where she could influence war policy and voted for benchmarks and oversight legislation. She also won a seat on the Agriculture Committee, from where she could deliver for her rural constituents. Both would be crucial to her reelection. Win she did, with 62 percent of the vote and a campaign theme that placed her above petty party politics. She refers to herself as an "independent leader" in Congress and posts a "Sunlight Report" of her daily schedule, which includes meetings with any lobbyists.[22] In 2009 she was appointed to Hillary Clinton's vacated seat in the Senate, and the Republicans determined to reclaim her House seat.

Having chosen a specific goal or a policy component to work towards, the political task begins—building a voting majority behind the goal/program. Defense policies represent jobs and have specific support groups. Foreign policy carries the highest stakes but has the fewest support groups. A new program or policy will need acceptance by the public,

---

22. Hernandez, "Frantic Start in Congress for One Democrat, Class of '06."

the Congress, the White House, and the relevant departments. Shaping preferences into a symbiotic policy community within that quadrangle is the holy grail of policy making.

This proves difficult, for Congress is a world of egos, populated as it is by people with ambition, purpose, and determination. Longevity in Congress also develops a sense of entitlement, especially for deference by rookies, and prerogatives of position. Simply getting "into the room" can be a privilege. For the leaders, the politics of the House is for new members to be deferential to them and "realistic" about achieving anything. "For you freshmen," Ralph Hellmann, former legislative director of Speaker Dennis Hastert, told a group of new members,

> ... my advice is don't try to think you are going to have the perfect solution. Don't set your sights (too high). That's not how the system works. Sometimes you just need to figure out how to get into the room and play a constructive role.[23]

Election to Congress provides a platform from which a member can reach for impact on policy. If "waiting your turn" seems wrong in a time of crisis, then a member must find a base of power. The best place for influencing policy is a committee, and getting appointed to an appropriate committee is the highest priority.

Committees. Four committees comprise the front line of influence on legislation and therefore policy, but they are not equal. The committee on Foreign Relations is the "home" committee for foreign policy issues and the Armed Services Committee for military policy and procurement. While they hold hearings and pass resolutions and legislation, the House Appropriations Committee is far more powerful since it decides what programs are funded and at what level. That is the key committee for influence. The Permanent Select Committee on Intelligence is the fourth committee of importance since is has oversight responsibility for the U.S. intelligence community. The work of all four is done in their subcommittees, distributing power and initiative to the chairs of the main committee to the subcommittees. Senior members of those committees have routine access to senior officials of the foreign policy bureaucracy, as well as to White House staff if not the president, so teaming with them goes beyond simply being involved in the work of the committee.

---

23. Quoted in Gavel, "A Different Kind of Freshman Orientation at KSG."

At one time power was held by committee chairs; not any longer. Power is held by chairs of subcommittees, which are widely dispersed. Subcommittees have discretion on what they want to investigate and oversee, giving great potential power to the chairpersons, and to even junior members. Their hearings are often updates on crisis areas, a forum for education and oversight, and a platform to pursue a new initiative.

For example, in 1973, at a time of growing concern over Secretary of State Henry Kissinger's foreign policy, Congressman Donald M. Fraser (D-MN), chairman of the Subcommittee on International Organizations and Movements of the House Foreign Affairs Committee, held hearings on nations who abuse their own citizens while receiving U.S. foreign and military aid. From that came a coalition of liberals who wanted the United States to stop giving aid to repressive governments and conservatives who wanted a lever to reduce foreign aid. Together they passed legislation that established an Office of Human Rights in the State Department, which became one of the "sign off" locations to approve foreign aid for countries. It also tasked the State Department to provide annual reports on human rights conditions in nations receiving American aid.

Resolutions. Members can use nonbinding resolutions to publicize an issue or make a political or legal point. It may be introduced and die, simply meeting a need to do something for an interest group, or it may gain support among members and pass the House. Even without legal authority, given the right issue and wording, they can have the potential to disrupt policy. In 2007 Rep. Adam Schiff (D-CA) did just that with a resolution that was "a bizarre mix of frivolity and moral seriousness, of constituent pandering, far-flung history and front-line foreign policy."[24] His Armenian Genocide Resolution reflected the demography of his district with 70,000–80,000 ethnic Armenians and for whom the slaughter of Armenians remains a focus. The Foreign Minister of Turkey spent several days in Washington lobbying against it while friends of Turkey lobbied Congress. It involved Congress in Turkey's national self-identity as well as brought into question Turkey's future willingness to let the United States use its Incirlik Air Base.

A resolution may also be a serious political warning by Congress to assert its legal and political prerogatives, such as a resolution expressing "grave concern" over an issue regarding another nation, or requiring congressional authorization before attacking Iran (HJ Res. 14).

24. Diehl, "The House's Ottoman Agenda," 15.

Plus ups. Budgets force decisions. The military services want more equipment than is wise to request, even though that equipment has been studied and approved as meeting an important need, a process and decision known as Program Objective Memorandum (POM). When the decision is made not to include such an item in the budget request, the item becomes known as an Unfunded Requirement (UFR), and military officials are not allowed to lobby Congress to add it to the budget. But a member may, and defense industries that would produce that equipment can attempt to get a member to do that. A "plus up" is the addition of such an item to the budget. A member can also lobby for items that were not designated in the POM or as a UFR, personally believing it necessary for the security of the nation, or the solvency of an industry, or for the economic health of his or her district. The military despises that effort.

"All politics is local," said former House Speaker Tip O'Neill (D-MA). True, but the national connection sustains the local connection. Rep. Joe Courtney (D-CT) narrowly defeated Rob Simmons in 2006 over the latter's inability to get the Navy to double the production of nuclear submarines, which is important to the economy of his district. It was crucial to prevent further lay-offs at the submarine production facility Electric Boat, a division of General Dynamics. Such defense firms as Electric Boat normally support incumbents but stayed in regular contact with Courtney. Once in office, Courtney reached out to Rep. John Murtha, chairman of the Defense Appropriations subcommittee, to push the Navy to build the additional submarines, while House Armed Services Chairman Rep. Ike Skelton (D-MO) tried to help all the new Democratic members.[25] In July of 2008 Murtha's subcommittee included funding for a second nuclear submarine to be built at Electric Boat as well as additional funding for a continuing program of six additional submarines, an acceleration beyond the plans and requests of the Navy.[26] Courtney won reelection in 2008.

An emerging corollary activity is the power of a member to contest a decision of the Defense Department that awards a contract to one defense firm over a competitor's proposal. Todd Tiahrt (R-KS), a graduate of Evangel College and who serves on both the House Appropriations Committee and the Permanent Select Committee on Intelligence, waged a war in partnership with representatives and senators from Kansas and

25. Tiron, "Courtney Gets Democrats' Support," 8.
26. Grogan, "Sub Funding Increase Advances."

Alabama over the Air Force's choice of a European firm to build the new KC-X air refueling tanker rather than Boeing. Boeing has a plant in Wichita, and Tiahrt worked there before running for Congress.

Earmarks. An earmark is an action by Congress within the Pentagon budget to direct the Defense Department to spend its funds on a specific program, or direct the department to select a specific firm, making the award outside the normal competitive or merit-based acquisition process. When a member of Congress tours an area such as Iraq and asks generals what they can do to help, and a general says we need more Predator unmanned vehicles, that member goes back home and attempts to put in the Defense budget an earmark for more Predators. This is an earmark rather than a plus up because it does not add additional spending to the budget but directs the department to spend funds for the Predator program. Or the member may direct the department to use a specific firm, usually located in his or her home district and the source of campaign contributions.

Foreign Policy Shop. A member can build an office staff that specializes in a topic, though at risk to other topics. Senator Henry Jackson built such a shop with his staff, headed by Richard Perle and dedicated to opposing Henry Kissinger and détente. The staff included such later top officials as Douglas Feith, Elliott Abrams, and Jim Woolsey. Each military service has a legislative office, which can assign an intern to a congressional office or committee. They learn "politics" and in turn can explain (or find out) why a particular budget issue or weapon system is so important, giving the member an important piece of leverage. Members or their staff can make study trips abroad, distribute provocative memos or position papers, offer leaks in friendly media, and make trades with other members and subcommittee chairs. Here, as in election campaigns, keeping a firm line between being too provocative and too deceptive or untrue has to be maintained.

Caucuses. Committees are not the only platform of influence. A normal technique of politics is to build a circle of allies into a policy caucus as a power base. In politics it is "not who you know; it's who you get to know."[27] Take the initiative; seek out a circle of allies and become its leader. A caucus of likeminded members can build expertise, develop a strategy, coordinate their actions, target other members, and provide its leader with exposure and a player that has to be courted by the lead-

---

27. Matthews, *Hardball*, 23–46.

ers. South Carolina's Joe Wilson (R-SC) organized the thirteen-member Victory in Iraq caucus in opposition to the seventy-four member Out of Iraq Caucus chaired by Maxine Waters (D-CA).

POLITICS IS PERSONAL

Persuading other members outside one's own party is hard work and requires finesse. Playing politics means courting them with praise and leading them to see that what you want is what they want. Congress is large, but it's personal. You meet, network, and expand your relationships. Just like targeting precincts in an election, members are identified and classified as to who will be hard-line opponents or supporters of your proposal, and who might be persuaded. How do members of the latter group think, what are their priority issues and district needs, who do they respect, and who are in their electoral coalition back home? Armed with those and many other pieces of information, a legislator will know how to craft an argument.

Since both the House of Representatives and the Senate are running the same processes from their different perspectives, new initiatives sometimes get killed. In 1979 the House placed country-by-country restrictions on the use of U.S. funds by international lending institutions like the World Bank, which would have prevented the bank from accepting any U.S. funds. The Senate struck out the restrictions.[28]

Some of the legislative process relates to top-tier issues, normally the preserve of the leadership. Members who are not fully on board can get caught here. Some party leaders have allowed members discretion in their votes on these issues, while others enforce compliance. If the reluctance is based on opposition from the member's district, discretion is usually allowed. If the opposition is based on a member's best judgment or principles, the leader will insist that party unity take precedence over a member's scruples. When the vote is close on a major bill, the majority party will demand unity to insure its passage, and the minority party will demand unity in the hopes that a majority member will vote with them and defeat the bill. Such processes of unity on either/or issues can involve hypocrisy as a party that votes on specific issues one way when in the majority will vote against it when in the minority. A recalcitrant member risks his or her future. Character will shine—or not.

28. Lyons, "On Capitol Hill," A4.

Other legislation is like making sausage, because there is less top-down pressure, more opportunity for local, ideological, and deontological assertiveness from multiple sides. Some of the legislative process is called earmarks, when specific members insert specific grants to groups, including faith-based groups.

Finally, given the right confluence of political skill and opportune time to build a majority, individuals can take the initiative and shape a new policy or program. The lasting achievement of Congressman Donald M. Fraser (D-MN) in taking the first step to insert human rights issues into American foreign and military aid is an example. Congressman Chris Smith (R-NJ) is another example. Smith authored three laws fighting global human trafficking with punishment for violators, shelters and rehabilitation for victims, and State Department action and reports. The first bill culminated nearly a decade of work, with the second coming in 2003 and the third in 2005. One member of Congress can use the institution of Congress, its structures and procedures, to lay the foundation for building a coalition that can impact foreign policy. The system is "open" for such initiatives; making an impact is not impossible.

"Charlie Wilson's War" demonstrates the impact one member may have on policy. Just a few months after Wilson was elected to Congress and won a seat on the Foreign Relations Committee, Arab nations attacked Israel in the Yom Kippur War. Wilson quickly requested a briefing at the Israeli Embassy and arranged a trip to the war zone. Wilson championed underdogs and he saw Israel in that light and became a strong supporter of its needs. The Jewish community in America then helped him win a seat on the Appropriations Committee, where he could help insure the annual $3 billion a year in aid to Israel.

In Latin America Wilson was distraught over President Carter's effort to remove the dictator Anastasio Somoza of Nicaragua, who Wilson saw as a strong U.S. ally against the Soviets. Despite Wilson's efforts, the committee cut funding to Somoza. In a stunning political maneuver Wilson took the issue to the Floor of the House and threatened to hold up Carter's whole foreign aid bill if the Somoza funds were not restored. He won that one, though later lost in the two-house conference committee. Later, when he was convinced the CIA was not doing enough to support the Afghan resistance against the Soviet Union, he pushed a stronger policy on the CIA and arranged a funding scheme to make it happen.[29]

Serving in the House to impact policy for the good of the nation is a great privilege. That service also brings members into direct dealings with the highest levels of the corporate world, where officers and lobbyists want something that will benefit them. What may seem minor to the overall picture can be very lucrative for the firm.

ETHICS IN CONGRESS

A Christian lives in eschatological tension between the "now" and the "not yet." In Congress a Christian lives in the political tension between the desirable and the possible, between the district and the nation, and between merit and "deals." Waiting for the expected Lord's return generates hope, a desirable trait when consulting, negotiating, battling, losing, compromising, and winning partial victories in the quest for that better world of foreign policy he or she sees. Nothing happens without a majority, so members must collaborate and defer to colleagues whose values he or she may only partially share.[30] They also live in the tension between self-interest and public duty.

Effectiveness as a congressional operative depends on good relations with other members. That has become more difficult since the 1994 "revolution" in Congress that sought a more ideological rather than congenial legislature. Furthermore, the pervasiveness of gerrymandering has moved the real election to the primary, where activists rather than the general public votes. Therefore, discounting fringe and nut-case candidates, a Republican must be the more conservative and the Democrat the more liberal to appeal to their activist bases. The result is the lack of a vital center, a polarized legislature where politicians form alliances, not wide circles of friendship.

Effectiveness also depends on "deals" or vote-trading and vote-buying. The maze and number of issues preclude equal priority for all. At the same time there are significant issues for a district that are low priority for all the other members. In a crunch, members can trade votes to support each other's needs and policies. When votes are close, and every vote counts toward passage or defeat, one's resistance to an issue can be traded

---

29. Crile, *Charlie Wilson's War*.
30. Thompson, *Political Ethics and Public Office*, 96, 101.

or "sold" for the district's benefit. Sometimes even trading and buying are not enough, and the seriousness of the issue can lead to intense if not politically coercive lobbying by the party leaders in the House. "Around here," one writer reported about a battle over a welfare bill, "it sometimes requires browbeating, blackmail, mixed metaphors and guts to feed poor children."[31] The lines between political skill and unethical politics can move, given sufficient significance of the broader issue.

Christians in Congress live in a social world as targets. They are accorded honor and deference, but usually for entirely utilitarian reasons. Hearings are augmented by receptions and dinners and other social events where members mingle with the highest levels of American society, but they are there not because of their person but because of their position. They are targets for solicitations because their office gives them influence; they remain important in power circles only so long as they have influence. Influence even among colleagues demonstrates that politicians have a short shelf life. Don Young (R-AK) chaired two important committees during the years of Republican control of the House, and when the Democrats took the majority in 2006, he lost his position. "My good friends are still with me," he once said, and others, "I knew they would not be there when I was no longer chairman. This is a very cold business."[32]

These processes of representation and legislation require institutional and personal integrity—that members are making decisions on the basis of merit and not personal reward. Members cannot be "selling" their votes to lobbyists and firms who will benefit for specific provisions of the legislation, nor can they be extorting funds from those benefiting from the legislation. The same is true of enrichment for themselves or their family and friends through gifts and fees.

Rep. John Murtha (D-PA) is Chairman of the Subcommittee on Defense of the House Committee on Appropriations, a position of enormous influence in the acquisition decisions of the Department of Defense. Paul Magliocchetti, a former staff member of the Appropriations Committee who worked closely with Murtha, left to found his own lobby group called PMA. That firm specializes in lobbying on defense contracts. In 2008 PMA clients received $299 million worth of earmarks, with a majority of the firm's clients in or near Murtha's district, which includes

---

31. Quote from a Tom Wicker *New York Times* article on the Phil Burton Machine, quoted in Jacobs, *A Rage for Justice*, 177.

32. Kucinich, "Young: There's Life after Lawmaking," 8.

many small firms as well as the giants like Lockheed Martin, General Dynamics, and Science Applications International (SAIC). PMA campaign contributions went to congressmen who either represented districts in Pennsylvania or to six members of the Appropriations Committee. The firm and its clients were among the top ten donors to Murtha's most recent campaign, together giving $183,700 toward his reelection. The most money given by PMA went to Rep. Pete Visclosky (D-IN), who tied Murtha in obtaining sixteen earmarks. Rep. Bill Young (R-FL), who formerly headed the subcommittee until control of the House changed and he became the senior Republican on the committee, received eight.[33]

Where is the line separating the political ethics of serving one's district and the political ethics of avoiding self-interest in the making of decisions? When Rep. Visclosky (R-IN), who is under investigation for receiving illegal contributions from a lobby firm seeking earmarks for a defense firm, said "I have represented the people of Northwest Indiana to the best of my ability," one understands the contextual dilemma.[34] A member of Congress needs to bring business to the district or the voters would assume he or she is a failure, as they implied with the defeat of Rob Simmons. Service on the Appropriations Committee puts the member in a position to create earmarks for his or her district. Lobbyists and defense firms donate funds to the reelection committees of Congress members. The nature of that donation may be legal or illegal, but a background question for any such donation is whether that money is a bribe by the firm, or a requirement by the member for a decision for an earmark (both unethical), a necessity by the firm simply to get recognition by a member, or a gracious or politically astute action of appreciation? One means of deciding is the ratio of the member's earmarks servicing the district as opposed to other districts.

Money is a political tool. Election to Congress is very expensive, and candidates have to raise it for campaigns. Each campaign candidate must raise it, and donors give it in anticipation of either support or at least access to the winner. That raises image problems during the campaign. The reality of two-year elections means that even while in office the search for reelection funds continues. There are five dangers in office. One is the donations that groups give in anticipation, and another is the fund-raisers organized

33. Crabtree, "Dems' Ethical Troubles," 6.
34. Tiron and Blake, "Amid Probe, Rep. Visclosky Steps Aside."

by members to which certain groups are expected to attend, what lobbyists call extortion. Third, each party has congressional campaign committees raise funds and give to candidates in their party in tight races, tightening the influence of party leaders over members. Fourth, there are "favors" that corporations offer—use of corporate jets, golf outings. Fifth, the disparity between congressional salary and the profits defense firms will make from decisions by Congress, and being around all the corporate money, encourages the question "where's mine?" That certainly was the case with Congressman Randy Cunningham (R-CA) who demanded kickbacks for leveraging decisions favorable to a couple defense firms.

Most members of Congress are honest, but Ron Wilcox, writing in *Forbes* magazine, noted well that "the American public gets the government they pay for, and right now they are trying to do it on the cheap." That is no excuse for corruption, but somehow, in the words of former Congressman Bob Edgars, "we need to encourage people to serve the public without the belief that they're going to get something out of it."[35] That takes character.

There is a code of ethics for members of the House. Can the House oversee itself? It has to, since the Constitution gives each chamber control of its members, so that one branch of government cannot interfere with another. There is a House Committee on Standards of Official Conduct with a manual on ethics, but there are weaknesses. The majority party will be tempted to protect its own, but not the actions of members of the other party. Can a nonmember bring an accusation, and will the investigation be open? Outside groups like Public Citizen and Citizens for Ethics keep watch over members and publicly accuse those they consider to have violated the rules.

For most of its history, members of Congress practiced civility, or "quiet collusion," to conceal their member's mistakes. It was a "political" tactic that is no longer viable in this era when the media and the other party are always present, looking for any misconduct; little is private anymore. Members of Congress are neither more nor less honest, but financial disclosures were increased to insure merit-based decisions. As one source put it, "No tycoon, TV pundit, professor, investigative reporter, or book editor is forced to reveal as much about his or her personal assets or private life as are members of Congress."[36]

35. Both quotes in Helling, "Temptation Exists for Politicians," 22.
36. Tolchin and Tolchin, *Glass House*, 12.

In the 1980s Newt Gingrich began using ethics as a political weapon, a tool in his arsenal of combative politics, publicizing unethical conduct by members of both parties. So successful was Gingrich that he unseated the Speaker of the House Jim Wright in 1987. In his resignation speech Wright predicted that Gingrich would eventually be consumed by the "mindless cannibalism" he had loosed. In fact, just a decade later, Gingrich, at this point the Speaker of the House, resigned over unethical financial practices, and he declared he was not willing to preside over "people who were mindless cannibals."[37] Neither was convicted of "selling votes" or extortion, but both leaders used books they had authored to side-step congressional rules about raising funds.

The fate of Wright and Gingrich represent bookends in a period of intense political use of ethics. In the past decades ethics and the ethics committee have vacillated between active and moribund. Since the political use of ethics cuts both ways and the public's concern varies, members feel caught in inconsistency.

Some members make mistakes, some find ways to "skim" funds, and others are crassly corrupt. Dan Rostenkowski (D-IL), a powerful chairman of the Ways and Means committee, was indicted in 1993 for $23,300 in mail fraud with the House Post Office. He lost his reelection campaign and pled guilty in 1996. The 2007 guilty plea of Congressman Randy "Duke" Cunningham (R-CA) for blatant corruption, $2.4 million in bribery from defense firms, represents an extreme failure of personal character. The conviction of the lobbyist Jack Abramoff in the legal system for widespread seduction of members of Congress took place in civil court, because the House Ethics Committee was moribund, representing the failure of institutional integrity and the substitution of political party interests over both institutional and personal ethics of its members.

Republican Majority Leader and outspoken Christian conservative Tom DeLay (R-TX) was the architect of the "K Street Project," a lobbying strategy to benefit members of his party and make issues more ideological, and which clouded the boundary between barely ethical and corrupt politics. In such a setting of loose boundaries and moribund oversight, even Tom DeLay himself got caught in the Abramoff scandal and resigned from his office, and then from Congress.

---

37. Ibid., 4.

CHRISTIANS AND CONGRESS

Power, policy, and self-defense come together, and it is the personal nature of this intrigue against others and the personal domination of a network and policy agenda that pulls one toward the boundaries of personal and political ethics. The ethics of humility and decent respect are at risk. Self-defense and self-promotion are normal attitudes in the world of politics, but always one's identity must be kept central—a Christian who happens to work in politics, not a politician who happens to be a Christian. First Love can live so long as it does not succumb to First Power or First Policy.

Why would ethically sensitive Christians, nonideological, nondeontological Christians, want to be there? It's dollars versus difference. Business can be cutthroat, even more so than politics, but people go into business because they want to make a dollar. People go into politics because they want to make a difference. When politicians become known for keeping their word on agreements, when their spiritual sense of self is strong, they will survive the cold, be regarded with respect while in the midst of political feuding and battles, and bring a positive impact to people and the system.

For example, Christians are deep in a world of image and image protection, where outside groups are all too willing to find and publicize any hint of corruption. Some members even have adversarial blogs formed against them. When a member gets caught in a scandal, most colleagues scatter. Friendship, Christian friendship, bonds closer than mere utilitarian alliances. Peter King (R-NY) remained a supporter of his colleague Vito Fossella (R-NY) who was exposed in scandal. They were close friends, and the Catholic Congressman King commented, "There, but for the grace of God go I."[38] Randy "Duke" Cunningham (R-CA) was convicted of bribery and extortion and sent to prison. His close friend Duncan Hunter (R-CA), a Southern Baptist who had urged Cunningham to run for Congress, continued to visit and pray with him in prison. "I think that as Christians, if we can forgive our enemies, we can certainly forgive our friends."[39]

It is also a world of money. Donated money complicates image and interest in an issue. It is likely that most issues have no deep ethical or Christian stakes, like the budget line item for the Fulbright program, or

---

38. Quoted in Rothstein, "Befriending the Fallen," 22.
39. Quoted in Martelle, "Duncan Hunter's Toughest Fight Yet."

one defense contractor over another. Still, some do, and they all call for individual decisions, and a Christian in Congress needs both faith and the strength that flows from personal access to the grace, strength, insight, and leadership of the Holy Spirit.

LEGISLATIVE EXAMPLE

The heart of all this is issues. Agreeing on solutions to those issues requires a majority vote, and building that majority requires building a coalition to close a "deal." This is an example of what individual members can do, and also the conflicts of policy and conscience such efforts create for individual members.

The near-unanimous vote that passed the International Religious Freedom Act was a coalition between members and parties. The Act established an independent commission, an Office of Religious Freedom in the Department of State, which produces an annual report on religious freedom around the world, a position on the National Security Council staff, and a toolbox of diplomatic tools.

The effort began in the mid-1990s when lone voices and various religious groups raised issues about religious persecution around the world, especially against Jews in the Soviet Union, Buddhists in Vietnam, Christian living abroad in such countries as Sudan, and China's effort to eradicate the underground Christian church at the time it was applying for admission to the World Trade Organization. High-level persons in the evangelical world began lobbying congressional members about the need for the United States to take action to protect religious minorities.

Congressman Chris Smith (R-NJ), who sat on the House Committee on Foreign Affairs, along with Tony Hall (D-OK) and Frank Wolf (R-VA), who was cochair of the Congressional Human Rights Caucus, introduced tough legislation to apply sanctions to nations practicing religious persecution. It was picked up in the Senate by Arlen Specter (R-PA), who wanted the support of the evangelical vote in his reelection, and Joseph Liebermann (D-CT). The Wolf-Specter bill, as it was called, ran into strong opposition because it defined persecution so tightly that only a couple regimes would fit, and it applied strong trade sanctions against nations that were identified as persecutors. Several members agreed it was a bad bill but would vote for it because it would be good for them and they knew the Senate would never pass it.

For the Religious Right, this was their bill, and since they considered their motives and purposes pure, the bill was immaculate. It was an emotional issue for them, and they mobilized support through their radio programs.

The Clinton administration opposed the automatic sanctions trigger in the Wolf-Specter bill, and the State Department expressed fear it would hinder dialogue with adversaries and harm relations with allies. Some Christian liberal groups made common cause with business interests opposed to disruption of trade, and Republican "realists" dismissed its idealism as dangerous to "stability." Some on the Christian Right supported the effort and some opposed it out of their disgust of working with the Clinton administration.[40]

By 1998 the Wolf-Specter bill was stalled, its leaders unable to build a majority coalition to support it. In response Congressman Chris Smith and Senator Don Nichols (R-OK) began quietly building support for an alternative bill that focused on violations of religious liberty rather than persecution and that provided flexible diplomatic responses. When it became known that an alternative bill was being developed by some staffers, leaders of the Right harshly attacked its authors and demanded they be fired. Non-Christians were amazed at the vitriolic attacks by Christians as righteousness became self-righteousness. As Dick Armey (R-TX), an evangelical and Majority Leader at the time, said of a different meeting with some big-name populist Christian Right leaders, "I am not tough enough to have Christians for friends. . . . I was never so wrongfully and viciously attacked in all my eighteen years in Washington as I was by the Christian leaders."[41]

Nevertheless, an unlikely coalition of liberals and conservatives, secular civil rights groups and religious conservatives, came together. Realizing Wolf-Specter was dead, the Christian Right dropped its antagonism and swung its support to the new bill and made it a priority, while the more liberal National Council of Churches (NCC) continued its opposition even against the new one. Christian staffers were baffled by NCC and their claims that the bill put religious minorities at greater risk and that it smacked of American imperialism. Some human rights advocates

---

40. This material is taken from a variety of sources, especially Hertzke, "The Faith Factor in Foreign Policy"; and Hertzke, *Freeing God's Children*, chap. 6, and personal interviews.

41. Lindsay, *Faith in the Halls of Power*, 65.

opposed separating out religious issues while others supported it, because religion was being overlooked as a human rights concern.

Congress members and their staffers worked hours and hours with administration officials to find compromise language. In the last hours before the vote they worked feverishly to stop "killer amendments" that would split the coalition. The amendment strategy failed and the coalition held. Unwilling to vote against a bill opposed to religious persecution, especially just weeks before the 1998 elections, the Senate passed it 98-0, and the House passed it by acclamation.

One of the ethical morals of the story of this coalition effort is the need for Christians, especially staffers, to transcend the "warfare" element of political disagreement. Christian interest groups in this instance confused morality and politics. When entering into policy issues, they must dispel their assumption that their group's position is the only moral one and take seriously the secondary diplomatic consequences of enforcing a bad policy. Michael Gerson wrote, "When I served on Capitol Hill, staffers dreaded the organized call-in campaigns of religious groups, because the comments were often the most vicious and hurtful. Religious Right leaders developed habits of certainty, which became indistinguishable from arrogance."[42]

The motives and preferences were good, but the political style that Christian groups used in this instance was a sorry spectacle. Christian staffers caught in the middle have an important role to play in "sanctifying" the process with their tone in their conversations.

The second note about this story is the key role staffers played in shaping and advancing legislation. There would not have been an international religious freedom bill if staffers had not worked the system to craft a bill that would inaugurate a policy that would be effective, pass the Congress, and be signed by the president. Building a workable coalition for such bills is hard. Legal battles are not easy; business deals are not easy. But in politics, the outcome of this hard effort is an improvement in the lives of people.

Thirdly, age. While one of the three staffers was in his mid-forties, the other two were in their mid-twenties. Young people are found throughout the congressional and White House staffs. The decade after graduation can be a career-making time.

---

42. Gerson, *Heroic Conservatism*, 118.

THREE KEY WORDS

Three signposts can help Christians navigate in Congress: true, tone, and transcend. Members of Congress live on two tracks, local and national, and in a maze of domestic and foreign issues. In their midst, the Christian in Congress must always be *true* to himself or herself. Foreign policy is not the only issue about which members feel strongly. Walter Jones (R-NC) was a member of the Armed Services Committee when the Republicans controlled the House of Representatives and was opposed to the war in Iraq, which cost him the chance to be chairman of a subcommittee. When he attracted national attention as a cosponsor of a nonbinding resolution to disapprove of President Bush's "surge" request, he was approached by some Democrats with the suggestion that he switch parties. He declined. "I'm guided by my faith. Quite frankly, I'm strong pro-life. . . . I think at the present time, because of the pro-life issue primarily, I am where I need to be."[43] True to self.

Politics is strategy, combat, compromise, winning, and losing. The *tone* with which one does those can be an important means of grace in the situation, one that will be widely appreciated and respected. The public "Christian witness" of many Christians on the Left and Right is seriously compromised by the way they engage in public life. A commitment to a decently respectful tone will help prevent one from slipping into combat zealotry. Demeanor ought to reflect God's embracing grace. Win or lose on a vote, win or lose on a local versus national issue, grace in the world of politics must be a force that elevates relationships.

A life embraced by grace will be a transcending life. Within the campaigns and in the struggles of congressional policy making, a Christian's identity and actions must *transcend* the immediate time zone, keeping in view both the mosaic of our lives and the sweep and mysterious providence of God in history. Sometimes that transcending may take the form of self-sacrifice for a principle of faith or national interest. Other times it takes the form of the wisdom Job finally found—releasing inflated goals and pretentious claims to be God's soldier with clear knowledge of providence. Those distort the profound sense of history that comes through God's embracing grace.

---

43. Kucinich, "Anti-War Jones Wooed by Dems," 4.

NO GUARANTEES

The word *transcend* is an appropriate segue into our final consideration. Christians do not define themselves exclusively by Congress or issues, for defeat on either can create a downward spiral of exclusion and alienation. The Christian must have life beyond Congress. John Dellenback was a Republican congressman from Medford, Oregon, a Presbyterian elder, Yale graduate, and former law professor. Dellenback said his faith led him to run for Congress to help solve America's immense national problems. A member of a Bible study group in Congress, Dellenback felt Congress was where the Lord wanted him to serve at that point in his life, but he understood there were no guarantees for reelection and nothing is easy. When the time comes to make that vote, he said, you just "hope and pray that your judgment is right." He did what he thought was right to do for four terms, but the shadow of Richard Nixon haunted Republicans in the election of 1974, and he was defeated for a fifth term.[44] When it was over he traveled around Oregon, thanking people for the privilege of serving in Congress. Dellenback went on to serve as the director of the Peace Corps and president of the Coalition of Christian Colleges and Universities.

Jim Wright grew up in Texas, son of an itinerant salesman during the Depression and member of the Church of Christ. He was bright and skipped grades, growing up in a family committed to personal honor and high expectations. The paradox of being one's own man while worrying about the world's opinion was resolved in achievement. Politics was the route to achievement. He attended the University of Texas and supported a group of young liberals who wanted anti-lynching laws and an end to the poll tax. He won election to the Texas state legislature, but his reelection campaign was a brutal street-fight, his opponents calling him a commie dupe who wanted every African American (referred in slang) to go to the University of Texas Law School. In the midst of that pressure, Wright made his first compromise—he took out a last-minute newspaper ad saying he supported the "Southern way of life" but still lost by thirty-eight votes. It was a time for introspection. Who needed the pain of campaigning? But running a business and making good money was not satisfying. He wanted to be able to do things. He won election as mayor and in 1954 ran successfully for the U.S. House of Representatives.[45]

---

44. Hefley and Plowman, *Washington: Christians in the Corridors of Power*, 125–26.
45. Barry, *The Ambition and the Power*, 44–51.

Wright hoped to move to the Senate and then run for president. When Lyndon B. Johnson became vice president and his Senate seat opened, Wright saw his chance. He lost and settled back into a career in the House. While the issues facing America were difficult, and even though he believed God had a plan for each person and nation, Wright expressed: "I don't know how to reconcile the omnipotence of God with the free will of man. I just know I must try to cultivate the kind of relationship with the Creator that will let me know and follow his plan."[46] Wright was elected to national leadership as Speaker of the House in 1987, but politics can be a "blood sport," and ethics charges were brought against him. The House Ethics Committee found violations of congressional rules, and he had to resign. Today Wright teaches courses on Congress and the Presidents at Texas Christian University.

A MEDITATION ON JUDGES 9

Gideon was a great war leader against the Midianites and Amalekites, who also tore down the alter of Baal, had seventy sons from his many wives, and one from a concubine in Shechem, whose name was Abimelech. The monarchy had not been established in Israel, and the seventy sons repudiated their father's loyalty to God and reestablished Baal worship. In the power vacuum Abimelech determined to compensate for his status by becoming ruler over Israel—success is the best revenge. He appealed to the men of Shechem to support him as their "brother" in a campaign for power, conquest, and rule. It made sense to them, so they funded his initial step to hire "worthless and reckless men" to kill his seventy brothers, after which he put together a fighting force and began expanding his area of control. He was successful for several years, but he alienated some of his followers who then acted treacherously again him. Some percentage withdrew their support, limiting Abimelech to his surviving forces. He tried too much, and they were defeated in battle and Abimelech killed.

This story is not unlike that of Shakespeare's Richard III, who connived and assassinated his way to power to compensate for his deformed body. Politics is about winning and losing, which is also about change for justice and modernization versus status recovery by those losing social place; it is about power for regional groups and social conquest for "values" interest groups. It can also be very personal, reflecting great social

---

46. Ibid, 132–33.

gifts or compensation for some need or deficiency. It is easy to lose one's way in campaigns involving personal ambition, interest-group power, and values-group conquest. All this is important to understand because the power of the media and computer networking means the Christian will be under pressure to make the initial campaign effort a strongly negative portrayal of the opponent—in effect a political assassination—for the initial portrayal of a candidate in the voters' minds tends to last and determine their votes.

Running for office in a primary in a gerrymandered district, or in the general election in a truly competitive district, is always done in an atmosphere of negativity. An election campaign is democratic warfare, and one's victory comes by way of another's defeat, so open attacks and subtle undermining are common. The psalms of David are full of his cries to God for protection and the destruction of his foes, but while one may feel strongly that important issues are at stake, it is presumptuous to apply the prayers of David to a democratic election. So, to candidates, three pieces of advice:

First, remember who you are: you are a fully engaged democratic participant. Other prophets of doom will cry "fear" from the sidelines to allies and the already persuaded, bask in the personal glory of White House invitations and presidential commissions, and then sulk when their favored presidential candidate loses and they lose access and adulation. You, on the other hand, are willing to enter the fray, to submit yourself and your ideas to the voters, to be questioned by the media (how many so-called religious leaders ever submit to a press conference of the regular media?), to fight hard the battles of persuasion to diverse groups, to be kicked and bruised and get dirty, to make very little salary if you win, and to have to do it all again two years later. Few are willing to commit their lives and reputations and service to that much democracy. There will be mistakes and regrets as quick decisions are made. Words once uttered cannot be recalled and may live on in opposition advertising in e-mail blasts and YouTube. One's reputation may suffer, but win or lose, you have been the one with Esther's moral courage.

Second, remember whose you are, and keep your first love first: you are a Christian who is a candidate, not a candidate who is a Christian. Priorities are a good definition of integrity, and life in Christ is the first priority. Election campaigns are not virtual reality; they are a flesh and blood reality. Hurts will come from campaign attacks, and even deeper hurts from friends who do not support you and your effort. Rapid prayers for grace, and deep prayers for grace and guidance will be indispensable. And it will be grace that sustains you and keeps you open to the very love of God that gets you through victory or defeat.

Third, embrace the process of being a Christian vote-hustler. No one's base is ever large enough to carry an election; candidates have to reach out, with important consequences. On the outside the campaign should have more balance as the candidate meets a wider range of people when they move beyond the comfort zone of their "brothers and sisters" in their regional or class or values group and their normal circle of supporters. On the inside there should be a softening of attitudes as one experiences the diversity and needs of real people. Abimelech understood the need for a base of supporters and the need to expand that base (in his case by force), but he, like Joseph, did not understand that politics is a means of service, a reflection of a mature individual, not one compensating for physical or psychological deformity. Voters and nonvoters are people not statistics. Their understandings may seem deficient and narrow, but to enter into their worlds of needs and fears and hopes and social ceilings is an act of courage, designed by the theory of electoral democracy and one's own humane character to broaden one's moral imagination.

Moreover, without mutual understandings that cross and transcend the diverse needs of a diverse people, this country could come to resemble the Tower of Babel. Democratic processes can hold this diverse country together only if there is sufficient social capital (such as tolerance and trust and self-discipline among those who are different or differ) to withstand its baser campaign tactics. This country has closed-minded people; it needs good people who will enter the fray and be truly democratic politicians. They will be Christian vote-hustlers, but they will also be people who take the risk to offer themselves to the scrutiny of others as a means to serve the country, to take the risk to both restrain themselves and to enlarge themselves and their ideas in a primary contest, and to be persons of principle in a context that requires multiple loyalties.

7

Beyond the Campus Culture

THE SKILLS OF DIPLOMATS, the strategies of generals, and the shadowy world of the assassins of 1914 represent the factors of national interest, the rise and decline of nations, and the calculations, uncertainties and failures not far distant from those of today. Nations (leaders, voters, and values) make large and small changes and choices with dimly perceived consequences on national decline or renewal. Our life in Christ is a journey of prayer, Scripture, and thought. It is a life of stages and grace, hope and moral courage, openness and closure, guidance and silence. Those involved in foreign affairs bring such political and theological frameworks to their careers where they face multiple choices represented in part by patience or resignation, a step over or a step back, the engineer's hat or the manager's hat, a vote for budget restraint or for district jobs.

These are issues of applied ethics in areas that are sometimes dark but often gray, with close calls between choices on issues not faced by those behind pulpits and podiums. Young men and women in the arena of foreign affairs work with leaders and people of different cultures and values, do the routine and the significant, here and abroad. In the personal "updrafts" of their careers and in times of pressures of immediacy and consequences, they will face individual choices of great national import and historical fate, whatever policy and organization factors may be in play. Choosing engagement is a personal decision made in the pursuit of a worthy cause, with success and failure both known and unknown. There are no "great answers" in these choices and sometimes dilemmas; choices are personal, and in their midst is grace.

In the next decades of challenge and response America needs the highest caliber young people to enter and engage in foreign affairs. We need men and women in policy, action, and scholarship. Careers in foreign affairs are beyond the ordinary choices made on campuses where students give little deference to government leaders in this era of hostile politics. To choose national service means choosing to respond to the broader national interest, and it begins a demanding career in the midst of a historical era of high importance if not a pivotal point in history. That choice also reflects the realization that one can be an agent of grace in history and to the nation through public service in foreign affairs. Such a choice is personal, and the remainder of this chapter addresses you personally, using second-person pronouns. So, if the nation needs the best and you plan to become engaged, then reach beyond the ordinary and the local campus.

THE LOCUST YEARS

In the first volume of his history of the Second World War, Winston Churchill refers to the four years between 1931 and 1935 as the locust years, the years the locusts have eaten. Four years of a college education pass quickly, and for a student aspiring to positions of impact on foreign affairs those years must not be locust years but years of significant accomplishment and development. College should be a time of great friends and fun, but also years of aspiration and involvement in research and organizations on campus and off.

Accomplishments, aspirations, involvement—what can one do during the four years of a college education? Consider these three students who won prestigious scholarships. The first student at Rice University developed a research agenda on gender issues and Islam. She wrote a senior thesis on veiling Muslim women in Houston, Texas, comparing attitudes of people living in Karachi, Pakistan, with Pakistani American immigrants living in the United States. She interned at Amnesty International U.S.A., the Office of Senator Carl Levin (D-MI), the Baker Institute Energy Forum, the Middle East Institute, and spent a semester in Cairo, Egypt, pursuing coursework in Arabic language and gender studies.

Another student, a political science major at Wheaton College in Norton, Massachusetts, worked extensively with the 1000 Friends of Oregon organization to preserve natural lands by studying the impacts of urban sprawl and advocating for better land-use planning. He spent a semester in a rural Ugandan village to teach soil conservation to rural communities, but after seeing a need for better early childhood education he raised the funds and developed the village's first nursery school program. He served as student body president and led a successful effort to create student representatives on the Wheaton Board of Trustees. His honors thesis addressed ways public transit can better be used to promote environmental goals.

With summers and a study abroad program, a third student volunteered in Romanian orphanages and was inspired to investigate international trafficking in persons. She traveled around the world researching the work of nonprofits in providing victims services and plans to develop a policy to curb the illicit trade through a financial approach. She co-founded a middle-school Model United Nations program, presents economics programs to high schools, and serves in party politics. She hopes to work in diplomacy and international security.

What can a student do in four years? Quite a lot.

Christian liberal arts colleges are a bottom rung on any ladder leading to positions of impact on foreign affairs. They have no graduate programs or independent research centers in international affairs, and their value systems promote the concept of community and servant leadership. Community is an important value for uniting and sharing with others on your common quest for spiritual depth. Community is also good for the administrative goal of harmony on campus, a value to which they can appeal when wanting student acceptance of a new policy. It leaves little room for students wanting more than moderate-level goals or seeking significant change on campus—both of which are important for developing leadership skills and reaching for high post-graduate goals. Community precludes strong groups with purposes other than service or ministry and tries to moderate social and electoral competition to low and highly controlled levels. Under such circumstances, running for student body office is not a training exercise in learning the realities of politics and leadership. Students intending more for their lives and to be recognized as potential leaders must push those boundaries or break out of them, and demonstrate an ability to make change.

Christian campuses often adopt the concept of servant leadership, though the meaning varies among colleges and universities, secular and Christian. It generally means giving first priority to the needs of others as a means of building community and infusing warmth and care for others in large hierarchical organizations. Across the spectrum of Christian universities its meanings range from no more than volunteering in community organizations to an emphasis on mentoring others and to more transformational meanings of breaking down hierarchy and sharing power. Some confine it to Christian community, while others apply it to business or recognize it in public service occupations. But servanthood and service are not the same. Servanthood has its most relevance within the confines of a community lacking danger and severe disagreements. There, warmness in leadership skills brings a positive atmosphere to common efforts and purpose reflected in caring for others, and dampens the intensity of ambition and spreads the definition of success.

The model is congruent with the values of contemporary youth culture wanting group leadership and is invaluable in helping a college shape the quiet community of campus culture. The values of helping others and sensitizing students to needs they have never seen before should be promoted. Yet will that model ever prepare students for the rigors of an election campaign for any office higher than those of student government? Will the model disarm a person under serious pressure from others to change their mind in a policy issue? College years are years of identity formation, and a student needs a good sense of self before sublimating to serving others. If not, the authentic self may never become firm. The identity and authenticity are important, for Jesus said in the Farewell Sermon that what he wanted was not servants but friends who know him and therefore know about the Father (John 15:15).

Community and servant leadership are fine kingdom values, but they do not define the extent of a Christian life nor do they prepare students for the worlds they will soon enter. Christian colleges work hard to create and maintain an explicit Christian community, but that engineered community does not exist off campus, and students who lived with the blessings of a high spiritual tide on campus can often find themselves in shallow spiritual tide pools a year after graduation. If one's virtues flow from habituation in a virtuous community with few moral conflicts, what happens when students move to a corporate or political community with their own values and standard operating procedures? Habituating behavior does not create a pure heart. The individual student must develop his or her own sense of self and authenticity.

In addition, where is an emphasis on success? Is ambition a value tolerated on campus? Should career ambition and success even be tolerated on campus? A crass answer is to ask a development officer seeking endowment donations from alumni and finding how few have reached positions making such donations possible. A better answer is that "it depends." Ambition is meaningless in some majors, but meaningful for others like business and political science. Foreign affairs take place in an atmosphere of national danger and self-interest and require people who are determined to win, rise, and prevail. Those attributes need to be developed in the process of identify-formation in college as students develop their spiritual life in Christ and their sense of their own authentic self.

While ambition and success have to be restrained, servanthood is not the means. A self-centered and self-promoting approach to success is no worse a model than a meek and deferential servanthood approach to foreign policy success, and neither provides a foundation for Christians in foreign affairs. The concept of service is a more traditional Christian college ideal, and is more relevant to realities. It is also one within which one can aspire to the highest positions, develop a career roadmap, connect with possible mentors, and make the most of "updraft" opportunities. Service is also the more appropriate approach to a public career, for public service is the purpose of those involved in U.S. foreign affairs and the national interest.

In diplomacy or intelligence or politics a person with a public service mentality combined with Christian character and virtues that come from the flow of grace in one's life can be humble but with moral courage, can have moral imagination but remain linked to realities, and can deal with moral boundaries within the interplay of conflicting contenders, even those exhibiting fury. A public service mentality means one serves the public, but one is not a servant either to the public or to leaders when they insist on shortsighted policies. Resistance, lobbying, or resignation are more plausible options for professionals than servants. The distinctions between servanthood and service are important. Leadership and ethics are more relevant to service than to servants, as are individuality and creativity. Servanthood would seem to have little use for breadth and depth in personal development, but pursuit of excellence in service to the nation in a world of diverse cultures and determined enemies needs the very best foundation of personal development.

Do not let the college years be the years the locusts have eaten.

THE RHODES IDEAL

There is an ethic of personal seriousness, to be our best and do our best. It may be helpful to have an ideal type to shape ideas of what one could and perhaps should become as a person to reach for the highest opportunities. The Cecil Rhodes Scholarship at Oxford University is the most prestigious and most arduous of the elite scholarships. Thirty-two students from the United States and ninety students from around the world are selected to be Rhodes Scholars and given two to three years of support for study at Oxford University. The purpose of the scholarship is not to support research but to support the emergence of future leaders. As such, the Rhodes is a key that opens doors to high circles of society. George Stephanopoulos, a 1982 Rhodes Scholar, wrote that "the Rhodes is a passport to the Establishment. While it may not assure success, it guarantees opportunities to interview for great jobs."[1]

The type of person selected by the Rhodes is a fine model to adopt. The scholarship has four criteria: scholarship, athletics, leadership, and the care and protection of the weak. Athletics is no longer identified with sports but in terms of personal vigor and the energy to participate in the Oxford experience (and to survive the Rhodes crunch week of interviews and cocktail parties) and there are no priorities among the four criteria.

What do these mean in practical terms for an aspiring applicant? First, scholarship must be outstanding but more than depth in a narrow research topic. Rhodes/Oxford is for people who not only have the best projects but who also understand how their project relates to the highest levels of discourse in their field, and where they integrate that project with the tough burning issues of public affairs, understood both philosophically and practically. That is valuable educational achievement.

Second, a Rhodes person is passionate about something in their field, or is not detached and neutral. This type of person must care deeply about a subject and what it means for the larger issues of society, and the person must have the moral force of character to be a leader in fighting for the right.

Social confidence and grace are required. Again, the Rhodes is not about the best project but about people, future leaders, persons who are engaging in informal settings with persons of high caliber. Students need to be comfortable at those levels and be able to explain their project in understandable terms in conversation. Grace is the opposite of presumptive arrogance and schmoozing. Think of it—being a person smart enough and humble enough to be confident and graceful, and to be an authen-

---

1. Stephanopoulos, *All Too Human*, 19.

tic person aiming to have an impact on the greater good of humankind. These qualities ought to define students at Christian colleges and universities. Recently students from St. Olaf College and Augsburg College received Rhodes Scholarships.

The breadth of the Rhodes ideal makes it valuable for absorbing the art and science, hope and fear in the four perspectives of chapter 1. It is a very good model for being the kind of person who would make a good member of Congress or a great diplomat and later a career policy maker. But is it a model for Christians? Not for those with a prepackaged set of absolutes that must be protected, or who believe Christians should be meek and humble, renouncing self-improvement and achievement. As argued in chapter 1, there is no single truth about the nature of international politics, so we rely on theoretical models that seem to most persuasively describe and explain the multiple perspectives of international politics and foreign policy and give guidance to scholars and practitioners. Likewise there is no single theology that captures the full range of God and humanity. Rather than asserting a few foundational assumptions or concepts that are then used to construct a tight theological architecture to answer any and all issues, chapter 2 developed a theological model to explain and guide. Given that, there is no final theory or theology, no final Great Answer to these issues. Hence, it is the role of Christians to seek their best understandings in depth and breadth, which these scholarships promote. How does intellectualism glorify God? It does so by ever-richer understandings of the Trinity, the cosmos, the social world, and the values to be promoted in their interconnections.

If you want to go beyond the typical university culture and graduate school, if you want to enter this world of the elite, then start focusing on it now. If you are not that four-sided person yet, then consciously begin to reinvent yourself by developing those traits that will lead you to the most advantageous opportunities for making a difference at the highest level.

TO REINVENT YOURSELF

University students have their own internal time clocks. Some come to campus as serious and goal-oriented students, and some do not reach that point until their junior and senior years. If you are ready to start now to become more like the ideal, here are five suggestions.

First, get yourself together. Think deeply about who you are as a person and a Christian, what you care about (as evidenced by . . .) and what you want to do in foreign affairs. Many students do not have answers to those questions. They see their futures with an optimistic glow but in terms that are not significantly different than their present world. Others put off serious thought about their future while they enjoy "college life." Get serious about yourself. Your university years at a liberal arts institution constitute a key time of reflection. Spend time with yourself, finding your deepest cares and foundational assumptions.

Second, do not think of the college years as a self-contained period. Your college years and your career years should flow together. Bring what you want to be into your college years and use these years as preparation for a career. Make a time chart that works backward. Start at the end point, such as admission to a prestigious graduate school or getting a select political job or winning a distinguished scholarship, and then work backwards in time to identify what needs to be done and when. A Truman Scholarship has to be won during the junior year, so all the steps toward a successful application have to be done in the freshmen and sophomore years. Become aware of opportunities for presenting papers at conferences, finding depth in a topic but also noting how that topic relates to broader issues.

Develop your own research agenda—this is crucial for bringing a unity to your college years and impressing graduate school admission committees. Find a cause, a concern, an idea that is compelling to you, and stay with it through all your research projects. Explore it; develop it; refine it; relate it. Make it the tie that binds the classes and the four years together and gives them meaning.

Third, choose friends well. One of the most important factors in academic success is your circle of friends. Choose likeminded and supportive friends. Get into an honors program of some kind that allows you to see your subject in the widest philosophical and social terms. Get to know well one faculty person a semester, and have them get to know you. Find out what they care about, what they are working on, and why they are "here" instead of "there." Learning about them should lead to them getting to know you as a person. This is crucial, for it is fundamental, fundamental, fundamental (yes, three times for emphasis) for them to be able to write a winning recommendation letter for graduate school or a distinguished scholarship.

Fourth, recognize that your grade point average is your most important asset in college, an asset to be built and protected. Universities are intellectual institutions. Reviewers will want to see that you have made full use of your academic opportunities here before they invest in you for further academic study elsewhere. So, you must either be, or be prepared to make yourself, academically competitive. At the same time you must build a context for it. Outside the scholarly campus the issues of foreign affairs are personal, and developing social skills needs to continue in these years. Deepen your understanding of theological issues by taking upper division religion or theology and philosophy classes, and learn to write creatively. You may take such classes without jeopardizing your grade point average if the university has a pass-fail option for classes outside a major or the general education curriculum.

Careers in foreign affairs are not bureaucratic office jobs; they require creativity, the ability to mobilize other people in a topic, and team leadership, so learn to be what the Truman Scholarship program calls "change agents." Neither talking nor writing about an issue is enough; demonstrate leadership in an area of your cause or concern. Create something new that has an impact, even something that is controversial in the sense of calling into question an existing campus policy or program. Joining is not leadership and neither is just presiding for a year; doing something new and getting others to join you is leadership. Finally, follow the news—science and the arts as well as political events. Be well rounded at a high level.

Fifth, do not say, "I can't." There are three categories of excuses that are often spoken and that must be resisted. Do not say, "My parents were only . . . , so I can't." Raise your sights and move beyond them. Do not say, "I don't have time." Priorities and time management are important skills and when mastered leave time for all you need to do. An interviewer may ask what television programs are your favorites. Do not have too many. A third negative to avoid is to say, "It's too late." If you blew off your freshman year and your grade point average suffered, move beyond it. Make up for it. Some of the scholarships and some of the jobs do not have academics at their highest level—but be aware that they will note academics and what that implies.

There are two common protests to all of this. College years are for fun; your social life is just as important as your academic life. Fit in and be cool; experience all the facets of college life. That is the right path for many students who want a fun and normal life, not too much exertion, and a nice "comfort zone" of similar friends. The second protest is that college is for exploring, so don't tie yourself down too early. Both are true, but to a minor extent. Fun is very important in college, but it is not equal in priority to grades. Enjoy college, participate in sports or musical groups, go skiing or hiking or white water rafting. You need the release of time, energy, and focus, but fit it in to your academic priorities. Explore and change your mind about careers, just do not avoid making a decision. Time passes and so do opportunities.

GENDER ISSUES

Women should be full participants in developing attributes of the Rhodes ideal and in seeking careers of impact. The fact that three of the last four Secretaries of State have been women should be symbolic of the fact that women can and should find career roles in foreign affairs and national security. Women are finding places in practice but seem to be missing in the world of scholarship.

In the congressional world there has been a significant change in the participation of women in the professional staff of the four main committees. In 2006 the Senate Armed Services Committee had 18 women out of 45 staff members, while the Senate Foreign Relations Committee had 16 out of 45. In 2008 that percentage dropped as the numbers changed to 2 out of 50 and 4 out of 25. In the House the numbers also changed between 2006 and 2008. In the Armed Services Committee the number dropped from 26 women out of 65 staffers to 12 out of 62, and the House International Relations Committee dropped from 12 out of 35 in 2006 to 8 out of 50.

Women have become increasingly involved in the Foreign Service. In 2003, 34 percent of Foreign Service Officers were women, though only 25 percent were in the senior service. The Clinton administration appointed 116 women to senior posts in eight years, and George W. Bush appointed 69 in his first four years. Still, of the 175 Chiefs of Mission posts, only 27 were women. Since 1975, 6 women have served as Assistant Secretary of State for regional bureaus and 45 in functional bureaus, and 8 have served as Undersecretaries of State.[2]

The world of scholarship shows the greatest gender discrepancy as reflected in this select list of book and authors.

---

2. Wright, "Breaking through Diplomacy's Glass Ceiling."

American Defense Policy has been a central text on security studies, with changing authors and articles over the years. In its first edition in 1965 there were no women authors. In the current eighth edition there are 4 chapters by women writers.

The Use of Force, with Robert Art and Kenneth Waltz as editors, is a standard text of readings. It was first published in 1983 and had 1 woman writer, Roberta Wohlstetter, who coauthored a chapter with her husband. The sixth edition has just been released, and only 1 chapter out of 32 chapters is by a woman.

Beginning in 1979 a series of Eagle books have been published: *Eagle Entangled, Eagle Defiant, Eagle Resurgent,* and *Eagle Rules*. In the 1979 book there was 1 woman writer who coauthored with her husband. In 1983 there were two female coauthors. In 2002 there are 2 female authors out of 16 chapters.

Handbook of War Studies II, edited by Manus Midlarsky, represents the second generation of empirical studies of war, with only two of thirteen chapters by women.

Avoiding War: Problems of Crisis Management, edited by Alexander George, is a 1991 book of readings with only 1 of 22 chapters written by a woman.

Transforming U.S. Intelligence, edited by Jennifer E. Sims and Burton Gerber, has fifteen chapters with 4 women authors or coauthors.

Strategic Intelligence, edited by Loch K. Johnson and James J. Wirtz, has 39 authors and coauthors, none of whom are women.

Ethics of Spying, A Reader for the Intelligence Professional, edited by Jan Gloldman, has 23 authors, among whom 3 are women.

Turbulent Peace, published by the U.S. Institute of Peace with Chester A. Crocker, Fen Osler Hampson, and Pamela Lall as editors, has 49 chapters, only 8 of which are authored by women.

Gasping the Nettle, Analyzing Cases of Intractable Conflict, the latest of the U.S. Institute of Peace books on peacemaking with Chester A. Crocker, Fen Osler Hampson, and Pamela Lall as editors, has 16 chapters with 4 female authors or coauthors.

A fine foreign policy book with a woman coeditor is *Good Judgment in Foreign Policy*. Stanley Renshon and Deborah Welch Larson are the editors, and Larson has 3 chapters and another woman has 1 chapter.

There are three premier journals in the field: *Foreign Affairs*, the more establishment oriented, had 43 articles in 2005, with 6 women authors, and 39 articles in 2008, with 4 women authors or coauthors. *Foreign Policy* is a more popularized publication and had 63 articles, with 13 female authors and coauthors in 2005, and in 2008 had 13 women authors or coauthors out of 53. In 2004 *International Security*, the most scholarly of the three, had 30 articles with 6 women authors and coauthors, and in 2009 had 4 women authors among 22 articles.

The country needs the presence, energy, creativity, and values of women in all areas of foreign affairs. There will be little place in official circles for those women who believe men are congenitally defective, that the world needs to be reconstructed on vastly alternative values, and the function of committees is not to reach decisions but to make all members feel empowered. On the other hand, women do not need to try to prove they are tougher than men. Like men they need to understand the essential reality of foreign affairs and the margins of opportunity to move policy toward the twin goals of national security and international cooperation. The corridors of power need the talents and wisdom and the formidable yet nurturing values of women as individuals and as females; young women need to raise their sights and goals beyond nongovernmental organizations and bring their advantages to the rationality of policy and the art of politics.

Young women should be aware and involved in organizations specifically for their gender. One is WIIS—Women in International Security, a network of women in all areas of security policy that encourages and facilitates women in the multiple disciplines and topics as they intersect with security issues.[3] Women are also involved in the corporate world of defense, from women-owned defense-related firms to scientists and program managers in large defense industries. Women in Defense is an organization that cultivates and supports the advancement and recognition of women in all aspects of national security.[4]

EXAMPLE

The absence of women in security scholarship can be overcome. An example is Jennifer Sims, currently Director of Intelligence Studies in the Center for Peace and Security Studies at Georgetown University. While growing up, Jennifer's mother was the mayor of Greenwich, Connecticut.

---

3. See http://wiis.georgetown.edu.
4. See http://wid.ndia.org.

Her election was a big upset for the mayoral race and for the Democratic Party, but when party activists came to her on election night and suggested a march to City Hall, her mother said, while amidst balloons and applause, "No, that would not be the gracious thing to do." Then she turned to Jennifer and said, "Remember this, Jennifer, always with grace."

Sims received her BA at Oberlin College and her MA and PhD at Johns Hopkins University, School of Advanced International Studies (SAIS). She served as the U.S. Coordinator of the Nuclear History Program (1988–1990), became a legislative aide to Senator John Danforth, and then a staff member on the Senate Select Committee on Intelligence (1991–1994). In 1994 she was appointed Deputy Assistant Secretary of State for Intelligence Coordination and then Intelligence Advisor to the Under Secretary of State for Management and Coordination for Intelligence Resources and Planning at the State Department (1998–2001). After the election in 2000 she taught as a Research Professor at SAIS (2001–2003) and then moved to Georgetown University.

For Sims the most important thing when dealing with the world of intelligence and its secrecy and action is integrity. There were times when the pressure to "change my position was extraordinary," she said, and one can bend and go with the flow, or hold your own with grace in the face of fury. Grace in the face of fury. Whether "you can do it a second time is equally important as to whether you can do it the first time." She made her reputation as she staked out her positions and has continued to expand her reputation with books on intelligence theory and reform, technology and arms control, and currently in counterterrorism and the use of advanced technology to intelligence missions.[5]

INTERNSHIPS

Any student planning a career in foreign affairs must again reach beyond the campus and bring that career into the college years with an internship. Internships are the first open door to political careers, and it would be valuable to have two internships, one during the sophomore year at a public office and a second or summer internship in a professional location like the Department of State or the Central Intelligence Agency. There are

---

5. This material is taken from the faculty directory of Georgetown University and an interview with Harry Kreisler as part of the "Conversations with History" at the Institute of International Studies, University of California, Berkeley. See globetrotter.berkeley.edu/people2/Sims/sims-con1.html.

also career internships with agencies that include funding for tuition and a guaranteed placement after graduation.

The Political Internship. Internships in the office of a state legislature or member of Congress provide an inside look at a public career and sensitize you to how political offices work—the demands, dilemmas, and decency of political leadership. Legislatures fund all programs, and that knowledge of the legislator's world will be important at later interviews and foreign policy careers. Moreover, internships offer introductions to people who can be contacts and influentials later in your career. When it is over, stay in touch and keep yourself available.

Before going to the interview, research the organization so you know about it and where you might fit in, and think about what you could provide for them. Make sure you have attire appropriate for a professional office, and dress like a professional for the interview.

Be prepared. If they are looking for someone to do specific tasks, be sure you know something about those tasks. If you are applying for an internship in a city council office, be sure you know such basic facts as the boundaries and demographics of the council district, the names of the council committees and on which committee the member sits, and a couple issues facing the city. I once had a student interviewing for an internship in the mayor's office, and a person came into the room (the mayor) and the student did not stand up to greet him—she didn't know who he was. Don't be that unaware. If you are interviewing at a campaign management firm, know the kinds of candidates the firm works for and the specialties that firm provides a candidate. If you are interviewing for an unadvertised internship because someone has set it up for you, keep the interviewer's perspective in mind—what can you do for them?

Finally, loyalty. These internships are not like a job at a retail store or local restaurant. Whether you want to or not, you represent the office you work for 24/7, and that will be assumed. You have to be loyal to the reputation of the office and the people in it.

The Professional Internship. There are internships in several foreign affairs agencies, including the State Department and CIA. State has a summer internship program, and students can choose to work in Washington, DC, or overseas at a U.S. embassy. Interns at both State and CIA will research, analyze, write, and brief others on their findings.

Once you get such an internship you will enter the professional world. Be on time and dress for that world. You may still be a student, but do not bring the campus culture with you. Even better advice is to dress for the job you aspire to land. Offices will vary in their casualness, but don't ever under-dress. They will also vary in personality types—from laid back and friendly to "snooty girls and Napoleon-complex guys."[6] Learn how to move in that world.

Always ask for more work to do; don't ever be without something to do. If your task is completed, look for something else to do. Ask to learn something new about the office. If there is an office policy of not assigning work to interns which is normally done by paid workers to avoid taking advantage of interns, suggest your willingness to do so since it would be for "educational purposes" only, and you want to learn as much as possible.

Make a buddy or mentor. Find someone you can trust. Develop an informal relationship with that person to get his or her perspective on office policy and politics, but also advice on what it takes to be successful as a political staffer. Ask the person to remain in contact after the internship, to talk once in a while and to let you know when your or other offices have an opening. Also important, an internship during the year does not cost you much. A summer internship in Washington, DC, will involve housing and living expenses. Success in a legislator's or congressional member's office could lead the office holder or the chief-of-staff to contact one of their major donors about investing in a top quality up-and-coming student by helping with your summer internship expenses.

The Career Internship. There are special programs to attract and support high quality students. The intelligence agencies have special college programs that lead to careers. The Central Intelligence Agency offers summer internships, and students who interned at the agency the previous summer are eligible to apply for the Pat Roberts Intelligence Scholars Program, a semester and summer combination with a stipend of up to $25,000 a year for the senior year. The CIA has an Undergraduate Scholar Program, and the Defense Intelligence Agency has a similar program called UTAP—Undergraduate Training Assistance Program. Students who are accepted are given $18,000 tuition assistance, intern at the headquarters for two summers, and then move into a career position.

These internships require security clearances, which can take many months. Once you get notification, make up a business card with your name, contact information, Student Intern and State Department (not the

---

6. Rothstein, "Intern Flops," 39.

CIA). Give those out as you meet people during the summer, or, if you can afford it, wait until you are there and add the office you are assigned to and your office e-mail. A security clearance is becoming so important in the career world in foreign affairs that the ability to get such a clearance while a student will greatly aid and speed up your job search after graduation.

Depending on the year and the office, you will find morale high or low. The arrival of a young person full of enthusiasm helps an office. Remember that you are not brought in by that office but by a central personnel office, and that specific department may or may not even know you are coming. If not, it may take several days before they have developed a task for you. Ask for work, but don't be a pest. They will be tied up for endless hours in committee meetings, so in the down time and for the rest of the summer, meet people.

Since FSOs are reassigned every three or four years, you will see people come and go, perhaps even your supervisor. Meet as many people as you can, taking their business cards, knowing the title will shift every couple years but not their State Department e-mail address, and give out yours.

Two more tips: Write thank you notes or letters, even to the security office who did the interviews of your friends and faculty. Also remember, people love food, and bringing snacks every once in a while will make you a favorite person of the day.

The Presidential Management Fellowship program is for those who hold a master's degree. The program is a two-year fully paid internship designed to fast-track an annual cohort of young professionals into management positions in government agencies. They enter the program as a level 9 and are promoted to a 12 in two years. Then a career fair is held for them to apply to specific agencies. There are no guarantees, and top agencies privilege elite institutions, but fellows who have finished a well-done internship can find that the department they served will make a position for them. This is an incredibly valuable internship that is relatively unknown to the vast majority of graduate students.

DISTINGUISHED SCHOLARSHIPS

Distinguished scholarship are a prize for your reputation. More than that, they are an entrance into higher circles of theory and practice, an important networking opportunity with other future leaders, and an important edge in securing a valuable placement when a career begins. There are elite scholarships that will support a student planning a career in foreign affairs, including the Rhodes, the British Marshall, and the George Mitchell scholarships. There are difficult but distinguished scholarships one step down, including the Harry Truman, the David Boren, the William Fulbright, and the Thomas Pickering scholarships. Generally there are three factors at play in the selection process. Candidates need to demonstrate high scholarship, evidence of leadership, and commitment to the larger issues of society; different scholarships have different priorities among the three. The scholarship awards for study overseas are growth opportunities, and the application process itself is the chance to grow and dream and discover one's best self.

These scholarships reflect the highest in liberal arts-educated persons. Liberal arts help students rise above their time and place, see issues from various viewpoints, and become persons who are more comfortable with both/and rather than either/or thinking. Liberal arts promote personal moral reflection and humane social values, and these scholarships seek persons who have a personal vision of what they want to do to improve society. In the words of the Truman Foundation, successful applicants are people who want to make a difference, not a dollar. Liberally educated students are able to integrate or synthesize the fields of life, and in the process develop their own personal creativity. Students who win these scholarships see beyond their specialized fields.

Under the pressures of education for all, institutionalized in large organizations built around academic specialization and "turf," students are rarely called upon to integrate their multiple classes and specialized fields with their own personal selves. The preparation of applications, particularly the personal statements for these scholarships, is the one time this integration will happen in your college experience. Win or lose, this exercise in itself is more than worth the effort.

The Rhodes Scholarship. The Cecil Rhodes Scholarship at Oxford University is the most prestigious and most arduous of the elite scholarships. A Rhodes Scholar can pursue either a second undergraduate degree or graduate degree. As explained above, its four criteria are scholarship, athletics, leadership, and the care and protection of the weak, adding athletics to the normal three. For the Rhodes, there are no priorities among the four.

Applications go first to a selection committee in each state where the reader wants to see what motivates and inspires you, what you know about the field and where it is going, and what you want to do with your life. Each state can forward two applicants to one of the eight districts, and four students are chosen from each district. The interviewers want to be sure you will be comfortable at those levels and be able to explain your project in understandable terms in conversation. To that end there are cocktail parties at the state and regional level of interviews.

As part of that motivation the applicants must have a higher ambition than the prestige of having Oxford on their résumé. The applicant must show how the project fits at Oxford, that is, why Oxford and not Harvard or Johns Hopkins. More than a good answer to that question, an applicant also needs to show how he or she will contribute to, as well as be affected by, Oxford, Europe, and the invisible college of scholarship.

Are you a potential candidate? Are you at the top of your class academically? If so, and you are reading this book because you care about contributing to improving the humane nature of the world, then go for it. Be prepared to focus on it from now on—and use the goal to broaden and deepen your college years. Take honors classes, study abroad, and do a senior research project.

The Marshall Scholarship. The George G. Marshall Scholarship was established by the government of England in appreciation for the Marshall Plan and its humane ideals. It funds student study for two years at any British university. This scholarship is usually used at Cambridge, but can be used at any British university. All that is relevant to applying for the Rhodes could be repeated here. It is next to the Rhodes in prestige and rigor of application, so all that is true of applying for the Rhodes applies equally to the Marshall.

The Mitchell Scholarship. The George J. Mitchell Scholarship was established by the government of Ireland in honor of the work of George Mitchell in bringing an agreement on peace to Northern Ireland. The scholarship funds one year of post-baccalaureate research or study in the Republic of Ireland or Northern Ireland. Students from any field may apply, but it is certainly relevant to a student interested in foreign policy and peacemaking. Its priorities are scholarship and leadership, and a student is expected to have an impressive record of prizes, scholarships, offices held, extracurricular activities and the like. Only twelve Mitchell Scholarships are awarded each year.

The Mitchell conducts its interviews on the same day as the Marshall, forcing students to decide between them.

The Rhodes, Marshall, and Mitchell are the most elite of the non-science scholarships. The next four represent a second tier of scholarships, competitive but doable for students preparing correctly, and more relevant to a career in foreign affairs.

The Truman Scholarship. The Harry S. Truman Scholarship was established by the Congress of the United States to honor the former president and to support students who intend a career in public affairs. It provides $2,000 for the student's senior year and $24,000 for graduate study.

The Truman Foundation is looking for public leadership. For example, a key phrase is "change agent." This scholarship wants to support those who, by evidence of what they have done in college, will likely improve the way public entities serve the public—demonstrated evidence, not potential. What do they mean by "change agent"? Someone who will mess up the system and make it better. As conservative and tightly controlled as some private colleges and universities are, the opportunities to mess up the system in order to make it better might well be minimal. If so, go off campus. Serve the larger public.

What do the reviewers look for? Answer this question: "What ticks you off?" Something should, and this scholarship is about public service, about your public mission. Public service is hard, so the interviewers want to assess if your heart and compassion are deep enough to sustain commitment to your mission.

Second, they look for leadership. To be a leader means the applicant has worked on a significant problem. Participation on a team project is not leadership. The applicant must have done something defined and unique, achieved a specific outcome, and gained the participation of others to follow him or her. This is not a world in which "everyone is a winner." This is not a "be a part of the team" world. In this world there is a significant problem, a leader and persuaded followers, and a distinct outcome.

The Truman is not grade-driven. Its two priorities are leadership and service, so question 15, the personal background question, is key, more key than the policy statement. The readers want to see recognition of the ethical dimension of learning, that is, using higher education for the common good. Education is not an end in itself. The scholarship seeks to help winners broaden their ability to improve life by reaching higher levels of government. Leadership is more important than specialization;

to that end, the graduate program should broaden a student's education, not narrow it.

The scholarship has a service requirement. Congress funds this scholarship to promote public service and wants a return on that investment in the form of working in public service for three of the seven years following completion of a graduate program. Among its priority fields is international affairs.

The quality of students who reach the interview stage is reflected in the fact that they receive solicitation letters from major graduate programs. One hundred scholarships are awarded each year.

The Boren Scholarship. The David Boren Scholarship is also known as National Security Education Program scholarship. It was named in honor of former Senator David Boren by the U.S. Congress to fund students who will study the language and culture of countries of particular interest to U.S. foreign policy.

It is wise to consider locations other than Beijing, Cairo, and Moscow, for those are the three most frequently sought areas of study. Africa, Eastern Europe, and South Asia would draw higher interest from the reviewers.

The foundation prefers a one-year program to insure there is depth to the knowledge gained. Applicants should be able to describe what they have done already to prepare for the experience, what they intend to do abroad to expand their cultural understanding, and how they plan to use this knowledge and experience when they return to school.

The scholarship comes with a service requirement. Upon return or graduation, each fellow must apply for a job at the Department of State, the Central Intelligence Agency, the Department of Defense, or the Department of Homeland Security. If a job is not offered within one year, the obligation is ended. The requirement is only one year, and fellows are given preference in applications and on the Foreign Service Exam. Close to 150 scholarships are awarded each year.

The Pickering Fellowship. The Thomas R. Pickering Undergraduate Foreign Affairs Fellowship is the Department of State's scholarship program, although it is administered by the Woodrow Wilson National Fellowship Foundation (WWNFF). The Department of State seeks a Foreign Service that represents America in world affairs with citizens who reflect the diversity and excellence of our society. The program seeks to recruit talented students in academic programs relevant to international affairs, political and economic analysis, administration, management, and science policy. The goal is to attract outstanding students from all ethnic, racial, and social backgrounds who have an interest in pursuing a Foreign Service career in the U.S. Department of State.

The fellowship program is more than just a one-year scholarship. It funds a junior-year summer institute in international affairs and a two-year master's degree, and one paid internship at the Department of State and another at an overseas embassy. It also funds tuition and fees, board and room, books for the junior and senior years of college and the first year of graduate school. In return there is a service requirement of four and a half years in the Foreign Service.

The Fulbright Scholarship. The William J. Fulbright Scholarship was established by Congress to promote international understanding. There are two programs. One is for recent BA/MA graduates and graduate students who want to conduct a research project overseas. Students interested in this program must have a research project defined and a professor at a university in the country in which they wish to study who has agreed to supervise the project. The scholarship funds 1,500 projects a year of study and living abroad. The criteria are (1) feasibility of the proposed project, (2) academic record, (3) language preparation, and (4) personal qualifications. There is a fifth, which is that you need to have established contact with a sponsoring agency (university) and with someone who will supervise your project. That is not the same as being enrolled at that university.

Even better, if the research project involves a language of critical importance to U.S. foreign policy, a Critical Language Enhancement Award can be added to the regular Fulbright Grant. A second Fulbright Scholarship is the English Teaching Assistantship. Grantees will be awarded funds for transportation and living while teaching English in other countries. These two Fulbright grants provide a wonderful opportunity to study overseas and experience the globalizing world.

PERSONAL STATEMENTS

Personal statements are the secret code for admission into the competitive ranks of applicants for national scholarships. The reviewer must see the "real" person behind the application, the commitments and values that drive the applicant and the application and the breadth of understanding of the project's value, in order to judge the quality of the investment the applicant is requesting.

Keep in mind three principles: First, the statement should help reviewers know who you are. The first sentence tells them one thing right off—do you know how to capture their attention or are you another nondescript applicant? The most common fault of statements is that no one has proofread them. Almost two-thirds are mediocre. The personal statement is crucial and must be of excellent quality. That means many, many, many rewrites. The essay should present you as a person who engages the reviewer and makes him or her interested in what you have to say. The essay cannot be boring or sound self-absorbed. Do this in the context of the particular interests of the specific fellowship.

A personal statement is not a résumé in narrative form. Don't tell all you have done; that is found elsewhere in the application. The statement is also not an opportunity to "make your case" of why you should be awarded the fellowship.

What then is a personal statement? As described by Mary Hale Tolar, formerly with the Truman Scholarship Foundation, it is the selection committee's first impression of you, and it determines whether the committee finds you interesting enough to invite to an interview. Tolar suggests dealing with four questions about yourself: Who am I? What do I care about? What contribution can I make in this world? How can I get there?[7]

Those are four potent questions; they get to the core of your most basic values and goals. Writing about yourself in terms of those four questions gives a committee a clear impression of you. In understanding those four questions, scholarships advisor Cheryl Foster suggests you think about questions such as the following:

> What errors or regrets have taught you something about yourself? When were you so absorbed in something that time seemed to stand still? What ideas or books made a profound impact on you? How much are you a typical product of your generation, and where do you deviate from it?[8]

Second, the key to the statement is demonstrating continuity from your high school years through your college years to your career goal. A national scholarship is both rare and prestigious, and its officials are not interested in funding a "study abroad" experience for students. They want to invest in a serious student who will make a long-term pay-off to

---

7. Foster, and Tolar, "National Scholarship Competition," 4.
8. Foster, *From a Faculty Representative*.

society. They want to see how you understand what you were and what you are and how that connects to what you will be. To get at this, have someone keep asking you "why" as you tell them about yourself.

Here is an example: I want to go into the Foreign Service. Why? I want to do something good in the world. Why? It's important to help people. Why? That's what I believe. Why? At that question one begins to get a clear sense of who you are and the foundational assumptions of your life.

Do not stop there. Look back at what might have happened in your high school years. Did you have a protagonist or experience injustice or tragedy? Did a summer job suddenly appear meaningless to you, or did you hear a speaker and have an "epiphany?" What was the impact of 9/11 on you, or the failure of mathematical models to predict Hurricane Katrina? Did something like that make a decisive impact on your thinking about your future, or at least make you begin to think seriously about committing your life to something significant? Find that line which can then be drawn from there to what major and courses you are now taking, what clubs you belong to, what volunteer work you do, and from there to your career goals.

Such pre-college connections must be found to give credence to a career interest. This does not mean that you have to show how you decided in high school to be a diplomat or literature professor or a leading medical researcher. Rather, the connections show your foundational beliefs and values; they give assurance to reviewers of your commitment and dedication, and show your professed goals and career interests are really who you are as a person.

The third key to the personal statement is to know with some precision the job you intend to go after and where (professional grade level or geographic location) you expect to be in five or seven years. For example, Foreign Service Officers have no choice in the first two of their three-year assignments, but you should know what you will want to choose for your third assignment. When you can demonstrate that you know the inside of that position, the ladder and benchmarks of the career, then the reviewer will know you are serious enough to have thought about a career rather than a dream or a "job." Do your homework—get to know the assignment you want.

Given the depth of the task, start early and rewrite, rewrite, rewrite. A winning personal statement for a Rhodes Scholarship takes at least twenty rewrites; the application needs that depth. Write simply, have perfect spelling and grammar, and make it engaging and easy to read.

Religious Beliefs. What about being from a religious institution; should you include your religious beliefs in your proposal? It has to be handled well. Some advisors recommend students avoid dealing with religious issues. Others recommend dealing with your faith if you take deep meaning from it, and if you do, do so only under two circumstances. First, discuss it with the same level of rigor and depth of thought as the rest of the application; do not be superficial. These are academic scholarships, and religious faith is not exempt from scholarly understanding. Second, do not take strong positions on issues or appear closed-minded. If you include it in your statement, and make it to the interview stage, it will be fair game for the interviewers. If your faith is meaningful to you and your goals, *and* you have struggled with understanding it and can discuss it with sophistication, include it as a feature of who you are and what motivates you.

MATTHEW, THE PRODIGAL, AND THE PREACHER

How can a Christian feel comfortable with a system of inequality that not only rewards the talented but provides them an accumulation of advantages whereby one scholarship leads to another and to other forms of support in building a career? That is "the Matthew Effect" (Matt 13:13).[9] Should merit be privileged over equity on a campus committed to Christian community and servant leadership? Perhaps it is not inconsistent with the principles of calling and gifts (Eph 4:1–13). Still, the answer may reflect basic religious traditions. The intellectual is important for those traditions emphasizing doctrine and the need for an alternative Christian worldview, but suspect for experience and revivalist-based traditions. The alternative community tradition represented by Stanley Hauerwas dismisses the individual developing their own intellectual outlook, arguing that "most students in our society do not have the minds well enough trained to be able to think," so the church must train them "through submission to authority that will, if done well, provide people with the virtues necessary to be able to make reasoned judgments."[10] That is an orientation of fear, with consequent suspicion, division, and intellectual imposition. That is not developing the mind of God and finding peace with God and self.

9. Merton, "The Matthew Effect in Science," 56–63.
10. Hauerwas, *After Christendom?* 99.

A better orientation is that of hope, for university students have a gift of the mind, and some the gift of a strong mind. Coupling those gifts with the gift of grace and a stage 5 maturity will never lead to a universal agreement on the "great answers" for applied ethics. But that coupling does mean students can reach for their most creative and passionate selves. The dynamics of God's continuing creation, the dynamics of grace and the dynamics of international politics means we use our mind to recognize the totality of experience and bring together the reality of facts, values, and action. Efforts to define the Christian mind and box it into a tight intellectual package have been useful and instructive but always partial, as various Christians have found their applied ethics in pacifism, or realism, or idealism, or liberal justice, or conservative justice, and the list can go on. The intersecting dynamics of mind, grace, and history empower mature Christians to develop new insights, to commit themselves to a cause, and to become artful in their efforts to impact the ideas, policies, and consequences of U.S. foreign policy. The world needs the minds of Christians.

Some Christians have great intellectual power and can seek and reach these scholarships. Injustice would seem to reside in not using that power for a greater good. If you can be special, who are you cheating if you aim for less? The answer is not singular; not God alone, but also yourself and those aspects of foreign affairs that could be impacted by the benefit of your insights and creativity. The soul and the mind are characteristics of humans, and one ought to seek their highest and best through growth in grace and growth in intellect. The Rhodes ideal is not about bureaucratic or technical knowledge but about breadth and service. There are new insights, new theories, new approaches as events change conditions. To seek growth in grace and intellect, in breadth and in service, and in the interplay of art, science, hope, fear, freedom, and fate are fitting and worthy goals of Christians.

Having come this far have we wandered with the prodigal son into the far country? From a deontological or "Christian worldview" point of view, the perspectives of these chapters may seem like we have wandered into a far country and begun cavorting with harlots. Let's change the image from harlots to enemies and dangers. Dealing with them is not prostitution, for while clean hands and a pure heart may be achievable in a cloistered world, our world is much more turbulent, risky, uncertain, and shadowed. A Christian embraced by grace, empowered with education, and committed to doing good in the world can find traction for personal choices when ethical issues arise in complex situations regarding ethical principles, the dark, and shadows.

Why should Christians enter this far country? We have discussed "diplomacy in the dark," the "dark side," and the "dark future." We need the moral imagination and the moral courage of Christian young people embraced by grace to engage this darkness and help insure light emerges. The priesthood of all believers means we can live "in Christ" and face decisions when all choices stab the conscience, confident in the real, active, and personal leadership of the Counselor in face of the decisions to step over or step back. If there is silence, we move with moral courage either ahead or not, based on the gift of the mind, the art and craft of our career, our understanding of the probabilities inherent in the situation, our definition of public service, and our personal definition of the moral boundaries. While in the background may be fear for the future of the country, the foreground is our personal life based in hope of God's good graciousness to his friends.

To be a university student with opportunities for excellent education and national scholarships is a great privilege, one not available to many other young people in other regions of the world. To use that privilege for building wealth or fame or church congregations is fine, yet using it in service to a country that makes such opportunities possible is commendable and important and does not make the Matthew Effect unjust.

Again, why should Christians enter this world, this far country? They are needed! It is easy to pray for peace from pulpits and shrines, as if God in response will came down and stand between warring factions and allow us to watch from afar with clean hands and self-satisfaction. It is easier to find purity in ethical principles when looking down from moral heights than for a person facing complex choices with major high consequences. It is easy to devise essays of what better policy should be pursued from the confines of a campus, but policies only gain traction in the world through the politics of people making decisions within the context of the pressures and constructs of allies and adversaries. It is easy from the comforts of our prosperous and technological society to decry the self-interest of the nation as if the conditions of our lives are natural and need neither thought nor protection. We need more than that. We need an aroused generation of young people who will find service and satisfaction through engagement with the challenges and opportunities of American foreign affairs.

Beyond that, this generation of young people is a unique generation. For the first time in nearly sixty years they are present at the dawning of a creation, that is, the Cold War world is gone, and a new world is in the process of creation. For the first time since the late 1940s a generation of foreign affairs leaders will help shape a new world order by the quality of their ideas and strategies, the quality of their implementing operations and actions, and by their successes and failures. To let a new creation merely evolve is too dangerous. Others with no good intentions toward the United States will be neither silent nor still, and the failed policy of U.S. hegemony and hubris is neither a means of grace nor a policy for building a world of self-restraint and global values. This nation needs a renewal of ideas and commitment from this new generation of young people.

Why should a Christian enter one of these fields? To be means of grace in the processes and policies of foreign affairs by exhibiting moral courage. Breaking the chain of threat saves lives and reduces fear, giving room for the grace of hope. Acting ethically validates ethical boundaries even if one is close to the moral margin. Negotiating in a way that builds trust and affirms higher values in appropriate settings moves counterparts beyond black-and-white dualism in situations of complexity. Using political office for serving the national interest demonstrates freedom of choice and inspires or strengthens a sense of service in others. A person embraced by grace can bring creativity to the world of risk and to the world of dialogue between freedom and fate. Grace is dynamic and renewing without being crusading or daydreaming. Those are attributes that can help shape the new creation to be safer, more cooperative, and more humane.

God is not an American; God's presence exists among us in the social and political institutions we create, and in the resulting opportunities and troubles. His holiness is not defined in law but in grace and mercy and righteousness, and those are given definition in the margins of opportunities that foreign policy creates. By engaging those troubles and opportunities, the demands of righteousness and margins of opportunity, the Christian can find his or her life in Christ and in the world, and find personal fulfillment and meaning.

Meaning? Vanity or meaningless, meaningless, all is meaningless says the Preacher. There is no justice in life, for the just die young and the wicked get rich. Whether a person is wise or not, the writer of Ecclesiastes admonishes his hearers to not try too much, not to engage the world.

Enjoy life is his advice, narrow our focus to enjoying life since none of us know when we will die and afterwards be forgotten.

Not so! Pakistan in early 2009 is facing a pivot point in its history, and its collapse into a radical Islamic state with access to nuclear weapons will have enormous consequences for the Islamic world, India, and the United States. Challenge and response—responding to that and similar challenges in the decades ahead will not be meaningless, whatever its success or failure. What happens abroad will have important consequences not only for the United States but also for neighboring nations as they respond on the basis of their analysis for their national interests, and for the hopes and fears and normative values of global politics.

Whether striving for a prestigious scholarship or running a clandestine intelligence operation or discussing American policy with reporters in another country—who will turn out to be successful cannot be fully answered early. The impact of your contribution to this country or to people in distress elsewhere in the world, or to the human family as a whole, cannot be fully evaluated early. All our lives will be forgotten as the world moves on, but we can walk worthy of our gifts and callings.

The Preacher is right, but also wrong. Life is meaningless if "under the sun" means a life detached and devoid of God. Within a context of life in Christ, however, multiple layers of meaning can be found in the time zones of life—the immediate, the mosaic of one's life, the sweep of history, and God's providential leadership and movement.

A MEDITATION ON JEREMIAH 4:19-22

"I cannot keep silent," Jeremiah wrote as he heard the alarms of war and disaster approaching. He was in despair because his people seemed so unaware of the approaching future, so foolish (so stupid in some versions), so lacking in understanding, so consumed in their own affairs. Isaiah's concern was warped understanding; Jeremiah's was the lack of understanding. Jeremiah wrote for his own time and circumstances, so what do his warnings about foolishness and lack of understanding mean for us in school and the early years of our careers? How do we not be foolish?

First, wrestle with issues. "O Lord," Jeremiah wrote, "I would speak to you about your justice: Why does the way of the wicked prosper? Why do the faithless live in ease?" (Jer 12:1-2 NIV) We are all aware that the world is full of tragedy, poverty, abuse, danger, repression, refugees. A deep spiritual life requires struggling with such issues, so we are neither dualists nor apocalyptics. A deep spirituality requires living in openness to God, close enough to be honest, devoted enough to listen, secure enough to speak and act. You need to wrestle with God over those issues until you find a framework that relates theology and theory, divine sovereignty and human freedom, divine grace and human evil, hope and fear—a framework that is persuasive for you and can be the foundation for your career.

Second, commit yourself and your career to prophetic values. Fear over issues is not enough; from your framework and wrestling with issues must come an appreciation of hope, of prophetic values of justice and righteousness that can function as means of grace in this world of international politics (Jer 22:2-3, 13-14). Foreign policy is about development of nations as well as diplomacy between them, about detecting evil that is developing in the dark as well as defending against it. Develop a research agenda as a normative unifying force in your college studies and scholarship applications and a normative policy agenda in your career.

Third, focus on three aspects of your learning to "get yourself ready" (Jer 1:17). Jeremiah lamented the lack of understanding in his people; the message for us is to study for understanding rather than for just knowledge or daydreams. Simplistic views become daydreams, which when turned into national policy can become nightmares. University education should not be indoctrination or memorization of "great answers" from authority figures; it is expansion, depth, and creativity in understanding. College is not grade 13 but a different culture, one that should force you to transcend and challenge the views common to your social/economic/status group. So don't "master" your text but instead use it as a new world of learning beyond boxed-in thinking and certainty. Understand backgrounds and dynamics and priorities and in so doing move toward stage 5 of integration and maturity. Make your major your "intellectual home."

As a second aspect of understanding, take a study abroad semester. See and talk and feel a different culture. Transcend textbooks and the campus. Visit the U.S. embassy and ask about any events you might be able to attend. Take a political officer or program manager to lunch and ask about career insights and a summer internship.

Third, add an elective course or two on management or administrative communication or proposal writing. A high state department official told me, "We get too many people who can name the six seas that surround

Turkey but can't manage an office." In your career you will have to "do" as well as "know"; produce "briefings," not term papers; and work with budgets, not books—so add some professionalism to the liberal arts.

Fourth, take yourself seriously. Think about your future, and whatever your aspirations may be, raise them. College years are not self-contained years but preparatory years for your career. I worked with a sophomore student on an application for the Boren Scholarship. Up to that time he lived in the present. When I said we needed to lay out his next year and a half of classes he looked at me and said, "You mean I have to grow up?" In the next three seconds he did. He got the scholarship, studied in Cairo, interned with the State Department, and now is a graduate student at Columbia University studying international security policy. Take yourself seriously and begin to think in terms of two five-year increments, and the potential steps, routes, ladders, and fast-track opportunities that will move you toward your goal. Then, assess what you need to qualify for them and begin to develop your capacities to achieve them.

To take yourself seriously also means recognizing how few Rhodes Scholars are named each year and the astronomical odds against being selected. Accept the Rhodes ideal and then find the scholarships and career routes for which you can be or become competitive and prepare yourself to reach for them. Allow for flexibility and failure, but don't give up or plateau early. Find advisors at your school or agency, talk with recruiters and human resources personnel, find good alternative routes to a goal of serving the nation in the field of foreign affairs.

This country and the world have passed the era of fear and danger of nuclear annihilation, but the patterns of 1914 are reemerging. There are the hopes of Richard Falk and the fears of Winston Churchill. Again the world needs an increase in the means of grace and a resistance to closure dynamics as well as skill in the art of diplomacy and understanding of the science of probabilities.

From the diplomatic front lines and clandestine operations to research centers and congressional committees, this country has benefited from the qualities of its youth—their energy, imagination, courage, and their capacity for love, loyalty, and perseverance. They will work in the world between Prometheus and Sisyphus, between hopes and high values and the ambiguities and frustrations that arise in a world of armed freedom. Young men and women serious about God and the flow of grace in and through their lives can be serious and valuable participants in the multiple careers in foreign affairs. They can be embraced by grace as they engage the personal, political, and ethical complexities and close calls of foreign policy. These are the young people the nation needs to engage events of international politics and foreign affairs with their scientific understanding of probabilities and processes (steps to war), their art of diplomacy, their background fears of the future, and their prophetic hopes, all in the service of the nation and the greater good of us all.

To be engaged in matters of state and history while embraced by the grace of God is a full life. Involvement in the renewal of the nation and executing its policies can and must include the parallel continuing renewal of one's own soul. Promoting diplomatic consensus, penetrating the shadows, negotiating the "wheels within wheels" of decision making, applying creative reason to the unreasonable forces of history, or finding solid grounds of integrity while simultaneously serving self, one's elector district, party leaders, and the national interest in the exercise of electoral responsibility—all these are the opportunities and tests of a Christian life well-lived.

Bibliography

Abella, Alex. *Soldiers of Reason: The RAND Corporation and the Rise of the American Empire.* New York: Harcourt, 2008.
Ackerman, Robert K. "Defense Intelligence Assumes More Diverse Missions." *Signal,* April 2007, 17–22.
Aldrich, Richard. "Dangerous Liaisons: Post–September 11 Intelligence Alliances." *Harvard International Review* 24, no. 3 (2002) 50–54.
Allen, Cathy. "Are You Really Ready to Run? *Campaign and Elections,* January 1988, 30–38.
Allison, Graham. *Essence of Decision.* Boston: Little, Brown, 1971.
American Association of Political Consultants. *Code of Ethics.* Online: http://www.theaapc.org/about/code.
American League of Lobbyists. *Code of Ethics.* Online: http://www.alldc.org/ethicscode.cfm.
"Anthropology Ass'n Blasts Army 'Human Terrain.'" November 7, 2007. Online: http://blog.wired.com/defense/2007/11/ anthropology-as.html.
Arkin, William. "The Secret War." *Los Angeles Times,* October 27, 2002.
Barry, John M. *The Ambition and the Power: The Fall of Jim Wright, A True Story of Washington.* New York: Penguin, 1989.
Barth, Thomas J. "Reflections on Building an MPA Program: Faculty Discussions Worth Having." *Journal of Public Affairs Education* 8, no. 4 (October 2002) 253–61.
Bassett, Paul M., and William M. Greathouse. *Exploring Christian Holiness,* Vol. 2: *The Historical Development.* Kansas City, MO: Beacon Hill, 1985.
Bauckham, Richard. "Theology after Hiroshima." *Scottish Journal of Theology* 38 (1985) 583–601.
Bean, Elizabeth A. "Down in Generation Gap: The Junior Foreign Service Office Looks at the System." In *The Annals of the American Academy of Political and Social Science,* edited by Smith Simpson. Philadelphia: American Academy, 1968.
Boren, David. *A Letter to America.* Norman: University of Oklahoma Press, 2008.
Bowden, Mark. "The Point/Pentagon Spy Effort Serves a Purpose." *The Philadelphia Enquirer,* March 18, 2007.
Brachman, Jarret M. "High-Tech Terror: Al-Qaeda's Use of New Technology." *Fletcher Forum of World Affairs* 30, no. 2 (2006) 149–64.
Bremer, Stuart A., and Thomas R. Cusack. *The Process of War: Advancing the Scientific Study of War.* Luxembourg: Gordon and Breach Publishers, SA, 1995.
Brodie, Bernard. *Strategy in the Missile Age.* Princeton: Princeton University Press, 1965.
Bronowski, Jacob. *Science and Human Values.* New York: Harper Torchbooks, 1965.
Brown, William P. *Character in Crisis: A Fresh Approach to the Wisdom Literature of the Old Testament.* Grand Rapids: Eerdmans, 1996.
Brueggemann, Walter. *Hope within History.* Atlanta: John Knox, 1987.

Butler, Amy. "Truth and Consequences." *Aviation Week and Space Technology*, January 19, 2009, 22–23.
Cahill, Lisa Sowle. "Christian Character, Biblical Community, and Human Values." In *Character and Scripture*, edited by William P. Brown. Grand Rapids: Eerdmans, 2002.
"Campaign Takedowns." *Politics*, June 2009, 28–32.
Cavas, Christopher. "Showdown Ends in Cancellation." *Navy Times*, April 18, 2007.
Christopher, Warren. *Chances of a Lifetime: A Memoir*. New York: Scriber, 2001.
Churchill, Winston. *The World Crisis: An Abridgement*. New York: Scriber's Sons, 1992.
Cogan, Charles G. "The In-Culture of the DO." *Intelligence and the National Security Strategist*, edited by Roger Z. George and Robert D. Kline. New York: Rowman & Littlefield, 2006.
Cohen, Carol. "Sex and Death in the Rational World of Defense Intellectuals." *Signs: Journal of Women in Culture and Society* 12, no. 4 (Summer 1987) 687–718.
Cohen, Raymond. "Negotiating across Cultures." In *Turbulent Peace: The Challenge of Managing International Conflict*, edited by Chester A. Crocker, Fen Osler Hampson, and Pamela Aall. Washington, DC: U.S. Institute of Peace, 2001.
Conant, Eve. "Faith under Fire." *Newsweek*, May 7, 2007.
Cooley, William, Brian Ruhm, and Adrian Marsh. "Building an Army: Program Management in Afghanistan." *Defense AT&L*, July/August 2006, 14–15.
Costigliola, Frank. "Unceasing Pressure for Penetration: Gender, Pathology and Emotion in George Kennan's Formation of the Cold War." *Journal of American History* 83, no. 4 (March 1997) 1309–39.
Crabtree, Susan. "Dems' Ethical Troubles Reminiscent of GOPers' Headaches as Majority." *The Hill*, February 11, 2009.
Crile, George. *Charlie Wilson's War: The Extraordinary Story of How the Wildest Man in Congress and a Rogue CIA Agent Changed the History of Our Times*. New York: Grove, 2003.
Curry, Dean C. *A World without Tyranny*. Westchester, IL: Crossways, 1990.
Daalder, Ivo H., and James M. Lindsay. *America Unbound: The Bush Revolution in Foreign Policy*. Washington, DC: Brookings Institution, 2003.
Dallek, Robert. *An Unfinished Life: John Kennedy, 1917–1963*. New York: Little, Brown, 2003.
Davis, Michael. "Thinking Like an Engineer." Illinois Institute of Technology, 1991. Online: http://ethics.iit.edu/publications/md_te.html.
Dean, John Gunther. *Danger Zones: A Diplomat's Fight for America's Interests*. Washington, DC: New Academic Publishing, 2009.
DeLay, Tom, with Stephen Mansfield. *No Retreat, No Surrender: One American's Fight*. New York: Sentinel, 2007.
Devlin, Larry. *Chief of Station, Congo: A Memoir of 1960–67*. New York: Public Affairs, 2007.
Diehl, Jackson. "The House's Ottoman Agenda." *Washington Post*, March 5, 2007.
Donley, Michael, and Norton Schwartz. "Moving beyond the F-22." *Washington Post*, April 13, 2009.
Doran, Charles F. "Confronting the Principles of the Power Cycle." In *Handbook of War Studies II*, edited by Manus I. Midlarsky. Ann Arbor: University of Michigan Press, 2001.
Dulles, Allen W. *The Craft of Intelligence*. Guilford, CT: Lyons, 2006.

Dulles, John Foster. "How My Faith Helped in a Decisive Hour." In *The Spiritual Legacy of John Foster Dulles*, edited by Henry H. Immerman. Princeton: Princeton University Press, 1990.

Elman, Colin, and Miriam Fendius Elman. "How Not to Be Lakatos Intolerant: Appraising Progress in IR Research." *International Studies Quarterly* 46, no. 2 (June 2002) 231–62.

Elshtain, Jean Bethke. *Just War against Terror*. New York: Basic Books, 2004.

———. "Just War as Politics: What the Gulf War Told Us about Contemporary American Life." In *But Was It Just? Reflections on the Morality of the Persian Gulf War*, edited by David E. Decosse. New York: Doubleday, 1992.

———. *Women and War*. Chicago: University of Chicago Press, 1995.

Enloe, Cynthia. *Bananas, Beaches and Bases: Making Feminist Sense of International Politics*. Berkeley: University of California Press, 2001.

Erickson, Erik. *Identity and the Life Cycle*. New York: International Universities Press, 1959.

Erwin, Sandra. "Despite SecDef Pleas, Pentagon Is Losing the Innovation War." *National Defense*, June 1, 2008, 10.

Falk, Richard. "Reforming World Order: Zones of Consciousness and Domains of Action." In *Planning Alternative World Futures*, edited by Louis Rene Beres and Harry F. Targ. New York: Praeger, 1975.

———. *Religion and Humane Global Governance*. New York: Palgrave Macmillan, 2001.

Falk, Richard, Samuel Kim, and Saul H. Mendlovitz, eds. *Toward a Just World Order*. Boulder, CO: Westview, 1982.

Faucheux, Ronald. *Running for Office: The Strategies, Techniques and Messages Modern Political Candidates Need to Win Elections*. Lanham, MD: National Book Network, 2002.

———. *Winning Elections*. Lanham, MD: National Book Network, 2003.

Feith, Douglas J. *War and Decision: Inside the Pentagon at the Dawn of the War on Terrorism*. New York: Harper, 2008.

Fisher, D., and W. R. Tolbert. *Personal and Organizational Transformation*. London: McGraw Hill, 1995.

Flamm, Kenneth. "Post–Cold War Policy and the U.S. Defense Industrial Base." National Academy of Engineering Web site 35:1 (Spring 2005): http://www.nae.edu/NAE/bridgecom.ns/MKEZ-6AGPFS?OpenDocument.

Forstchen, William R. "The Eye of God—The Finger of God." In *Beyond Shock and Awe: Warfare in the 21st Century*, edited by Eric L. Haney and Brian M. Thomsen. New York: Caliber, 2006.

Foster, Cheryl, and Mary Hale Tolar. "National Scholarship Competition as Educational Experiences." The Harry S. Truman Scholarship Foundation. This is available in the Faculty Representative section. Online: http://www.truman.gov/usr_doc/beyond_comp.pdf.

Fowler, James W. *Stages of Faith: The Psychology of Human Development*. New York: HarperOne, 1995.

Fowler, Robert Booth, and Allen D. Hertzke. *Religion and Politics in America*. Boulder, CO: Westview, 1995.

Frank, Thomas. *What's The Matter with Kansas?* New York: Metropolitan, 2004.

Freeman, Charles W. *Arts of Power: Statecraft and Diplomacy*. Washington, DC: Institute of Peace Press, 1997.

———. "Can American Leadership Be Restored?" *Foreign Service Journal*, November 2007, 44–48.

Furnish, Timothy R. "Beheading in the Name of Islam." *Middle East Quarterly* 12, no. 2 (Spring 2005) 51–57.

Gates, Robert. *From the Shadows*. New York: Touchstone, 1996.

———. "Speech Delivered to the Association of American Universities, April 14, 2008." Department of Defense. Online: http://www.defenselink.mil/speeches/speech.aspx?speechid=1228.

Gavel, Doug. "A Different Kind of Freshman Orientation at KSG." *Harvard Gazette*, January 18, 2001. Online: http://news.harvard.edu/gazette/legacy-gazette/#.

Geller, Daniel S. "Explaining War." In *Handbook of War Studies II*, edited by Manus I. Midlarsky. Ann Arbor: University of Michigan Press, 2000.

Gellman, Barbara. *Angler: The Cheney Vice Presidency*. New York: Penguin, 2008.

Gerson, Michael. *Heroic Conservatism: Why Republicans Need to Embrace America's Ideals*. New York: HarperOne, 2007.

———. "A New Social Gospel." *Newsweek*, November 13, 2006.

Gerstein, Daniel M. *Securing America's Future: National Strategy in the Information Age*. Westport, CT: Praeger, 2005.

Gibbs, Nancy, and Michael Duffy. *The Preacher and the Presidents: Billy Graham in the White House*. New York: Center Street, 2007.

Gingrich, Newt. "Rogue State Department." *Foreign Policy*, July/August, 2003, 42–48.

Global Security. "A. Q. Kahn." No date. Online: http://globalsecurity.org/world/pakistan/kahn.htm.

Godfrey, J. E. Drexel. "Ethics and Intelligence." *Foreign Affairs* 56, no. 13 (1978) 624–42.

Gregory, William H. *The Price of Peace: The Future of Defense Industry and High Technology in a Post–Cold War World*. New York: Lexington, 1993.

Grogan, Jennifer. "Sub Funding Increase Advances." *New London Day*, July 31, 2008.

Gropman, Alan. "Balancing Act: Uncertainty about Budgets, Workforce Shape Future of U.S. Weapons Industry." *National Defense*, May 2008, 24–25.

Grose, Peter. *Gentleman Spy*. New York: Houghton Mifflin, 1994.

Halper, Stefan, and Jonathan Clarke. *America Alone: The Neo-Conservatives and the Global Order*. New York: Cambridge University Press, 2004.

Harrington, Mona. "Feminists and Foreign Policy." *Ideas and Ideals: Essays on Politics in Honor of Stanley Hoffmann*, edited by Linda B. Miller and Michael Joseph Smith. Boulder, CO: Westview, 1993.

Hasenclever, Andreas, and Volker Rittberger. "Does Religion Make a Difference? Theoretical Approaches to the Impact of Faith on Political Conflict." In *Religion and International Relations: The Return from Exile*, edited by Fabio Petito and Pavlos Hatzopoulos. New York: Palgrave, 2003.

Hass, Richard. "The Dilemma of Dissent." *Newsweek*, May 2, 2009.

Hauerwas, Stanley. *After Christendom? How the Church Is to Behave If Freedom, Justice, and a Christian Nation Are Bad Ideas*. Nashville: Abingdon, 1991.

Hayden, Michel V. "CIA Director's Address at Duquesne University Commencement." Central Intelligence Agency, News-Information, Speeches. May 4, 2007. Online: https://www.cia.gov/news-information/speeches-testimony/2007/cia-directors-address-at-duquesne-university-commencement.html.

———. "The Influence of Richard Helms on the American Intelligence Profession." *Intelligencer: Journal of U.S. Intelligence Studies* 16, no. 1 (Spring 2008) 61–64.

Healy, Rita. "Is Dobson's Political Clout Fading?" *Time*, January 24, 2008.
Hefley, James C., and Edward E. Plowman. *Washington: Christians in the Corridors of Power*. Wheaton, IL: Tyndale, 1975.
Helling, Dave. "Temptation Exists for Politicians to Use Powers for Personal Interests." *Kansas City Star*, December 14, 2008.
Helms, Richard. *A Look over My Shoulder: A Life in the Central Intelligence Agency*. New York: Random House, 2003.
Hernandez, Raymond. "Frantic Start in Congress for One Democrat, Class of '06." *New York Times*, February 20, 2007.
Hersh, Seymour M. "The Coming Wars." *The New Yorker*, January 24, 2005, 40–47.
Hershberg, James. *James B. Conant: Harvard to Hiroshima and the Making of the Nuclear Age*. New York: Alfred A. Knopf, 1993.
Hertzke, Allen D. "The Faith Factor in Foreign Policy: Religious Constituencies and Congressional Initiatives on Human Rights." In *Extensions*, published by the Carl Albert Congressional Research and Studies Center, Spring 2001.
———. *Freeing God's Children: The Unlikely Alliance for Global Human Rights*. New York: Rowman & Littlefield, 2004.
Herzog, Arthur. *The War-Peace Establishment*. New York: Harper & Row, 1963.
Hildreth, Reed C. "Code Name CYNTHIA." *Intelligencer: Journal of U.S. Intelligence Studies* 14, no. 1 (Winter/Spring 2004) 23–25.
Hill, David. "Religious Right and the GOP." *The Hill*, February 6, 2008.
Hoffmann, Stanley. *Duties beyond Borders: On the Limits and Possibilities of Ethical International Politics*. Syracuse, NY: Syracuse University Press, 1981.
Holbrooke, Richard. *To End a War*. New York: Random House, 1998.
Holmes, William R., and Robert A. Seraphin. "Munitions Industrial Base: Trouble on the Horizon." *National Defense*, June 2007, 39.
Holsti, Kalevi, J. *Peace and War: Armed Conflicts and International Order, 1648–1989*. New York: Cambridge University Press, 1991.
Hostler, Charles W. *Soldier to Ambassador: A Memoir Odyssey*. San Diego, CA: San Diego State University Press, 2003.
Huntington, Samuel P. *The Clash of Civilizations and the Remaking of World Order*. New York: Touchstone, 1996.
Ignatieff, Michael. *The Lesser Evil*. Princeton: Princeton University Press, 2004.
Imbler, Norman B. "Espionage in an Age of Change: Optimizing Strategic Intelligence Services for the Future." In Roger Z. George and Robert D. Kline. *Intelligence and the National Security Strategist*. New York: Rowman & Littlefield, 2006.
In the Spirit of '76: The Citizen's Guide to Politics. Washington, DC: Third Century, 1975.
Jacobs, John. *A Rage for Justice: The Passion and Politics of Phillip Burton*. Los Angeles: University of California Press, 1995.
Jaffe, Greg. "Gates Sharpens Rhetoric in Dispute on F-22 Funds." *The Washington Post*, July 17, 2009.
Jakes, Lara, and Vijay Joshi. "Gates: North Korea Nuke Progress Sign of 'Dark Future.'" *The Seattle Times*, May 31, 2009.
Jarecki, Eugene. *The American Way of War*. New York: The Free Press, 2008.
Jean, Grace V. "Economies of Scale: Analysts Predict New Wave of Industry Consolidation." *National Defense*, January 2009, 18–19.
Johnson, Loch K. "Ethics of Covert Operations." In *Ethics of Spying*, edited by Jan Goldman. Lanham, MD: Scarecrow, 2006.

Bibliography

Johnson, U. Alexis. "Memorandum on Planning-Programming-Budgeting (PPBS)." In *Planning-Programming-Budgeting, Hearings before the Subcommittee on National Security and International Operations, 90th Congress, Second Session, Part 4.* Washington, DC: Government Printing Office, 1968.

———. *The Right Hand of Power.* New York: Prentice-Hall, 1984.

Jones, L. Gregory. "Formed and Transformed by Scripture: Character, Community, and Authority in Biblical Interpretation." In *Character and Scripture*, edited by William P. Brown. Grand Rapids: Eerdmans, 2002.

Jurkiewicz, Carole L., and Kenneth L. Nichols. "Ethics Education in the MPA Curriculum: What Difference Does It Make?" *Journal of Public Affairs Education* 8, no. 2 (April 2002) 103–14.

Kahn, Herman. *On Escalation: Metaphors and Scenarios.* New York: Praeger, 1965.

———. *On Thermonuclear War.* Princeton: Princeton University Press, 1960.

Kambrod, Matthew R. *Lobbying for Defense: An Insider's View.* Annapolis, MD: Naval Institute Press, 2007.

Kaplan, Fred. *Daydream Believers: How a Few Grand Ideas Wrecked American Power.* Hoboken, NJ: Wiley, 2008.

———. *The Wizards of Armageddon.* New York: Simon & Schuster, 1983.

Kennan, George. *American Diplomacy, 1900–1950.* New York: Mentor, 1957.

Kennedy, Paul. *The Rise and Fall of the Great Powers.* New York: Vintage, 1987.

Kenney, George. "On Dissent: My Resignation from the Foreign Service." *Foreign Service Journal*, October 1992, 20–22.

Kessler, Ronald. *Inside the CIA: Revealing the Secrets of the World's Most Powerful Spy Agency.* New York: Pocket Books, 1994.

Kiesling, John Brady. *Diplomacy Lessons: Realism for an Unloved Superpower.* Washington, DC: Potomac Books, 2006.

Kissinger, Henry. "Domestic Structure and Foreign Policy." In *Power, Action and Interaction*, edited by George H. Quester. Boston: Little, Brown, 1971.

Kreisler, Harry. "Intelligence and National Security in a Democracy," broadcast interview with Jennifer Sims in *Conversations with History*. Institute of International Studies, University of California, Berkeley (February 11, 2002). Online link to index: http://Globetrotter.berkeley.edu/conversations.

Kristof, Nicholas D. "Make Diplomacy, Not War." *New York Times*, August 9, 2008.

Kucinich, Jackie. "Anti-War Jones Wooed by Dems, But Plans to Stay in GOP for Now." *The Hill*, March 8, 2007.

———. "Young: There's Life after Lawmaking." *The Hill*, June 26, 2008.

Kugler, Jack, and Douglas Lemke. "The Power Transition Research Program: Assessing Theoretical and Empirical Advances." In *Handbook of War Studies II*, edited by Manus I. Midlarsky. Grand Rapids: University of Michigan Press, 2001.

Kuklick, Bruce. *Blind Oracles: Intellectuals and War from Kennan to Kissinger.* Princeton: Princeton University Press, 2006.

Lafore, Laurence. *The Long Fuse.* 2nd ed. New York: Lippincott, 1971.

Lauren, Paul Gordon. *The China Hands' Legacy: Ethics and Diplomacy.* Boulder, CO: Westview, 1987.

Lawlor, Maryann. "Reconnaissance Task Force on Target." *Signal*, February 2009, 59–62.

Leacacos, John P. *Fires in the In-Basket: The ABC's of the State Department.* Westport, CT: Greenwood, 1977.

Lee, Matthew. "Diplomatic Critics of Policy Honored." *Washington Post*, June 28, 2007.

Lefever, Ernest. *Ethics and United States Foreign Policy*. New York: Meridian, 1957.
Lerche, Charles O. *The Cold War . . . And After*. New York: Prentice-Hall, 1965.
Lieber, Keir A. "The New History of World War I and What It Means for International Relations Theory." *International Security* 32, no. 2 (Fall 2007) 155–91.
Lindsay, Michael. *Faith in the Halls of Power*. New York: Oxford University Press, 2008.
Lyons, Gene M., and Louis Morton. *Schools for Strategy: Education and Research in National Security Affairs*. New York: Praeger, 1965.
Lyons, Richard. "On Capital Hill." *Washington Post*, September 26, 1979.
Macmillan, Margaret. *Paris 1919*. New York: Random House, 2001.
Macomber, William B. "Change at Foggy Bottom: An Anniversary Report on Management Reform and Modernization in the State Department." *Department of State Bulletin*, February 14, 1972, 206–13.
Magnuson, Stew. "Cyber-Attack: U.S. Plans to Destroy Enemy Computer Networks Questioned." *National Defense* 95, no. 668 (July 2009) 22–23.
Mann, James. *The Rise of the Vulcans: The History of Bush's War Cabinet*. New York: Viking, 2004.
Marchetti, Victor, and John D. Marks. *The CIA and the Cult of Intelligence*. New York: Knopf, 1974.
Marsden, George. "Why No Major Evangelical University? The Loss and Recovery of Evangelical Advanced Scholarship." In *Making Higher Education Christian*, edited by Joel Carpenter and Kenneth W. Shipps. Grand Rapids: Eerdmans, 1987.
Martelle, Scott. "Duncan Hunter's Toughest Fight Yet." *Los Angeles Times*, July 13, 2007.
Martin, John Barlow. *Overtaken by Events: The Dominican Crisis from the Fall of Trujillo to the Civil War*. Garden City, NJ: Doubleday, 1966.
Matthews, Chris. *Hardball*. New York: Simon & Schuster, 1988.
McClure, George F. "Is Aerospace Worth Saving?" *Today's Engineer*, July 2003,. Online only: http://www.todaysengineer.org/2003/Jul/aerospace.asp.
McIntosh, Elizabeth P. *Sisterhood of Spies*. New York: Dell, 1998.
McNeil, Phyllis Provost. "The Evolution of the U.S. Intelligence Community: An Historical Overview." *Report of the Commission on the Roles and Capabilities of the United States Intelligence Community*, March 1, 1996. Online: http://wwws.gpoaccess.gov/int //int022.pdf.
McNeill, William H. *Arnold Toynbee: A Life*. New York: Oxford University Press, 1989.
Mee, Charles L., Jr. *The End of Order: Versailles 1919*. New York: Dutton, 1980.
Merton, Robert. "The Matthew Effect in Science." *Science* 159 (January 1968) 56–63.
Morgenstern, Oscar. *The Question of National Defense: A Critique of Our Military Preparations and Policies*. New York: Random House, 1959.
Morgenthau, Hans. Introduction to *Ethics and United States Foreign Policy*, by Ernest Lefever. New York: Meridian, 1957.
———. *Politics among Nations*. New York: Knopf, 1960.
———. *Scientific Man Versus Power Politics*. Chicago: University of Chicago Press, 1946.
———. "We Are Deluding Ourselves in Vietnam." *New York Times Magazine*, April 18, 1965.
Morris, Dick. *The New Prince*. Los Angeles: Renaissance, 1999.
Morris, Roger W. *Uncertain Greatness: Henry Kissinger and American Foreign Policy*. New York: Harper & Row, 1977.
Murphy, Nancy, and George F. R. Ellis. *On the Moral Nature of the Universe: Theology, Cosmology, and Ethics*. Minneapolis: Fortress, 1996.

Murray, Craig. *Dirty Diplomacy*. New York: Scribner, 2006.
Nelkin, Dorothy. *The University and Military Research: Moral Politics at M.I.T.* Ithaca, NY: Cornell University Press, 1972.
Newsom, David D. *Witness to a Changing World*. Washington, DC: New Academic Publishing, 2008.
Nitze, Paul H. *Tensions between Opposites: Reflections on the Practice and Theory of Politics*. New York: Scribner, 1993.
Olsen, James M. *Fair Play: The Moral Dilemmas of Spying*. Washington, DC: Potomac Books, 2006.
O'Sullivan, Jim. "The Divided Faith." *Campaigns and Elections*, August 2006, 30–32.
Pae, Peter. "Northrop Grumman-TRW Whistle-Blower Case Settled." *Los Angeles Times*, Business Section, April 3, 2009.
Pfaff, Tony. "Bungee Jumping off the Moral Highground." In *Ethics of Spying*, edited by Jan Goldman. Lanham, MD: Scarecrow, 2006.
Power, F. Clark, Ann Higgins, and Lawrence Kohlberg. *Lawrence Kohlberg's Approach to Moral Education*. New York: Columbia University Press, 1991.
Powers, Thomas. *Heisenberg's War: The Secret History of the German Bomb*. Cambridge, MA: Da Capo Press, 2000.
Public Papers of the Presidents of the United States, John F. Kennedy. Washington, DC: United States Government Printing Office, 1964.
Ramsey, Paul. "A Political Ethics Context for Strategic Thinking." *Strategic Thinking and Its Moral Implications*, edited by Morton Kaplan. Chicago: University of Chicago Center for Policy Studies, 1973.
Reardon, Betty. *Sexism and the War System*. New York: Teachers College Press, 1985.
Reeves, Richard. *President Kennedy: Profile of Power*. New York: Touchstone, 1993.
Remak, Joachim. *The Origins of World War I: 1871–1914*. 2nd ed. New York: Harcourt Brace, 1995.
Rice, Condoleeza. "Transformational Diplomacy: Remarks at Georgetown School of Foreign Service." January 18, 2006. Online: http://www.unc.edu/depts/diplomat/item/2006/0103/rice/rice_georgetown.html.
Rich, Ben R., and Leo Janos. *Skunk Works: A Personal Memoir of My Years at Lockheed*. New York: Little, Brown, 1994.
Riemer, Jeffrey. "Top Ten Rewards for Being a Program Manager." *Defense AT&L*, November/December 2006, 40–41.
Rosenberg, Emily. "'Foreign Affairs' after World War II: Connecting Sexual and International Politics." *Diplomatic History* 18 (Winter 1994) 57–70.
Roth, Toby, and Allen D. Hertzke. *Freeing God's Children*. New York: Rowman & Littlefield, 2004.
Rothstein, Betsy. "Befriending the Fallen." *The Hill*, May 20, 2008.
———. "Intern Flops." *The Hill*, June 26, 2007.
Rusk, Dean. *As I Saw It*. New York: Norton, 1990.
Schlesinger, Arthur, Jr. *Robert F. Kennedy and His Times*. New York: Ballantine, 1978.
———. *A Thousand Days*. Boston: Houghton Mifflin, 1965.
Schroen, Gary. *First In: An Insider's Account of How the CIA Spearheaded the War on Terror in Afghanistan*. Novato, CA: Presidio, 2007.
"Secretary Rogers Announces Management Reform." *Department of State Bulletin*, July 24, 1971, 103–8.

Serwer, Adam. "How Tom Perriello Showed Virgil Goode the Door." *The Prospect*. Online: http://www.prospect.org/articles?article=how_tom_perriello_showed_virgil_good_the_door.

Shaw, Gaylord, and William C. Rempel. "Billion-Dollar Iran Arms Search Spans U.S., Globe." *Los Angeles Times*, August 4, 1985.

Shulsky, Abram, and Gary J. Schmit. *Silent Warfare: Understanding the World of Intelligence*. Washington, DC: Potomac Books, 2002.

Shultz, George. *Turmoil and Triumph: My Years as Secretary of State*. New York: Random House, 1993.

Silk, Mark, and John C. Green. "The GOP's Religion Problem." *Religion in the News* 9 (Winter 2007) 2–4.

Simon, Stephanie. "In Political Ads, Christian Left Mounts Sermonic Campaigns." *Wall Street Journal*, July 2009. Online: http://online.wsj.com/article_email/SB12465772631198209.html.

Simpson, Howard R. *Bush Hat, Black Tie: Adventures of a Foreign Service Officer*. Washington, DC: Brassey's, 1998.

Singer, P. W. *Wired for War: The Robotics Revolution and Conflict in the Twenty-first Century*. New York: Penguin, 2009.

Smidt, Corwin. "Religion and American Public Opinion." In *In God We Trust?*, edited by Corwin Smidt. Grand Rapids: Baker, 2001.

Smith, Robert W. "Teaching Public and Private Sector Ethics: Some Fundamental Differences and Surprising Similarities." *Teaching Ethics and Values in Public Administration Programs: Innovations, Strategies, and Issues*, edited by James Bowman and Donald Menzel. Albany: State University of New York Press, 1998.

Snyder, Jack, and Keir A. Lieber. "Defense Realism and the 'New' History of World War I." *International Security* 30, no. 1 (Summer 2008), 174–94.

Solomon, Jay, Siobhan Gorman, and Matthew Rosenberg. "U.S. Plans New Drone Attacks in Pakistan." *The Wall Street Journal*, March 28, 2009.

Stephanopoulos, George. *All Too Human: A Political Education*. New York: Little, Brown, 1999.

Stevenson-Yang, Ann. "Anatomy of an Office Corps: The Foreign Service of the 1960s." *Foreign Service Journal*, March 1993, 26–32.

Swearengen, Jack C. "Arms Control and God's Purpose in History." *Perspectives on Science & Christian Faith* 44, no. 2 (1992) 25–35.

———. *Beyond Paradise: Technology and the Kingdom of God*. Eugene, OR: Wipf & Stock, 2007.

Swearengen, Jack C., and Alan P. Swearengen. "Comparative Analysis of the Nuclear Weapons Debate: Campus and Developer Perspectives." *Perspectives on Science & Christian Faith* 42, no. 2 (1990) 75–85.

Taylor, Maxwell D. *Responsibility and Response*. New York: Harper & Row, 1967.

———. *Swords and Plowshares*. New York: Norton, 1972.

Tenet, George. *At the Center of the Storm: My Years at the CIA*. New York: HarperCollins, 2007.

Thomas, Evan. *The Very Best Men*. New York: Simon & Schuster, 2006.

Thompson, Dennis F. *Political Ethics and Public Office*. Cambridge: Harvard University Press, 1987.

Thomson, George Malcom. *The Twelve Days*. New York: Putnam's Sons, 1964.

Tickner, J. Ann. "Hans Morgenthau's Principles of Political Realism: A Feminist Critique." *Millennium: Journal of International Studies* 17, no. 3 (1998) 429–40.

———. "What Is Your Research Program? Some Feminist Answers to International Relations Methodological Questions." *International Studies Quarterly* 49, no. 1 (March 2005) 1–21.

Tiron, Roxana. "Courtney Gets Democrats' Support on Submarines." *The Hill*, March 7, 2007.

Tiron, Roxana, and Aaron Blake. "Amid Probe, Rep. Visclosky Steps Aside from Approps Bill." *The Hill*, June 3, 2009.

Tolar, Mary Hale. "A Path Revealed: Reflections of a Former Scholarship Advisor." *Beyond Winning: National Scholarship Competition and the Student Experience*, edited by Suzanne McCray. Fayetteville: University of Arkansas Press, 2005.

Tolchin, Susan J., and Martin Tolchin. *Glass House: Congressional Ethics and the Politics of Venom*. Boulder, CO: Westview, 2001.

Toward a Modern Diplomacy: A Report to the American Foreign Service Association. Washington, DC: American Foreign Service Association, 1968.

Toynbee, Arnold. "The Meaning of History for the Soul." In *Civilization on Trial and The World and the West*, essays by Arnold Toynbee. New York: Meridian, 1958.

———. "Why and How I Work." *Saturday Review*, April 5, 1969, 22–27, 62.

Tuchman, Barbara. *The Guns of August*. New York: Dell, 1962.

Tully, Andrew. *CIA: The Inside Story*. Greenwich, CT: Crest, 1962.

Tyson, Ann Scott. "Applying Diplomacy to Conflict." *Washington Post*, September 29, 2006.

Ullman, Harlan K., and James P. Wade. *Shock and Awe*. Charleston, NC: Bibliobazar, 2007.

Van Geest, Fred. "Deepening and Broadening Christian Citizenship: Going Beyond the Basics without Succumbing to Liberal and Communitarian Ideals." *Christian Scholars Review* 34, no. 1 (Fall 2004) 91–118.

Vasquez, John A. *The War Puzzle*. New York: Cambridge University Press, 1993.

Vos Fellman, Phil, and Roxana Wright. "Modeling Terrorist Networks—Complex Systems at Mid-Range Networks." *Intelligencer: Journal of U.S. Intelligence Studies* 14, no. 1 (Winter/Spring 2004) 59–66.

"Voting Religiously." A Pew Research Publication (November 5, 2008). Online: http://pewresearch.org/pubs/1022/exit-poll-analysis-religion.

Walker, William. "Nuclear Enlightenment and Counter-Enlightenment." *International Affairs* 83, no. 3 (May 2007) 431–54.

Warrick, Joby, and R. Jeffrey Smith. "Latest CIA Scandal Puts Focus on How Agency Polices Self." *Washington Post*, March 20, 2009.

Weber, Theodore R. *Politics in the Order of Salvation*. Nashville: Kingswood, 2001.

Weigel, George. *Witness to Hope: The Biography of Pope John Paul II*. New York: Cliff Street Books, 1999.

Weigley, Russell F. *The American Way of War: A History of United States Military Strategy and Policy*. New York: Macmillan, 1973.

Wenhold, Dave. "It's Not All Fun and Games." *The Hill*, May 11, 2008.

Whitlock, Craig. "After a Decade at War with West, Al-Qaeda Still Impervious to Spies." *Washington Post*, March 20, 2008.

Wildavsky, Aaron. "What Is Permissible So That This People May Survive? Joseph the Administrator." *PS: Political Science* 22 (1989) 779–88.

Willard, Dallas. *Hearing God: Developing a Conversational Relationship with God*. Downers Grove, IL: InterVarsity Press, 1999.
Wilson, Joseph. *The Politics of Truth: A Diplomat's Memoir*. New York: Carrol & Graf, 2004.
Wise, David, and Thomas B. Ross. *The Invisible Government*. New York: Vintage, 1974.
Wolterstorff, Nicholas. *Until Justice and Peace Embrace*. Grand Rapids: Eerdmans, 1983.
Woodstock Theological Center. *The Ethics of Lobbying: Organized Interests, Political Power, and the Common Good*. Washington, D.C.: Georgetown University Press, 2002.
Wright, Ann. "Breaking through Diplomacy's Glass Ceiling." *Foreign Service Journal* 82, no. 12 (October 2005) 53–62.
Wurmser, David. *Tyranny's Ally: America's Failure to Defeat Saddam Hussein*. Washington, DC: American Enterprise Institute, 1999.
York, Herbert F. *Making Weapons, Talking Peace*. New York: Basic Books, 1987.

www.ingramcontent.com/pod-product-compliance
Lightning Source LLC
Chambersburg PA
CBHW050342230426
43663CB00010B/1952